Pier Giorgio Frassati

Pier Giorgio Frassati

Truth, Love, and Sacrifice

David C. Bellusci, OP, PhD

WIPF & STOCK · Eugene, Oregon

PIER GIORGIO FRASSATI
Truth, Love, and Sacrifice

Copyright © 2020 David C. Bellusci. All rights reserved. Except for brief quotations in critical publications or reviews, no part of this book may be reproduced in any manner without prior written permission from the publisher. Write: Permissions, Wipf and Stock Publishers, 199 W. 8th Ave., Suite 3, Eugene, OR 97401.

Wipf & Stock
An Imprint of Wipf and Stock Publishers
199 W. 8th Ave., Suite 3
Eugene, OR 97401

www.wipfandstock.com

PAPERBACK ISBN: 978-1-7252-5095-6
HARDCOVER ISBN: 978-1-7252-5096-3
EBOOK ISBN: 978-1-7252-5097-0

Manufactured in the U.S.A.   APRIL 16, 2020

All Scripture quotations are from The Catholic Edition of the Revised Standard Version of the Bible, copyright © 1965, 1966 National Council of the Churches of Christ in the United States of America. Used by permission. All rights reserved worldwide.

In memory of my beloved mother and father.

Dedicated to my nephews and nieces,
to my godchildren,
to my students,
to those whom God has put on my path.

Do not be conformed to this world, but be transformed by the renewal of your mind, that you may prove what is the will of God, what is good and acceptable and perfect.

—Romans 12:2

Contents

Acknowledgments | ix
Vocabulary | xi
Abbreviations | xii
Introduction | xiii

1. Father and Mother | 1
2. Growing Up—Luciana and the Extended Family | 30
3. Sacramental Life | 48
4. Studies | 69
5. Pier Giorgio's Culture and Travels | 92
6. Friendship | 111
7. Christian Society | 141
8. Pier Giorgio's Spirituality | 168
9. Love: Purity—Obedience—Sacrifice | 187
10. Pier Giorgio's Eschatological Vision | 204

Bibliography | 223
Index | 227

Acknowledgments

This book project on Blessed Pier Giorgio Frassati's letters began in 2011. I arrived late Sunday evening in Pollone spending my day connecting trains from Venice to Turin. Signora Wanda Gawronska warmly welcomed me into her home and graciously offered me the oratory where I could celebrate Mass. It was the vigil of Blessed Pier Giorgio's Memorial, July 4. Having received Pier Giorgio's *Lettere (1906–1925)* edited by Signora Gawronska's mother, Luciana Frassati, I made it my task to get to know Blessed Pier Giorgio by translating all his letters from Italian into English.

The project began in 2011 and providentially in 2015–2016 I was assigned as confessor to Santa Maria Maggiore in Rome for the Year of Mercy allowing me to meet with Signora Gawronska on a regular basis, and consult her library to help me with my research and writing. Signora Gawronska took time from her busy schedule to read each of my chapters; she was straightforward with her criticism and made corrections which I appreciated. Drawing from Signora Gawronska's personal discussions with her mother, our meetings gave me a better sense of Blessed Pier Giorgio's background. Any errors in the text are my own.

Signora Germana Moro, one of the Turin coordinators of the Pier Giorgio Frassati Association, kindly organized a detailed visit to Turin so I could acquaint myself with the places where Pier Giorgio spent his life. We met at the Turin Cathedral in front of the altar dedicated to Blessed Pier Giorgio where his remains are kept and where Blessed Pier Giorgio continues to intercede for us. Not far from the cathedral we visited the medieval Dominican Church where Blessed Pier Giorgio was received as a Third Order Dominican (Lay Dominican).

At the basilica, Our Lady Help of Christians, Signore Antonio Labanca, journalist editor, and a friend of the Frassati Association, explained the history of the Salesian Basilica. Of particular importance, Signore Labanca pointed out Turin's geographic position, from the northwest subjected to secular ideology from France and from the north receiving Calvinist influences from Switzerland. In response, Turin and the Piedmont region became the birthplace of numerous Blesseds and Saints. Blessed Pier Giorgio's first biographer was a Salesian, Don Antonio Cojazzi, and as Signore Labanca explained Don Cojazzi's *Testimonie* served as a didactic tool for the youth to help live a life of virtue. Not far from the Basilica, Signore Labanca brought me to the Cottolengo district where Pier Giorgio visited the sick. Continuing our walk, we entered in Turin's oldest Marian shrine, and Papal Basilica, *La Consolata*, where Pier Giorgio spent time in prayer. A painting of Blessed Pier Giorgio is also placed in this basilica.

Luca Manzon, friend and collaborator of Turin's Frassati Association, and a member of *Azione Cattolica*, "Catholic Action," generously spent his afternoon with me. He first accompanied me to the Church of Corpus Domini where Turin's Eucharistic Miracle took place in the fifteenth century. Blessed Pier Giorgio discussed the miracle in detail in one of his letters. We visited the Sacramentine church, Santa Maria in Piazza, where Blessed Pier Giorgio spent hours in all-night adoration. Luca also brought me to Massimo D'Azeglio where Pier Giorgio attended secondary school for several years. Walking on Corso Galileo Ferraris we saw Blessed Pier Giorgio's home and not far from his home we visited his parish, *La Crocetta*. Entering the church on the left wall a sizeable mosaic includes Saint John Bosco, Blessed Pier Giorgio, and a child. Our last stop was the Turin Polytechnic where Blessed Pier Giorgio pursued his university studies in mining engineering.

I went on several pilgrimages to Our Lady of Oropa in the Italian Alps, sixty-two miles from Turin, and very close to Blessed Pier Giorgio's Pollone summer home where I could celebrate Mass on different occasions. I am grateful for the warm and friendly staff of the Oropa guest house. I am thankful for Canon Don Michele Berchi and the canons and clergy of the basilica with whom I was able to concelebrate Mass during my visits, especially during the Easter Triduum. In the shrine where Our Lady of Oropa stands in her sacellum, Blessed Pier Giorgio spent hours kneeling in prayer.

Vocabulary

Italian	English
addolorato/a (adj.)	sorrowful/afflicted
affettuosissimo	most affectionate
babbo	daddy/papa
baci	kisses
cena	supper (around 8 p.m.)
corso	promenade/street
festa	feastday/namesday
lestofantesco/a [n., m./f.]	swindler
maccheroni	macaroni
Madonna	Our Lady
mammina	mommy/mamma
mille baci	thousand kisses
nonna	grandmother
papalino	daddy/papa
pranzo	lunch (around 1 p.m.: Italian "dinner")
proponimento	resolve
sfacciato/a (adj.)	bold
Signore	Mr.
Signora	Mrs.
Signorina	Miss
Tipi (adj.) Loschi (n.)	Shady Ones
zia	aunt

Abbreviations

Associations/Clubs

AC / Azione Cattolica — CA / Catholic Action

CAI / Club Alpino Italiano — Italian Alpine Club

D.d.g. / direttrice di gita — director of excursions

FUCI / Federazione universitaria cattolica italiana — Federation of Italian Catholic Universities

GC / Gioventù Cattolica — CY / Catholic Youth

GCI / Gioventù Cattolica Italiana — Italian Catholic Youth

GM / Giovane Montagna — Youth Mountaineers

PPI / Paritito Popolare Italiano — Italian Popular Party

Introduction

The objective of this book on Blessed Pier Giorgio is to show that sanctity, with the help of God's grace, is possible. As Pier Giorgio teaches us, the person's pilgrim journey is not meant to be alone. We are born into a family, we belong to a community, we participate in the sacramental life of the church, and we are called to bring the truth and love of the gospel, the teachings of Christ, into our society. Anyone who reads the letters and biographies on Blessed Pier Giorgio will be moved by his capacity to bring joy, his sense of purity, and his willingness to make sacrifices.

I have written this book in ten chapters as a "rising tide" where waves recede as they continue to rise. A citation at the opening of each chapter is relevant to the period/context of Pier Giorgio's life. While the letters in individual chapters are chronological, the movement from one chapter to the next, like the water receding from previous letters, only to bring forth the rising tide of new letters. Pier Giorgio's life does not have any rupture as far as his faith is concerned. The remarkable continuity in his life of faith is like these waves that continue to rise as he gets older, but always drawing from earlier experiences, so, the chapters, move forward, only by drawing from the past.

Blessed Pier Giorgio's journey of faith includes sacrifices which he chooses and suffering which he does not choose. His faith represents the realism of the sacramental life that builds from baptism, relies on parents to instill values in their children, and even depends on a community where the faith is visible and manifested. This is called Catholic culture; and this religious culture is an underlying theme of this book. The presence of Catholic culture in the early 1900s of Turin is clearly given the prominence of the Church in society and politics. But Catholic beliefs and practices in any culture may be challenged and threatened. Pier Giorgio understood that political choices need to be made in harmony with Catholic teaching; his politics translates into one reality: the gospel.

Chapter 1 explores in some detail the background to both Pier Giorgio's father and mother. I operate from the assumption that parents are the first educators of their children. But what is this education? This is where one discovers the differences and complementarity between Alfredo Frassati, the journalist, and Adelaide Ametis, the artist. They both instill values in Pier Giorgio, the father's sense of justice, the mother's sense of courage. The chapter shows that already as a child, Pier Giorgio expresses remarkable sensitivity toward those around him. He chooses to sit with a skin-infected boy and have lunch with him. He wishes to have the "Sister" bring flowers to Jesus at the chapel for him.

In chapter 2 the role of his sister, Luciana, and the extended family are considered, all those who have a formative role as Pier Giorgio grows—including pets and nature. Pier Giorgio learns especially to care. His desire to write, or to be in the company of his grandmother, Linda Ametis, or his Aunt Elena, his mother's sister, indicate that even as a child, Pier Giorgio sought friendship, to reach out, to share, and this he experienced with his own family members. At an early age, he recognizes the value of the "other." In his childhood years, Pier Giorgio develops a sense of nature, whether on the Riviera or in the Alps, nature is enjoyed, but also shared with others. Receiving a strict discipline, whether at home or on vacation, prayer or bedtime, negotiation is impossible. He learns obedience, respect and to follow rules. From his parents, Pier Giorgio acquires the sense of right and wrong, responsibility and neglect, but especially the virtuous behavior, values reinforced by his family at home.

Chapter 3 presents Pier Giorgio's Sacramental life which intensifies very quickly—and providentially. Pier Giorgio's Baptism prepares him for Confession and Communion and his desire for frequent reception of the Sacraments is prompted by his heightened spiritual experience with the Jesuits at the Social Institute in Turin. Having failed Latin Pier Giorgio is removed from the public school by his parents and placed into the structure, discipline, and spirituality of Catholic education. His involvement in Eucharistic Associations and Marian Confraternities nourishes his spiritual life. His devotion to Saint Mary the Consoler and Our Lady of Oropa continues to grow.

Pier Giorgio's "studies" are examined in chapter 4 starting with his home tutoring under Rosina Busatto; his Latin tutor, the Salesian, Don Cojazzi, follows; then, soon after being admitted to secondary school studies at Massimo D'Azeglio, the unexpected enrollment at the Jesuit-run Social Institute; and finally, the Turin Polytechnic where Pier Giorgio pursues studies in Mining Engineering. Already as a child, Pier Giorgio manifests more interest in knowing about Jesus than Latin, as he makes clear to his Latin tutor.

With his sensitive disposition to Christian values, the Social Institute where Pier Giorgio studies under the Jesuits, especially under the influence of Father Pietro Lombardi, Pier Giorgio's spiritual life blossoms. A significant development during his time at the Social Institute is Pier Giorgio's contact with the poor and suffering through the Saint Vincent de Paul Conferences. Finally, as a member of the Federation of Italian Catholic Universities, Pier Giorgio manifests his Christian faith through his political choices.

In chapter 5 Pier Giorgio's culture is explored starting with his journey to Rome, for the first time Pier Giorgio travels outside the Italian Riviera and Alps. The other part of Italy Pier Giorgio writes about is Umbria, specifically Assisi and Perugia, and a brief account of Our Lady's Shrine in Loreto. His numerous trips to Germany, especially to the capital Berlin where his father is the Italian ambassador to Germany, provide Pier Giorgio the opportunity to visit other Central European cultural centers such as Prague, Innsbruck, and Vienna. In addition to his extensive travels, chapter 5 also presents Pier Giorgio's impressive literary culture with his particular passion for Dante Alighieri and the *Divina Comedia* which Pier Giorgio knows remarkably well. He also reads William Shakespeare's *Hamlet* and Wolfgang Goethe's *Faust*. Pier Giorgio's artistic culture which he acquires from his mother, reveals his sense of the beautiful extending to cathedral architecture. Finally, in his brief visit to Poland, he explores the mines of Upper Silesia connecting him to his area of study, mining engineering. The visit to Polish Katowice offers Pier Giorgio's first experience of a non-German speaking people.

Pier Giorgio's network of friends is presented in chapter 6. His friendships include not only those he developed over the years at school, such as Antonio Villani but friends with whom he was involved through Catholic student movements in Italy and Germany, as well as the newly formed *Pax Romana*. Through these contacts, the Austrian Maria Fischer, the German Willibald Leitgebel, represent friends connected to the international Catholic associations. With his intimate group, *Tipi Loschi*, "Shady Ones," Pier Giorgio shares his passion for mountain climbing. The statutes and structure of Tipi Loschi are explored in detail to show Pier Giorgio's creativity with his friends promoting a group who enjoyed the mountains united in prayer and faith. Letters to Tipi Loschi friends in this chapter include Ernestina Bonelli and Marco Beltramo. All of Pier Giorgio's friends, Italian and non-Italian, Tipi Loschi and non-Tipi Loschi are committed Catholics who help each other grow in sanctity.

In chapter 7 "Christian Society" represents the numerous elements that come together in Pier Giorgio's own lifetime as reflected in the six letters of the chapter. The letters extend over four years, from 1921–1924. Pier Giorgio is aware of the critical condition of migrants in Turin and vulnerable university students, issues which Pope Leo XIII addresses in his encyclical *Rerum Novarum*. Pier Giorgio experiences the effects of the Versailles Treaty on the Germans, especially with the devalued mark and the occupation of the Ruhr. Pier Giorgio becomes a victim of aggression of Italian nationalists as Italian Catholic Youth process in Rome. Tension between Italian nationalists and faithful Roman Catholics reflect the divided allegiances, creating further political instability. The conflict is even felt within the Federation of Italian Catholic Universities. At his home parish of *La Crocetta,* Pier Giorgio establishes *Milites Mariae* and becomes a member of Catholic Action. In the midst of this chaotic climate Pier Giorgio takes an anti-Fascist position, works to combat Communism through the Savonarola Club, while he remains staunchly Catholic. He supports a "militant Catholicism" expressed in the Popular Party of Italy, founded by a Sicilian priest, Luigi Sturzo. Pier Giorgio's politics follow Girolamo Savonarola—based on the gospel of Christ.

Chapter 8 considers the different spiritual influences in Pier Giorgio's young adulthood and how they shape his spiritual life. The Dominican expression of his life of faith is reflected in the numerous Dominican figures who inspire him, especially, Fra Girolamo, Saint Thomas Aquinas and Saint Catherine of Siena. This chapter examines, in particular, the process that leads to Pier Giorgio's admission into the Third Order Dominicans.

"Love" is the topic treated in chapter 9 and how Pier Giorgio manifests his love. Unlike chapter 6 which looks at close friendship, chapter 9 presents Christian love fundamentally as sacrifice. The different relationships presented in chapter 9 all share a sacrificial love: his mother, Laura Hidalgo, his sister, Luciana, and Marco Beltramo. In each of these bonds, there is sacrifice.

Pier Giorgio's correspondence concludes with chapter 10, his "eschatological vision." Crucial letters are referenced as his writings relevant to final judgment are explored: peace, hope, and faith. Love is reexamined in relation to his rich discourse on charity. The chapter ends with Pier Giorgio's death and final act of charity.

Letters/Translations

The bulk of the primary sources on Pier Giorgio have been written in Italian. I worked from the Italian original of Pier Giorgio's letters, Luciana Frassati's Italian edition, published by Vita e Pensiero, *Pier Giorgio Frassati: lettere (1906–1925)*. I also consulted and made reference to the St. Pauls English translation, *Pier Giorgio Frassati: Letters to His Family and Friends*. The English translation, however, does not contain all of Pier Giorgio's letters.

For each letter section under consideration, I have included, for reference purposes, both the English (St. Pauls) and the Italian (Vita and Pensiero) editions. For letters referred to within sections, I give only the English edition, unless the letter is available only in the Italian edition. I have also made references to the English translation of Luciana Frassati's *Man of Beatitude*. In my own translations of Pier Giorgio's writings, I have remained as close as possible to the Blessed's use of Italian.

The numerous testimonies in Luciana Frassati's works, as well as Don Antonio Cojazzi's earlier testimonies, and other writing on Pier Giorgio in Italian, are my own translations into English.

For biblical references, I have used The Catholic Edition of the Revised Standard Version (1965, 1966). Passages from the *Summa Theologiae* are the 1920 translation, second revised edition of the Fathers of the English Dominican Province.

1

Father and Mother

> Honor your father and your mother.
>
> EXODUS 20:12

Chapter 1 explores the background to Pier Giorgio's parents, Alfredo Frassati and Adelaide Ametis. The significance of the Italian sociopolitical context is also considered in relation to Alfredo Frassati's moral convictions as a humanist. Adelaide Ametis's personality, her artistic skills, as well as her stoic spirituality, are treated in this chapter. Alfredo and Adelaide both share the suffering of having lost a sibling. Finally, significant personality differences anticipate a difficult marriage. Pier Giorgio's earliest letters to his parents will reflect from childhood the nature of his relationship with his mother and father which can be best described in terms of love and obedience.

1. Letter to His Father—Pollone, 1906?[1]

One of Pier Giorgio's earliest letters was written with an uncertain date, 1906? The five-year-old Pier Giorgio wrote the letter to his father whom he addressed with the adjective *bello*, "wonderful," literally, "beautiful." He also used the affectionate form, *papalino*, the diminutive form of *papa* as a term of endearment, "daddy." Four principal thoughts were expressed in

---

1. Frassati, *Letters*, 1; Italian edition, *Lettere*, 3 (henceforth: *Lettere* / Ital. ed.). Question mark indicates the uncertainty of the date.

this letter: first, to tell his father that he loved him; second, that he would behave—he would no longer hit his sister; third, he wished his father a happy namesday; and fourth, he assured his father he would pray to Baby Jesus for him.[2] Pier Giorgio kissed his father farewell, signing his name in the diminutive, *Dodo*, a nickname Pier Giorgio gave to himself.[3] These four elements reflected Pier Giorgio's affectionate ties with his father which seemed natural for the five-year-old. Pier Giorgio's letter already expressed remarkable religious and moral sentiment. His sense of guilt, hitting his younger sister, is also underscored in this letter. Finally, Pier Giorgio reinforced his father's namesday salutation by offering to pray for him.

In his postscript, Pier Giorgio found other words to qualify his short letter; again, addressing his "wonderful *papalino*," making a "promise" not to lie. Luciana was included in his short message by sending his kisses and Luciana's to their father. The note served to strengthen Pier Giorgio's short letter, reassuring the affection, religious and moral message already contained in his writing. The five-year-old showed his attachment to his father, his bond with his sister, and both moral and religious expression in the few lines that he had written. From this early letter, insight into Pier Giorgio's relationship with his father was transmitted, beginning with his affectionate and conscientious disposition.

1.1. Father: Alfredo Frassati

Alfredo Frassati was born in Pollone surrounded by the hills of Biella in the northwestern Piedmont region of Italy. Born on September 18, 1868, Alfredo was the third son of Pietro Frassati, a doctor in medicine. Alfredo's mother, Giuseppina Coda-Conati, was born in Genoa.[4] In 1886, Alfredo pursued studies in the Faculty of Jurisprudence at the University of Turin.

1.1.1. Journalism Career

With an increasing interest in politics and social ideals, Alfredo's career shifted toward journalism. He began contributing to the Biellese paper, *L'Eco dell'Industria*. Barely in his twenties, he already had articles appearing in three papers, *Gazzetta Piemontese*, *Gazzetta Letteraria*, and *L'Eco*

---

2. I use "namesday" instead of "feastday" (throughout) for clarity.
3. Frassati, *Calendario*, "Pollone, August 18, 1902."
4. Frassati, *Un uomo*, 3.

dell'Industria.⁵ Alfredo eventually became the co-owner with three other partners of *L'Eco dell'Industria*, but he ultimately detached himself from *L'Eco*. In 1891, Alfredo founded the biweekly *La Tribuna Biellese*, which expressed his political convictions.

Alfredo Frassati's views in nineteenth-century Italy were present in his first issue of *La Tribuna*, where the journalist expressed the intention of his paper: "In political matters we shall follow truthful and frank social progress. Society progresses and we must hasten so as not to obstruct its glorious cycle. . . . Social problems will be the object of our studies, to bring forth the solution one of the highest ideals in our mind the holiest and most dutiful task of our work as a journal."⁶

Alfredo added to these thoughts in the first issue a specific social program, "We think and believe that relief needs to be brought to human misery, help to honest families, to good farmers, to hard workers."⁷ The concern clearly expressed in this first issue of *La Tribuna* related to the well-being of the workers which he associated with the prosperity of industry. Alfredo was not indifferent to the misery in the streets of Turin. The relief of the poor for Alfredo was connected to prosperous industry, and not in terms of the dignity of the individual. The value of human life was not for its intrinsic value, but rather, for its productivity. The distinction is a significant one because the first meaning, "intrinsic value" is ontological, who the person "is," as opposed to the second, "productivity," the economic, which refers to the person's capacity to produce.

In 1888, Alfredo had decided to take a one-semester course perfecting penal law at the University of Heidelberg in Germany, giving him the opportunity to learn the German language. During this time of studies in Heidelberg, Alfredo developed an "admiration" for the German people, a respect which remained with him for the rest of his life as a Germanophile.⁸ Returning to Germany in 1892, Alfredo registered at the University of Berlin taking courses in penal law, and in 1897 he became a lecturer in penal law in Turin.⁹ Alfredo also won a competition to teach penal law at the University of Sassari.¹⁰ Due to the problems of defending guilty individuals in serious cases Alfredo abandoned his career in teaching believing that to

---

5. For the development of *La Stampa*, see Luciana Frassati's comprehensive work, *Un uomo*, vol. 1, pt. 1; Frassati, *I gorini*, 14. Also, Casalegno, *Pier Giorgio Frassati*, 26.

6. Frassati, "La Tribuna Biellese," July 5, 1891, *Un uomo*, 8.

7. Frassati, *Un uomo*, 8.

8. Frassati, *Un uomo*, 10, 108. Alfredo already expressed these Germanophile views in a letter written from Bigen am Rhein, July 6, 1897.

9. Frassati, *Un uomo*, 22–23.

10. Frassati, *Un uomo*, 10, 23. See also, De Biasio, *Alfredo Frassati*, 14–15.

teach and the law profession were not meant for him; instead, he pursued a career in journalism.[11]

In 1895 with help from his father's patrimony, and Luigi Roux, Alfredo became the co-owner of *La Gazzetta Piemontese*, and with its new name, *La Stampa*, he became the newspaper's director. Alfredo's direction for *La Stampa* is made evident in his article October 4, 1896, "Neither masons nor clerics, this is our flag."[12] In 1902, Alfredo purchased the entire paper from Roux.[13] With his sense of honesty, duty, and work, Alfredo proved himself to be a person who had vision, who was committed to the truth, and the coherency between thought and action.[14] *La Stampa* gradually increased in circulation from 1903 to 1915 during the Giovanni Giolitti years.[15] These dates also correspond to the gradual ascent to power of Giovanni Giolitti during the same period, 1903–1914. *La Stampa* proved to be a great supporter of Giolitti's social programs.[16] By 1913, Alfredo Frassati was nominated the youngest senator to the Kingdom of Italy.

Alfredo's post-Enlightenment humanist values harmonized with fundamental Christian social teachings, just as Aristotle's virtues play in Christian ethics.[17] Alfredo's secular humanism, therefore, contained Christian elements, namely, the convictions of a just society, even if Alfredo's beliefs were not driven by the gospel.[18]

In 1890, in *La Gazzetta Piemontese* Alfredo announced in the newspaper, "Saturday Charity."[19] Columns of donations offered were indicated in the newspaper by anonymous donors; Alfredo continued with the Saturday Charity in *La Stampa*.[20] During the same period of *La Gazzetta*, Alfredo's biweekly paper, *La Tribuna Biellese*, conveyed similar fundamental social values which Alfredo continued to promote. Alfredo's liberal political and economic views intended to improve the working conditions of the laborers

11. Frassati, *Un uomo*, 8.

12. De Rosa, *Introduction*, xiv.

13. Frassati, *Un uomo*, 134–42. It should be noted that Alfredo's brother, Pietro Frassati, from 1901 to his death was the administrator of *La Stampa*. Pier Giorgio would witness his uncle's deathbed conversion in 1923. See also Frassati, *Un uomo*, 3n10.

14. Siccardi, *Pier Giorgio Frassati*, 39.

15. Frassati, *Un uomo*, part 1. It should be noted, however, that Alfredo Frassati's "neutralist" position in WWI reduced the circulation of *La Stampa*.

16. Frassati, *I giorni*, 15–16.

17. Enlightenment humanism is briefly discussed in the following sections.

18. For a clarification of secular Christianity, see Pinckaers, *Sources of Christian Ethics*, 306–15.

19. In Italian, *Carità del Sabato*.

20. Casalegno, *Pier Giorgio Frassati*, 51.

as well as those of the migrants. The influx of Italians gravitating toward the industrialized cities of Italy's northern triangle, Genoa-Turin-Milan, needed to be resolved. Housing and transportation were two fundamental issues. Alfredo's concerns were focused on the more vulnerable in society, the neglected or marginalized, by encouraging laborers and entrepreneurs to work together. Alfredo did not keep these preoccupations with social justice to himself; they inevitably became part of dinner conversations, justice and equality between men and women, and the concern for equal rights as well.[21]

Alfredo had been described as agnostic.[22] The agnostic does not deny God's existence, nor does the agnostic claim any certitude about God's existence. A humanist could even be an atheist since an atheist may still seek the betterment of the human condition; being tolerant, peace-loving, and just do not require any belief in God. Nevertheless, seeking the good of the other has its source in God: only God is the source of all that is Good, whether the person acknowledges God or not; as Saint Thomas Aquinas states, "Therefore it is most necessary that, for us to perform the act of charity, there should be in us some habitual form superadded to the natural power, inclining that power to the act of charity, and causing it to act with ease and pleasure."[23]

In a letter written to the Ametis family on All Souls' Day, Alfredo expressed his view on death, the immortality of the soul, and God. In November 1894, Alfredo's thoughts went to two deceased souls, one of the Ametis family, Emilia, who died of a heart-attack in her twenties, and another, his own sister Emma, who was killed by an assassin. Alfredo's words were remarkably reconciled with the will of God, "God gave her to you, God took her from you, blessed be the name of God."[24] Echoing the book of Job, these were not the words of an agnostic, but the words of man who was spiritual, moved not only by humanist principles, but also Catholic beliefs. His thoughts—and tears—even turned to the Oropa cemetery, the deceased buried by the Marian shrine not far from Pollone.

While Emilia died premature, Emma, Alfredo's sister, suffered a tragic death. Emma had already noticed criminal tendencies in her future husband,

---

21. Frassati, *Beatitudes*, 50. Luciana Frassati makes these statements with a tone of irony since she points out some of her father's inconsistencies with such statements. See *Beatitudes*, 49–50.

22. Frassati, *Beatitudes*,17; Frassati, *I giorni*, 23.

23. St. Thomas Aquinas, *Summa Theologiae*, book II, part II, question, 23, article 2, *respondeo* (henceforth: *ST*, IaIIae, q. 23, a. 2, *resp.*). For the distinctions between natural love and charity, see *ST*, IaIIae, q. 26, a. 4; IIaIIae, q. 23, aa. 1–2.

24. Letter, November 2, 1894, Frassati, *Un uomo*, 15; see Job 1:21.

and admitted their engagement was a fatal error, which Alfredo knew about in a letter his sister had written. Alfredo in turn attempted to dissuade his sister from the marriage, but Emma, not wanting to display *la brutta figura*, "bad image," was apprehensive to cancel the engagement set for June 20, 1889, "I would already send to the devil the marriage, Rizzetti, and men altogether. What do you think?"[25] Blinded by jealousy when she cancelled the wedding engagement, Luigi Rizzetti threw Emma out the window of her home. Rizzetti was sentenced to eight years in prison, declared "a born criminal," "psychologically unstable," and therefore, not morally responsible for his actions.[26] With a positivist interpretation of the crime, and with the subsequent sentence, human nature and the justice of God both made an impact on Alfredo. These elements suggest his concern for the vulnerable, perhaps even a sense of a providential God. A family relative, R. M. Pierazzi, asserts that Alfredo did not criticize religion, nor did he express any problems with Catholicism.[27] With his moral principles defended, Alfredo instilled similar humanist values into Pier Giorgio.[28]

1.2. Italian Society and Politics

Giovanni Giolitti, who governed Italy from 1903–1914, promoted a social progress scheme that Alfredo supported; hence, Alfredo's critical liberal paper, *La Stampa*, became a supporter of Giolittan politics. The aim was transformation; instead of defending big business interests to the detriment of the economic rights of the workers and farmers, the government would mediate, defending labor rights and social order.

Both political movements and the Catholic Church sought to address the matter, industrial interests and labor rights. The serious social problem in Italy came with industrialization that increased the difference between the working class and the entrepreneurial class. Between 1907 and 1909, fifty thousand people were added to the population of Turin.[29] In addition to the material and psychological challenges deriving from the Italian migration from the rural areas, urban problems of cohabitation, disease and violence created a social crisis. Starting in 1904, urbanization paid a high

---

25. Letter, February 6, 1889, Frassati, *Un uomo*, 13.
26. Letter, February 6, 1889, Frassati, *Un uomo*, 13.
27. Pierazzi, *Così ho visto*, 33.
28. Siccardi maintains that Alfredo Frassati was someone "seeking," *in ricerca*. Siccardi, *Pier Giorgio Frassati*, 36.
29. Siccardi, *Pier Giorgio Frassati*, 49.

social cost exacerbated by the five thousand to six thousand migrants per year arriving in Turin from different parts of Italy.[30]

In 1891, Pope Leo XIII issued the encyclical *Rerum Novarum*, and a year later in Genoa the Italian Socialist Party was created.[31] Giovanni Giolitti's government was to find a solution to the working masses by instituting a series of measures in the defense of the working sector. In spite of Giolitti's policies, a prevailing problem existed in both the rural regions and the industrialized cities.

In 1898, Giovanni Agnelli, the founder of FIAT, had realized, "We are just at the beginning of a great movement of capital, of people, of work. I may be mistaken, but the automobile will be a sign of the beginning of a fundamental social renewal."[32] In 1906, the date of Pier Giorgio's letter to this father, Alfredo wrote in *La Stampa*, "Never was there in our city a more happy moment for the development of the public economy, for the remarkable flow of business, for the great creative work of its industry. Today, there is a lot of work in Turin, a lot is produced, a lot is earned. It is absolutely necessary that the city is capable of favoring such a rising movement. Work is in need of always improving moral and material conditions. There are questions on the table that urgently demand solutions: lighting, schools, operation of the railways."[33]

Alfredo's academic and professional career from law to journalism reveal the profound integrity of his character. While Alfredo may have pursued a career in law, given his academic competence and preparation, he recognized that social change in Italy was not only needed, but would come about through the press, as he made clear in *La Tribuna Biellese*. Alfredo's political convictions emphasized the freedom to offer a critical assessment of political events in the name of justice and truth, especially if change were to come about in Italian society. The depth of these beliefs were reflected in his career change, to promote political transformation in the name of social justice and welfare which Alfredo believed could be achieved through journalism.

1.2.1. Enlightenment Shift

When Renaissance humanism emerged in the Christian culture of Europe in the fifteenth and sixteenth centuries, the individual continued to

---

30. Castronovo, *Il Piemonte*, 250.
31. *Rerum Novarum* is discussed in further detail in chapter 7.
32. Castronovo, *Piemonte*, 192.
33. Castronovo, *La Stampa*, Year XL, January 27, 1906, *Piemonte*, 164–65.

believe and collaborate with a Creator God.³⁴ Instead, the Enlightenment project replaced God with man, divine law with human logic. If the Renaissance represented a cosmic shift from God to the human being, the Enlightenment was fixated on, and finally absolutized the individual. Earlier religious fragmentation was triggered by the Reformation: Martin Luther (1483–1546) placed individual conscience above papal authority; René Descartes (1596–1659) subordinated truth to the private world of a thinking being; and, David Hume (1711–1776), through doubt and skepticism, led the intellect down the path to a world without God.³⁵ In stages, religious disintegration, anticlericalism and positivism opened the Enlightenment to aggressive secularization.³⁶ Northern Italy experienced Swiss hostility toward Catholicism stemming from John Calvin (1509–1564) and the Calvinist stronghold Geneva which lay north of Turin. French aggressive secularization penetrated Italy on the northwest border through the Piedmont region.³⁷ Turin was especially hit in the practices of the traditional faith, while agnosticism grew.

Building a just society reflects Christian principles traceable to the social teachings of Jesus (Matt 25:35–40). In the same passage Jesus teaches that final judgment is contingent upon works of charity. These works cannot, however, be separated from faith in Christ, the Saviour of humanity (John 3:16). The difference between secular humanism and Christianity is that the former defines what is true and good, while in Christianity, good works are recognized to have their source in God and performed because of one's collaboration with divine grace.³⁸

The Catholic Church in Turin became the source of great saints precisely because individuals energetically and generously responded to

---

34. Among sixteenth-century humanists one finds the works of saints, such as St. Thomas More (1478–1535); those whose writings were suspect, such as Erasmus of Rotterdam (1466–1536) and Gasparo Contarini (1483–1542); then, among the sixteenth-century humanists (late fifteenth century) one also finds condemned writings, such as the Dominican preacher Girolamo Savonarola (1452–1498). These Roman Catholic Renaissance humanists all shared a deep spiritual life. For details on Renaissance humanism, see D'Onofrio, "Renaissance," chs. 3, 6, and 7. Savonarola will be taken up in chapter 8.

35. Jacques Maritain considers the "three reformers" to be Martin Luther, René Descartes, and the third contender Jean-Jacques Rousseau. See *Trois Réformateurs*, 1925. For a detailed discussion on secularization see Taylor, *Secular Age*, 2007. Don John Bosco and the Salesian teaching mission was precisely to bring forth truth and clarity starting with the young minds. See chapter 4 below.

36. See Taylor, *Secular Age*, esp. chs., 2, 6, 11 and 12.

37. Castronovo, *Piemonte*, 270–71.

38. For a treatment on the subject of "grace," see Aquinas, *ST*, Ia–IIae, q. 111. On "operating" and "cooperating" grace, a. 2, *resp*.

combat anticlerical and secular influences. At the spiritual level, in spiritual works of mercy as in teaching and catechesis, and at the social level, corporal works in hospitals and orphanages. John Bosco's congregation, the Salesians, took their name after the great Swiss Counter-Reformer Francis de Sales (1567–1622), Bishop of Geneva, reaffirming the Catholic faith of Turin. Saint Dominic Savio (one of Saint John Bosco's students) followed in his teacher's spirituality. Saint Maria Mazzarello, foundress of the Salesian Sisters, spread a congregation for religious sisters. Saint John Benedict Cottolengo founded a house for the poor and suffering. The founder of the Consolata Fathers, Blessed Joseph Allamano, focused on evangelizing mission lands.[39] Pier Giorgio was connected directly or indirectly to all these congregations and their churches.

2. Letter to His Mother—Pollone, November 7, 1907[40]

Pier Giorgio's letter was written in 1907 from Pollone, the family's summer home, forty-four miles from their residence in Turin. Pier Giorgio was six years old. His letter expressed his affection for his mother, *ti voglio molto bene*, "I love you so much." The six-year-old asked his mother whether she was enjoying herself in Venice. He expressed an interest in what the others were doing and was not only focused on his own sentiments. Pier Giorgio also had his sibling relationship on his mind. The two kisses he sent included his and his sister's, conveying the bond between Pier Giorgio and Luciana. Pier Giorgio did not only express an interest in his mother, but also his aunt, zia Elena, Pier Giorgio's maternal aunt with whom his mother had traveled to Venice. His thoughts also reached out to other members of the family.

In his letter he provided details of his daily activities, creating a sense of Pier Giorgio sharing what he was doing with others. This detailed "update" became a characteristic in his letters as early as six years old. He wanted his mother to know about his visit to the Burcina Park. Furthermore, the work he produced with the help of the domestic workers was sent to his mother so she would know that Pier Giorgio was thinking about her and appreciate his activities at home. Pier Giorgio did not just say he had done "this" work, but he added, "with the help of the Sisters," so as to be entirely truthful about his accomplishment.

He and Luciana would be doing a dictation as they had told their father in a postcard. Pier Giorgio also suggested in his letter they were not ignoring their studies, working conscientiously, while their mother was away

39. Castronovo, *Piemonte*, 272.
40. *Letters*, 1–2; Ital. ed., 3.

in Venice, and their father in Turin. The letter expressed Pier Giorgio's sense of moral responsibility as he kept his parents informed of their studies. A sense of reassurance was further transmitted, letting his mother know they were all fine, so, she had nothing to worry about. In fact, his letter created a comforting tone so his mother could enjoy her stay in Venice, and not have to worry about the family.

Pier Giorgio did not forget to include their cat, and their dog, Jor, when he mentioned that everybody was "fine." The household for Pier Giorgio included their pets, which revealed not only Pier Giorgio's love for animals but his sensitivity to nature, all of God's creation. When Pier Giorgio ended his letter, he sent greetings from "everyone" in Pollone and not just his own greetings.

Reading the letter of this six-year-old, certain personality traits begin to surface: his desire and capacity to express his love, in this instance in reference to his mother; his conscience by reassuring his mother he would be "good" with his sister; sensitivity expressed by including his sister's kisses; his value for the extended family, in this case his zia Elena; his desire to share, sending his "little work"; his sense of responsibility doing the "dictation" by informing his mother; and his love for animals, including his pets when he spoke of "everyone." These thoughts reflected Pier Giorgio's sense of "other": mother, sister, zia, Sisters, domestic workers, and animals.

2.1. Mother: Adelaide Ametis

Adelaide was the daughter of Francesco Ametis, a pharmacist. After combatting in the Crimean War, Francesco went to South America like many Italian adventurers of the nineteenth century hoping to find prosperity, which Francesco did in Peru.[41] Upon returning to Italy, he married the Genovese Linda Copello who bore three daughters, Elena, Emilia and Adelaide.[42] Francesco had a villa constructed when he moved to Pollone in 1875, and planted a sequoia he brought from overseas in front of his home.[43]

Adelaide remained attached to her older sister, Elena, throughout her life. She was an aspiring artist since her youth. According to the

---

41. Pierazzi, *Così ho visto*, 13. Francesco Ametis had the reputation of being generous and loved man.

42. Casalegno, *Pier Giorgio Frassati*, 26. Emilia died of a heart attack at twenty-four years old.

43. The sequoia Francesco Ametis planted stands to the southwest of the main entrance of the Frassati-Ametis residence in Pollone. Adelaide's bedroom has been transformed into a private chapel for pilgrims who wish to pray to Blessed Pier Giorgio, and from where the sequoia tree remains visible.

graphological study of Adelaide in the *Positio*, the following characteristics were identified,

> Gifted in the sense of proportion of color and in general many qualities of color, she possesses an artistic sensibility that imposes. Vibrant, need to live in a hurry and she becomes agitated if the life around her does not move and her day is not filled. Only a few words are needed to get to the bottom of the question; no frills; no circumlocution; decisively a modern woman, almost anticipating her time for absolute freedom of her ideas . . . Before illness and ill people she has the capacity to withdraw herself completely from her feminine nature . . . Cold in her reactions, so, she is capable of never losing her head, one could say, to see, more accurately than any other . . . Presumptuous, does not hesitate to be up-to-date on everything, more than anyone else. She feels deeply intellectual and before her interlocutor even has opened his mouth, she has already judged him, whether she is correct or not, that does not matter. Classical heroine, she remains in certain things rather cerebral; even for this reason, one might say, that she would go looking for challenges to be overcome.[44]

The graphological interpretation of Adelaide's handwriting can serve to shed light not only on her relationship with her husband, but more significantly, her relationship with Pier Giorgio. Subsequent letters will show the emotional relationship that existed between mother and son. At times, this relationship may have appeared rather asymmetrical; that is to say, Pier Giorgio, unlike his mother, never held back his affection.

2.1.1. Painting

Adelaide, drawn to painting since her childhood, dreamed of becoming a true artist. In her adult years she was taught by Alberto Falchetti, though Alberto may not have reached the reputation of his father, Giuseppe Falchetti.[45] Adelaide addressed her mentor as "Bertie." The close relationship between the two artists reflecting their artistic sensibilities had an impact on Pier Giorgio who sites Falchetti in his letters on numerous occasions when writing to his mother. Adelaide also led her son to a refined sense of beauty.

Pier Giorgio's letter made reference to "Venice," asking his mother whether she was enjoying her time there. Having learned at an early age

44. *Positio*, 45–46.
45. Frassati, *Un uomo*, 29.

the value of art, acquiring sensitivity to colors and texture, Pier Giorgio observed his mother paint, admired her works, and the seriousness of the artwork with her visits to Venice for the Biennale.[46] Art for Pier Giorgio was not only to be appreciated in the art gallery, but art was experienced in his own home, in the colors brushed by his mother, canvas after canvas. Between mother and son, aesthetics became a point of connection.

2.1.2. Prenuptial Exchange between Adelaide and Alfredo

Adelaide got to know Alfredo in the summers when Alfredo visited his relatives in Cossila.[47] Adelaide's relationship with Alfredo, and her sister's relationship with him, were expressed in a letter dated February 17, 1895. The letter offers further insight into Alfredo's personality, and the kind of lifetime relationship into which he and Adelaide were about to enter,

> On this day I ask you and Elena to always, always, but always be good and sincere friends to me. I need your affection. I am in need of your affection. Am I possibly too self-centered to take it? Life is so empty, so stupid, and so false, that it would not be worth living if there were not the ideal of friendship that sustains on the rugged journey. Will you promise me then, and will you also have Elena promise this, that we will remain always, but always friends whatever the world reserves for us in the future? From you, Elena I desire only one thing: do not judge me badly, even when the world, logic, reason, should all be against me.[48]

Alfredo's letter made a passionate appeal to Adelaide in the name of "friendship": this would help them through the times when their journey was difficult. But this desire for what was ultimately fidelity in friendship, besides giving the "foolishness of life" true meaning, suggested the human bond of love was truly more significant than anything else. Adelaide was invited to make a commitment—not only her, but her sister, also. Alfredo's letter had further implications: how the value of friendship that Alfredo so clearly emphasized as an over-arching value in human relationships would ultimately be transmitted to their son, Pier Giorgio.

---

46. The first Biennale di Venezia was held in 1895, only three years before Alfredo and Adelaide married.

47. Frassati, *I giorni*, 13.

48. *Positio*, 44–45.

2.1.3. Marriage

On September 5, 1898, the Biellese cousins, Alfredo Frassati and Adelaide Ametis, married in Pollone and a few days later moved into the Ametis villa Francesco had built.[49] Even before they married, however, differences manifested themselves between Alfredo and Adelaide, as expressed in a letter Alfredo had written to Adelaide two years before their marriage, "We have characters that are too similar to avoid these storms: I would need a good friend, who would be able to forgive me and my bad moods, my harsh words, who would give me back peace, not to increase the sadness and the causes of worry. And you would need a sweet friend, who could quickly forgive you. It is not without an infinite sense of sadness, what I say (in fact, repeat) these impressions of mine; but you will see that it will all be useless. Nevertheless, characters do not change nor will they ever change."[50]

The letter Adelaide received from Alfredo did not suggest they were about to enter a marriage with false hopes or expectations—that either might change their characters. Adelaide was being asked to accept him, as he accepted her, a mutual acceptance for who they were, and instead of change, to be willing to love and forgive. The existing tension between the two before marriage, Adelaide anticipated that it would not only repeat, but even get worse. Alfredo did not even suggest that things would change or improve after their marriage, perhaps reflecting an undeniable realism.

Adelaide's future spouse gave insight into their relationship before marriage, their personality differences, and what they might expect when they married, indicative of the relational dynamics existing between Pier Giorgio's parents. These dynamics Pier Giorgio would not only grow up with, but would also effect the relationship with his parents, especially his mother, and the difficult decisions confronting him.

2.1.4. Moral Values

When Adelaide remembered she was pregnant she realized she needed to slow down as she walked; she had even been tempted to slide down the hand railing in her home as she had been accustomed. Alone in Pollone she wrote to her husband in Turin working at *La Gazzetta Piemontese*, conveying a sense of her youthfulness and vitality, she expressed why she hoped to have a girl, "I would feel capable to educate her, to be good and honest.... With a

---

49. Biella is a provincial city, fifty-nine miles from Turin, in the Piedmont region. Pollone is administered from Biella.

50. Letter of Alfredo Frassati to Adelaide Ametis, April 23, 1896. *Positio*, 45.

boy I would be truly scared but although you would always be there to help me, what could you tell him one day to resist his passions, you who have no religion?"[51]

The letter revealed Adelaide's strong sense of moral rectitude: her primary preference of a girl over a boy focused on transmitting moral values, "good and honest." She believed this would be easier for her with a daughter, whereas a boy, it would be the responsibility of her husband, but then, with the absence of religious convictions, how would their boy learn to be "good and honest." This extraordinary letter conveys fundamental values of this mother-to-be in her twenties: first, the moral education of her children; then, the other significant feature surfaces: religious values. The letter anticipated that Adelaide would be the moral educator of her children, whether daughter or son.

Now pregnant she recognized her lifestyle had significantly changed as this lively woman was now refrained from the movements to which she had been once accustomed. One can identify in Adelaide's letter her views: there could be no true moral education without religion. Whether this view reflected her own education, or whether this manifested her own intuition, she was correct in associating religion with moral values. God is the source of all that is true, "good and honest": moral education has first, a religious end, God; and then, a human end, the human being. Adelaide's concern for their child's moral education revealed the fundamental difference between Adelaide and her husband, and it would also reflect the difference between Pier Giorgio and his father: religion as part of moral formation.

2.2. Pier Giorgio's Birth and Baptism

On June 3, 1899, Adelaide and Alfredo gave birth to their first child whom they named, "Elda." But eight months later, their first baby died. Soon after, Adelaide was pregnant once again, writing to her husband, "The other night, waking up, I thought so much about her; but when I feel truly desperate it seems as if the little one inside me knows and moves and is agitated until I am forced to think also about him."[52]

On April 6, Holy Saturday of 1901, the baby boy was born in Turin, at Via Legnano, N. 33. Born "third degree" asphyxiated the baby was immediately administered conditional baptism by the parish priest, Monsignor Alessandro Roccati of the local parish, *La Crocetta*.[53] Their baby boy

---

51. Frassati, *Un uomo*, 27; Frassati, *I giorni*, 53.
52. Frassati, *Calendario*, "Turin, April, 1901, Adelaide to her husband."
53. Frassati, *Calendario*, "Turin, April 6, 1901."

was baptized Pier Giorgio Michelangelo Frassati. The name "Pier Giorgio" was the result of a compromise of his parents: Adelaide accepted that baby boy be named after Alfredo's father, "Pietro," with the condition that to this name, another name outside the family would be joined, and so, "Giorgio."[54]

Five months later, the rite of baptism was celebrated on September 5, 1901, in Pollone, as registered in the baptismal certificate at the Church of Saints Fabiano and Sebastiano with Pier Giorgio's grandparents as his godparents, Francesco Ametis and Giuseppina Frassati.[55] His parents chose their anniversary date for the baptism day in Pollone. At Pier Giorgio's birth, a cousin on the mother's side, R. M. Pierazzi, found that the best exclamation to be made was, "He's like a fly in milk." The expression referred to the milk, "white and pure crib" and the "black" referred to Pier Giorgio's black hair.[56]

3. Letter to His Mother—at Home, December 19, 1909[57]

The language used in this letter reflects the eight-year-old Pier Giorgio's feelings in relation to his mother's illness: *mio cuore è addolorato*, "my heart is sorrowful."[58] An emotionally charged expression Pier Giorgio would have already heard in relation to suffering or misfortune or some other misery.

The letter underscored Pier Giorgio's empathy, already at eight years old, in this case, directed toward his mother in writing. Words of deep emotions reflected Pier Giorgio's state due to his mother's illness, weighing on him as if he were the one ill. Pier Giorgio used the verb "see" which is enough to have an impact on him: the visual sight of suffering caused him to suffer. Pier Giorgio's response conveyed the desire to reach out to the suffering that Pier Giorgio witnessed around him, whether in terms of sickness at home, or the misery in the streets of Turin. In this letter emerged the remarkable sensitivity of an eight-year-old.

Pier Giorgio continued as if reacting to his mother's illness was insufficient; somehow, he needed to offer more than the comments of his sorrowful heart. "Get well good and dear mama," meant that there was hope.

---

54. Caslalengo, *Pier Giorgio Frassati*, 30. Also, *San Giorgio*, "St. George" combats the dragon—Satan.

55. Frassati, *Calendario*, "Pollone, September 5, 1901."

56. Pierazzi, *Pier Giorgio Frassati*, 7; *Positio*, 47.

57. *Letters*, 6; Ital. ed., 6–7.

58. The English "very heavy" does not capture the emotional intensity of *addolorato*, a participial adjective commonly associated with the suffering of the Virgin Mary, *La Madonna Addolorata*, "Our Lady of Sorrow."

Getting well anticipated an improvement for her condition, and so, Pier Giorgio was hopeful and offered his mother words of hope that she was to get well. His words do not end with suffering but with hope.

Being his mother's namesday the following day, December 20, when the family celebrated Saint Adelaide, Pier Giorgio was already reflecting on the previous year, and with his mother ill in bed, he could not imagine the happiness of the previous year's celebration. The letter reflects the surprising reminiscence of a young boy who longed for the joy of the previous year. His looking back, Pier Giorgio's memory of past events, suggestive of his nostalgia, would have a powerful effect throughout his life, a characteristic of Pier Giorgio's letters. Through memory, Pier Giorgio would discover the value of prayer and make sense of his spiritual life.

The namesday meant to be celebrated showed the value of religious traditions observed in the Frassati home which by extension influenced Pier Giorgio's spiritual life because he took the religious traditions seriously. The family observance of namesdays and their related patron saints was something more than a ritual observance. For Pier Giorgio to seek intercessory prayer for his loved ones resulted not only praying to the patron saint, but also thanking God for the individual carrying the saint's name.

3.1. Empathy

Pier Giorgio made his feelings clear, "your namesday will not be happy as it was last year because you are suffering in bed." His emotional state was effected by his mother's health. The connection between the two, mother and son, illness and unhappiness, respectively, expressed in these few lines, became indicative of Pier Giorgio's personality as he matured: as long as misery existed around him, Pier Giorgio could not be truly happy. He would have to reconcile, somehow, misery and his own sensitivity, as his conscience continued to sharpen. While the eight-year-old felt limited in terms of what he could do for his mother, he conveyed his thoughts, feelings, and hope; "my heart will be happy when you get well." Pier Giorgio reiterated sadness and happiness, his mother's condition, impacted his own state. He reminded his mother that he was waiting for her to get better, "I wish you a speedy recovery," and with such words Pier Giorgio repeated the sequence of suffering with the hope of looking ahead to recovery. Pier Giorgio profoundly expressed that he shared in his mother's suffering: he was united with her.

While the letter seemed to define Pier Giorgio's relationship with his mother, the letter in fact revealed far more. Pier Giorgio's words expressed his intense empathy toward individuals around him who suffer. He responded to illness by expressing how it affected him. His reaction to his mother's illness compelled Pier Giorgio to do something, to write, and let his mother know how he felt: his experiences were somehow identified and acknowledged, but then, Pier Giorgio needed to act.

3.2. Prayer

When an eight-year-old boy said that he would "pray to God," did he understand what was being said? Or was he repeating something that he heard at home? Through prayer one is united with God; a child learns first at home. Pier Giorgio was baptized into the Catholic faith and his parents and godparents assumed the responsibility of "teaching" their child Catholic values and principles. The first religious act is prayer since this is the greatest act a human being can perform; what makes humans "human" is the capacity to kneel and pray before God. With his receptivity, whether he watched family members pray, heard them pray, he would have recognized the value of prayer by his own inquisitive nature. Typical of children asking questions, in his home in Turin, and vacation residence in Pollone, in the presence of parents, but also grandparents, aunt, and numerous domestic workers, including Sisters, certainly Pier Giorgio would have learned at an early age about prayer.

The testimonies of Pier Giorgio's prayer, already as a child, were observed by the domestic workers and in this instance, the housekeeper, Clara Baumgarten, "I knew Pier Giorgio Frassati from the time he was a little boy, from the age of seven to nine years. I remember clearly his surprising piety. I must confess, I remained confused the first time when I observed him in Church, at evening prayer. A visit to Our Lady of Oropa showed me again the depth of his piety."[59] Clara Baumgarten would have known Pier Giorgio at the time he wrote the letter of December 19, 1909, when he was eight years old. Clearly, besides his prayerfulness were his pious expressions of faith that Baumgarten observed, not only at church, but already the Marian piety Pier Giorgio developed for Our Lady of Oropa.

3.3. Action

Pier Giorgio continued his letter to his mother, "he will make you better," in reference to God as the healing agent: the use of the verb, "make," to heal

---

59. Frassati, *La fede*, "Testimony of Clara Baumgarten," 214.

his mother conveyed a God of action; God would intervene in his mother's life and restore her health.[60] Pier Giorgio informed his mother the intention of his prayer, and he knew God would "act." The faith in divine intervention already reflected Pier Giorgio's spiritual life: Pier Giorgio's prayers and God's action.

An incident occurred in Pier Giorgio's childhood requiring an immediate response. Luciana Frassati relates the incident, "They knocked on the door of our home.[61] It's summer; it's hot. Pier Giorgio runs to open it and he finds himself in front of a poor lady who asks for something. Our mother is out, the house personnel cannot make decisions on these matters, and Pier Giorgio, besides being a child, does not have a cent in his pockets. A moment of indecision, then, the solution is quickly, suddenly and marvelously found in his mind: he quickly takes off his shoes and socks and gives them to the poor lady for her children."[62] For Pier Giorgio action was not only present at this early age to respond to the needs of others, but action became a hallmark of his personality which went hand-in-hand with prayer and faith. Recognizing and responding to the urgency of the poor mother, Pier Giorgio acted. Could he already have been taught this in his home? Or was he already familiar with Saint James's Epistle, "What does it profit my brethren, if a man says he has faith but has not works? Can his faith save him . . . ? So faith by itself, if it has no works, is dead."[63] Or perhaps it was simply Pier Giorgio's intuition in this unexpected situation? The answer: God's grace was a work in Pier Giorgio's life, and Pier Giorgio showed constancy in his receptivity to divine grace.

This sensitivity responding to the needs of others was clearly present in his childhood; Pier Giorgio recognized love as Christian responsibility: helping others. On another occasion visiting a nursery school with his grandfather, Francesco Ametis, the children were at their tables eating their lunch. Pier Giorgio noticed one of the children sitting alone, isolated, due to an infectious skin disease. The disease, "somewhat repugnant," did not inhibit Pier Giorgio in any way, nor what the other children might have thought. Instead, he naturally walked toward the little boy, sat beside him, keeping him company, taking the spoon, "one for himself and one for the boy," sharing lunch with him. Sister Celeste Cavagna, worried about the

60. It should be noted that the Italian *faccia* is the subjunctive form of "make" used in the present (third person singular) to convey the request/hope of a future act.

61. The family moved three times, first from their home on via Legnano, N. 33, to corso Galileo Ferraris, N. 55 (previously corso Siccardi), then to corso Galileo Ferraris, N. 70. Their home on Galileo Ferraris, N. 70 still stands.

62. Frassati, *La carità*, 23.

63. Jas 2:14, 17.

infection being transmitted, was unable to distance Pier Giorgio from the little boy; Pier Giorgio seemed to almost want to embrace him.[64] He had a refined conscience, allowing himself to grow in conformity to truth and love.

3.4. Trust

Pier Giorgio completed his thoughts in his letter telling his mother with remarkable trust, "and God will hear my prayers." For Pier Giorgio God was not abstract, or "someone out there" or a name that he heard. Already, he expressed that God was a relational Being by the fact that he could turn to God in prayer. Moreover, and fundamental to the Judeo-Christian tradition was that God intervened in the life of the individual.[65] Finally, "he will make you better," reflected the little boy's complete trust in God. The three parts to this penultimate sentence of his letter can also be divided into the three theological virtues: faith (I will pray to God), charity (that he will make you better), and hope (God will hear my prayers).

The first two statements in this sentence, "I will pray to God so that he will make you better," are joined as an act of faith and love, a cause-effect that one anticipated from praying to God, but a significant point was that Pier Giorgio added the unexpected qualifying sentence, "and he will hear my prayers." The hope was expressed with certitude, "God will hear." This third part of the sentence revealed Pier Giorgio's spontaneous trust as an eight-year-old, anticipating Pier Giorgio's complete trust in God that would shape his spiritual life as an adolescent and adult.

Trust in oneself, trust in others, trust in God, develops from one's experience; positive or negative experiences have an effect on one's willingness to trust. The first experience that one has of trust relates to parents, their presence, their love and affection, their words of comfort, encouragement and joy. One would expect the converse effect in the case of parents who are absent, who show no or little love and affection, whose words are hurtful, critical, and discouraging. Pier Giorgio was described as having his own weaknesses as a child, "irritability" as well as "mischief," with little interest in being orderly, showing that virtue in Pier Giorgio was not something innate.[66] With God's grace, one grows in virtue, perfecting sanctity, by seeking

---

64. Frassati, *La carità*, "Testimony of Suor Celeste Cavagna," 134.

65. The liberation from slavery (Exod 14), and the fulfillment of the messianic promise in the incarnation (John 1).

66. Cojazzi, *Testimonianze*, 24.

to collaborate with God. For Pier Giorgio to trust God hearing his prayers began with God's grace, but Pier Giorgio also learned trust from his parents.

Pier Giorgio's letter of November 7, 1907, indicated that his mother had traveled to Venice for the 1907 Biennale. Although not expressed in the letter, the six-year-old Pier Giorgio would have felt his mother's absence and the question, "Are you having a good time in Venice?" conveyed his implicit desire to be with his mother. Pier Giorgio communicated feeling his mother's absence in this childhood experience of distance. Later letters would reflect the length and frequency of Pier Giorgio's absence from his mother, or his mother's absences, which were difficult for him.

The experience of trust is not just whether a parent is present or not, since presence does not always mean attentiveness. Whether Pier Giorgio's parents were present or absent, it was certain that both his mother and father took an active interest in Pier Giorgio's and Luciana's lives, if not directly themselves, through their domestic workers. This interest was followed by instilling a sense of accountability in the children, with what had been done, or not done, especially in terms of studies, and how they had used their time. This sense of duty did not exclude helping in the garden and other similar responsibilities.

At eight years old, Pier Giorgio's mother was actively present in his life, as Adelaide Frassati described a mountain trip with Pier Giorgio when he was still a young boy, a ten hour climb of Mount San Teodulo (10,900 ft.) and the Schwarzsee on Zermatt. Making these excursions with his mother, Pier Giorgio had no special training.[67] In Adelaide Frassati's memoirs, the relationship between mother and son, the stoic values she instilled in Pier Giorgio, emerge. But Adelaide's memoirs also reveal the influence of a mother who painted, her refined sensitivity toward nature transmitted to her son, "We climbed up the White Summits when the first light of dawn emerged. Everything, as almost always at that antelucan time, constant and still, without a shadow, without obstruction. In an enclosure on the right of a little valley, we noticed motionless sheep, asleep, lying like dogs with their mouths hidden under their legs, one next to the other, to shelter themselves from the cold of the night. . . . The crossing from the Teodulo with Pier Giorgio close to me by cord was rather tranquil. . . . We stopped for two days at the Schwarzsee. At the table all were interested in the beautiful little alpinist."[68]

---

67. Frassati, *Calendario*, "Fiery d'Ayas, September, 1909."
68. Frassati, *I giorni*, 29–30.

From Pier Giorgio's mother he had acquired the virtue of courage, learning from his mother not to surrender and also to overcome weakness.[69] Adelaide's detailed description unveiled a person who was receptive to people, to nature, and to events, descriptions found precisely in Pier Giorgio's own letters. With his mother present, Pier Giorgio developed a sense of trust. His confidence is echoed in the Gospel of Saint Matthew, "For every one who asks receives, and he who seeks, finds, and to him who knocks it will be opened. Or what man of you, if his son asks him for bread, will give him a stone? Or if he asks for a fish, will give him a serpent? If you then, who are evil, know how to give good gifts to your children, how much more will your Father who is in heaven give good things to those who ask him!"[70]

Adelaide Frassati's memoir provides not only the description of an artist, but also reveals Pier Giorgio at an early age, attached to his mother by a cord, as they climbed the mountain. From her he received a sense of trust, building his courage, overcoming fear and weakness.

A mountain excursion when Pier Giorgio was ten years old reflected similar stoic values: perseverance, resisting cold, and dealing with fatigue. In September 1911 he successfully climbed, for his age, the crossing of Bettaforca, in the Furggen and the ascent of Castore (13,865 ft.) in the Monte Rosa mountain range, as his mother recalled the event, "The boy, tied to a cord, was often dragged with the wide and swift steps of the men. He got mad a little because they did not leave him to 'jump well over the crevasses.'"[71]

Pier Giorgio experienced trust; his home was secure even if relations at times might have been difficult. He knew his parents loved him; they were involved in Pier Giorgio's life even if they felt distant at times. Pier Giorgio could only have developed trust, central to biblical teachings, through the relationship he experienced with his parents, and even if Pier Giorgio's religious instruction at home was shallow.[72] Moreover the instruction he and Luciana received from priests at this stage was "superficial." In the case of their Latin instructor, a Salesian priest from Venice, Don Antonio Cojazzi, Pier Giorgio even had to insist that he talk to him about the life of Jesus.[73] If parents in all their shortcomings are capable of seeking the good of their children, how much more God, the Father, answered prayers—the best for the individual. At eight years old Pier Giorgio expressed this trust in God.

---

69. Frassati, *I giorni*, 29–30.
70. Matt 7:8–11.
71. Siccardi, *Pier Giorgio Frassati*, 81.
72. Frassati, *Beatitudes*, 17.
73. Frassati, *Beatitudes*, 19.

Pier Giorgio's closing phrases in his letter would be consistent throughout his life, writing to his family members and friends to whom he sent kisses and best wishes. Closing this letter to his mother he repeated "very loving," *affettuosissimo*, and included his kisses.[74]

4. Letter to His Mother—Pollone, September 25, 1913[75]

The letter written when Pier Giorgio was twelve years old contains three characteristics of his letters: first, the very deep relationship of love he maintained for his mother; second, his preoccupation with school; and third, the structure of his letters. In terms of structure, Pier Giorgio's letters show with remarkable consistency three parts: preface: his gratitude or his apology; body: studies, social/political issues with an explicit or implicit spiritual purpose; and, farewell: typically with kisses, and always remembering to send his best wishes to family and friends, often on the behalf of others.

Sometime between September 20 and September 24 of 1913, Pier Giorgio received a letter from his mother, and he informed her in his reply he could not write sooner. Given that less than four days had passed, Pier Giorgio's letters show concern about his correspondence, not only replying immediately to his letters, especially when this letter came from his mother, but also offering an explanation for any kind of delay. Pier Giorgio conveyed this sense of duty by replying promptly to his letters.

On the day he wrote, his "half-hour free in the morning" meant Pier Giorgio used his free time to write. At home in Pollone, Pier Giorgio had a compact schedule with his studies, following the schedule plan arranged with his teachers, in preparation for his exams to be admitted to secondary school.[76] Already, a sense of discipline had been installed in relation to his studies which his family took seriously, and for which Pier Giorgio was accountable; even if his mother and father were away, they expected to know how he used his time and what he was studying.

Pier Giorgio informed his mother of his math exam and that he would be promoted, so he included events in his letter that he knew would please her. Pier Giorgio was delighted to make his mother happy. His exams were not finished, and he still had Geometry and Italian exams. The letter clearly provided his mother with an update, informing her of his satisfactory

---

74. In fact *affettuosissimo*, "most affectionate" in the superlative form, is repeated by Pier Giorgio.

75. *Letters*, 11; Ital. ed., 11–12.

76. Pier Giorgio's studies and the post-elementary school system in Italy are discussed in chapter 4.

progress. These updates would continue during all of his studies, keeping his mother and father connected with his progress.

Immediately after explaining why he did not write sooner, Pier Giorgio expressed the true nature of his letter: how he felt about his mother's distance. In fact, though Pier Giorgio engaged in his studies very seriously, they represented something secondary to him in comparison to his family relations, and in a special way, his bond with his mother. The core of this letter reflected Pier Giorgio's deep feelings, "These days are taking forever to go by and it seems like it's been a year since I've seen you." Twelve years old, Pier Giorgio expressed what truly moved his heart: his longing to see his mother. This desire to be united with his mother during prolonged absences did not change in his later letters.

4.1. Mother's Absence

The simple words conveyed deep emotions of attachment; absence reflected Pier Giorgio's desire to be reunited with his mother, "days are taking forever to go by," and then he qualified the statement by adding, "like it's been a year since I've seen you." Pier Giorgio conveyed the message that he performed his duty of a son, studying diligently, but his mind was more on his mother whom he missed.

Pier Giorgio felt his mother's absence the way a twelve-year-old would miss his best friend. In fact, to describe the feeling of absence in terms of time, Pier Giorgio stated, *passati eterni*, "forever." The subject-object dichotomy becomes clear: "that *I* have not seen *you*," *che non ti vedo*. Two people exist in the phrase: Pier Giorgio and his mother. And the obstacle between the two was time—and distance.

One would be mistaken to think that Pier Giorgio's desire to be with his mother was because she spoiled him or showered him with affection and kisses. Pier Giorgio's relationship with his mother was not that of a "mamma's boy." Such a relationship hardly described Pier Giorgio's ties with his mother, although Adelaide most certainly loved her son, and Pier Giorgio knew this. As far as emotional expression was concerned, the relationship was asymmetrical: Pier Giorgio showed an attachment to his mother, while Adelaide was less demonstrative. This became apparent in the consistency of Pier Giorgio's letters expressing the same yearning for his mother's presence, as he waited for her letters, while, Adelaide, on the other hand, was often late in writing or replying to her son. This "distance" already in the nature of Pier Giorgio's mother has often reinforced the perception of Adelaide's "austerity," which had been documented on numerous accounts, such as Don Cojazzi, "The mother was severe with the two children, until about sixteen years old, then, knowing they were well-taught, she left the two of them with a reasonable amount of freedom. . . . She was inflexible; no was no, and the children knew that tears or tantrums would not change her mind. Never sweets, never little gifts; only on special feasts."[77] One should note here that the mother approached her children's education and moral formation on the basis of their age: she was strict with them as children, to instill values, teach them virtues; and then, after their rigorous formation, she gave them reasonable freedom at an appropriate age, when their conscience would have been adequately formed. Adelaide did not transmit ambiguous messages to her children: "no was no." The importance of children knowing the boundaries meant there would be no attempt to "negotiate" with their mother, or even turn to their father who had left the education of the children to his wife. Pierazzi compares Adelaide's discipline of her children to "barracks"—regimental.[78] The few exceptions in changing his parents' minds involved spiritually-related matters when Pier Giorgio sought the intervention of a priest.[79]

Another significant point was the equality and justice in their discipline: privileges or deprivations were not the case for either Pier Giorgio or Luciana because one was a boy or one was a girl: the same rules applied to both. When they went on vacation at the beaches of Alassio, after dinner, their mother would tell them, "'Prayers and to bed,' and the children went to the closest Church, while other children of the hotel went with their families to have an ice cream or to hear music."[80] In other words, the disciplined childhood was not limited to their homes during the school year, but even during the summers while on vacation: their prayer life did not change, nor did their bedtime schedule. This discipline assured a sense of consistency, coherency and continuity. For Adelaide Frassati, virtue did not go on vacation. The two mountain excursions were concrete examples of the stoic values which Adelaide transmitted to Pier Giorgio, teaching him perseverance, resistance to fatigue, overcoming coldness and even hunger already as a child. Pier Giorgio adjusted to his mother's absence—or silence.

One could hardly think that Pier Giorgio's mother was emotionally fused to, let alone emotionally dependent on, her children. Pier Giorgio's attachment to his mother derived from his own need for her presence, and simply the devoted love that a son had for his mother. Yet, precisely because

---

77. Cojazzi, *Testimonianze*, 44; Frassati, *I giorni*, 22.
78. Pierazzi, *Così ho visto*, 43.
79. These exceptions are taken up in chapters 3 and 7.
80. Cojazzi, *Testimonianze*, 44.

Pier Giorgio expressed this yearning to be with his mother, Adelaide, even if unintentional, displayed wisdom ensuring emotional space for her son allowing Pier Giorgio to mature and develop early in life healthy and genuine friendships.[81]

5. Letter to His Father—Pollone, October 1913[82]

Pier Giorgio was twelve years old when he wrote a letter to his father expressing his state of torment: he failed his second year at Massimo D'Azeglio secondary school in Turin.[83] Pier Giorgio employed the word "confused," *confuso*, suggesting that he would have to repeat the year of Latin. "Confused" because he did not understand what happened and did not know what to tell his parents. Feeling miserable, or more specifically "heart-broken," Pier Giorgio informed his father he was not even capable of writing him.

The choice of Pier Giorgio's verbs to convey his emotional turmoil was precisely expressed with the Italian verb *addolorato* employed in an earlier letter concerning his mother's illness.[84] Pier Giorgio's pain was deeply felt. *Addolorato* is the same word used to grieve someone's death. Pier Giorgio did not take for granted his relationship with his parents, his duties toward them, or his responsibilities, bringing joy to them, and not causing them pain. His letter addressed to his father also acknowledged that he saw how "upset" his mother was. Pier Giorgio recognized and assumed the responsibility for disappointing them, and suffered this pain "miserably." The letter reflected the relational dynamic between him and his parents already at twelve years old, anticipating the depth of Pier Giorgio's relationship with his parents in his adolescence and early adulthood: he did not want to cause his parents disappointment or suffering. On the contrary, he desired to bring them joy, to make them happy, to please them. The last thing he wished to do was violate the fourth commandment, "Pier Giorgio was too faithful to the fourth Commandment to judge his father."[85]

81. The relationship between Pier Giorgio as a young adult and his mother is developed in chapter 9.

82. *Letters*, 12; Ital. ed., 13.

83. The Liceo Massimo D'Azeglio still stands at the same location, Via Parini, N. 8, corner of Via San Quentino in the center of Turin. The secondary school advances to the Italian liceo. Details on the Italian school system are given below, chapter 4, section 3.1.1, n22.

84. "Heart-broken," *addolorato*, expressed Pier Giorgio's emotional state knowing how his mother and father felt.

85. Frassati, *Beatitudes*, 54.

Pier Giorgio felt confused and heart-broken, tormented by the disappointment of his father and mother. He reflected on this matter at length, "I thought about you so much," that Pier Giorgio was led to one request: forgiveness. He was so ashamed for what had happened, his failure, and having hurt his parents, that he could not bring himself to even ask for forgiveness.

Nevertheless, he began by asking his father for forgiveness, but then he continued, why he felt such sorrow, not only he felt shame for repeating the year, but all his classmates, as well as his sister, would advance a year. This embarrassment was not only experienced by Pier Giorgio, but also his father and mother. While Pier Giorgio's parents were thinking about his future, they understood that their son studying at Massimo D'Azeglio was obliged to stay behind the year. His parents inevitably expressed concern, but also, the feeling of humiliation that could not be avoided. Pier Giorgio sensed all of this; he was aware of his parents' expectations in terms of diligence in studies and commitment to one's responsibilities. Both his father and mother had shown to be conscientious in their values, his father disciplined with his work, and his mother, dedicated to refining her artistic skills.

5.1. Proponimento "Resolution"

After Pier Giorgio asked for forgiveness, he then expressed his sorrow, and he told his parents why he was sorry. Pier Giorgio moved from forgiveness to apology, to promise and action: he promised to correct the situation by studying harder, hoping that he would be able to make up for everything. The last item proved significant: promise/action (3.3 above) because this became a central quality in Pier Giorgio's personality. Whether prayer or an apology, a form of action or "resolution," *proponimento* followed as Pier Giorgio had firmly stated.

Proponimento meant to assume responsibility, and propose concrete changes as a result. The intention reflected a course of action to increase virtue: in this case, diligence. Pier Giorgio could have responded quite differently. In his favor to justify himself he could have said that he did his best, he studied and did the most he could to prepare himself. Or he could have blamed, the common way of dealing with problems, finding others as the cause of his failure. He could have blamed the inadequate private teaching he had received at home; he could have blamed the teacher at Massimo D'Azeglio, claiming the teacher marked him unfairly. In other words, Pier Giorgio could have minimized his responsibility having failed Latin. Instead, Pier Giorgio apologized for the results, asked his parents forgiveness, and promised that things would change: Pier Giorgio assumed full responsibility for his actions—a sign of maturity. He was only twelve years old. The plea appeared to be focused on his parents losing trust in him, no longer believing in him, and this is what Pier Giorgio wanted to avoid: as if by disappointing them to the extent that he had, they might think he did not love them. Pier Giorgio did not want to hurt his parents because he loved them; nor did he want to lose their love.

The spiritual value of Pier Giorgio's *proponimento* was the product of Pier Giorgio's emotional experience: when someone is loved, it follows that the person does not want to hurt the beloved, and the fear of hurting the beloved, is also the fear of losing the beloved. The consequence is not punishment but being unable to live without love. This was precisely what Pier Giorgio discovered as he spiritually matured; he did not want to hurt God because he loved God, and in turn Pier Giorgio was nourished by God's love. The mutuality of love makes love not only relational, but that which sustains the relationship: sensitivity, respect, goodness, all expressing love: the desire not to hurt the beloved but to love. Pier Giorgio's letter captured the intensity of these relations, father-son-mother—ultimately, pointing toward God.

Pier Giorgio wanted his parents to believe in his sincerity—in his "resolution." For Pier Giorgio to mean that he was being sincere meant that his response reflected his awareness of the gravity of the situation, but not only in the material sense of repeating a year, but in the personal sense the emotional turmoil he caused his parents. For Pier Giorgio to be sincere meant that he understood their deep disappointment, and his "resolution" was a response to their pain—and his.

Having already received a letter from his father, Pier Giorgio made it clear that he replied, that he had not delayed in his reply, either; he was taking the matter seriously. Pier Giorgio received advice from his mother to write to the professor who failed him in Latin. Reading the teacher's letter, Pier Giorgio felt worse and he remained in a troubled state. The scenario conveyed in Pier Giorgio's letter was no doubt dramatic—it could not have been a worse situation for someone with Pier Giorgio's sensitivity. He had failed Latin and must repeat the year; his father was upset and wrote to him immediately; Pier Giorgio's mother was clearly distressed; his teacher made him feel worse. Pier Giorgio replied to his teacher with his mother's advice, *consiglio*. He had turned to his mother for help, and listened to her advice. He did not act on his own, nor was he indifferent to whatever advice his mother offered. He understood that his parents had wisdom they wished to communicate, and this wisdom derived from their experience.

Pier Giorgio's secondary school years were not just part of his parents' expectations, but Pier Giorgio realized his parents reacted as they did because his studies were fundamental to his human and personal development. To study did not mean the prospect of job opportunities since Pier Giorgio could follow his father's footsteps in the career of a journalist. Studies meant more than a career or a lucrative income; his parents knew that going to school and success in his studies meant Pier Giorgio's formation, cultural and intellectual, and then, opening possibilities to the career he desired.

This "confusion" Pier Giorgio felt suggested he could not comprehend how he did so poorly—as if he had been in a state of shock with his teacher's report. After all, he and his sister had received private instruction in the home since 1907 by Rosina Busatto, who prepared them for the final exams in July 1910 at the Salesian Institute at Alassio. But Pier Giorgio did experience difficulty, "In spite of continuous heroic efforts, the cry 'You can't write' became a source of continual humiliation."[86] Even though Don Cojazzi taught Pier Giorgio and Luciana Latin, his observation regarding Pier Giorgio's failure focused on Pier Giorgio's reaction to his father, noting that "each gentle admonition of the father produced in Pier Giorgio a profound impression."[87] This observation corresponded to the heartbroken letter Pier Giorgio wrote to his father. Don Cojazzi explained that Pier Giorgio's letter was not an attempt to save himself from some kind of punishment, but rather, Pier Giorgio wanted to remove this "stain."[88] The decision to fail Pier Giorgio did not come easily by his teacher, either, Mario Lobetti Bodoni. His teacher wrote to Alfredo expressing the trouble this had caused him, "Believe me, the pain in my heart continues that this good boy will not be among my students in the third year."[89]

Pier Giorgio ended his letter telling his father that his "love" will be "proven" by "facts," *fatti*. These "facts" or "deeds" belonged to Pier Giorgio's *proponimento*. The observation this twelve-year-old made was crucial: one might say "I love you," as often as the person wished, but love was ultimately demonstrated by deeds. These "facts" became concrete actions assumed by Pier Giorgio to signify his love for his parents; Pier Giorgio would "prove" his love with "deeds." Again, the movement was toward action referring to the accomplishment of these facts.

This association between "love" and "act"—as far as sacrifice—corresponds to the Christian Scriptures. Christ's fundamental teaching Pier Giorgio put into practice early in life: love ultimately manifests itself in sacrifice,

---

86. Frassati, *Beatitudes*, 24.
87. Cojazzi, *Testimonianze*, 33.
88. Cojazzi, *Testimonianze*, 33.
89. Frassati, *Calendario*, "Turin, October, 1913."

"Greater love has no man than this, that a man lay down his life for his friends."⁹⁰ Pier Giorgio discovered the relationship between love, responsibility and acts through his own experience with his parents, not wishing to hurt them, but to show he loved them. This love as act and sacrifice would continue to grow in Pier Giorgio as he reached out to others. Pier Giorgio's pre-adolescent experience led him to realize that one's relationship with God was based on concrete acts of love, and not only repeating the word "love": fundamentally, love is expression, action, sacrifice of what inhabits the person's heart moving outwards.

Pier Giorgio would be separated from his sister and classmates, putting him a year behind. While the whole matter saddened and disturbed Pier Giorgio, it constituted an experience from which he would concretely learn about love. Pier Giorgio applied these principles of love, responsibility and action, summed up in his *proponimento* not only in relation to his family, but with his friends, and ultimately to those who were in need. For Pier Giorgio, "action" became an integral part of loving God.

Questions

(Note: *ST* refers to *Summa Theologiae* of Saint Thomas Aquinas—part [I/II/III], question, article, response)

1. Why did Alfredo Frassati pursue a career in journalism (1.1.1)? How is Alfredo's humanism described (1.1.1) compared to Alfredo's spiritual beliefs (1.1.1)?

2. How is Adelaide Ametis portrayed (2.1)? What does painting say about her personality (2.1.1)? What are Adelaide's moral values (2.1.4)?

3. How is the relationship between Alfredo and Adelaide described before they marry (2.1.2)? What concerns does Alfredo express (2.1.2)? What family misfortunes do they share (1.1.1)?

4. What is the name of their first baby (2.2)? How is Pier Giorgio's baptism name chosen (2.2)? Why is Pier Giorgio conditionally baptized in Turin (2.2)? Where is Pier Giorgio baptized and who are his godparents (2.2)?

5. List four childhood qualities that Pier Giorgio manifests (§3; 5.1) in his letter to his mother (§3; December 1909).

6. How does Aquinas distinguish "natural love" from "charity"? (See note 22; *ST*, Ia–IIae, q. 26, a. 4; IIa–IIae, q. 23, aa. 1–2.)

---

90. John 15:13.

2

Growing Up—Luciana and the Extended Family

And as you wish that men would do to you, do so to them.

LUKE 6:31

Pier Giorgio's childhood is spent in the company of his sister and friend, Luciana, in Turin. Pier Giorgio and his sister remained in Pollone during the summer months with his family members including his grandmother, Linda Ametis, and his mother's sister, Elena Ametis. His final greetings in his letters when he wrote to his family, especially to the household in Pollone, included the names of the domestic workers, and his pets, even naming the individual cats and dogs. In his mid-adolescence, only Pier Giorgio could mount and ride his father's Irish horse, "Parsifal," for miles; and whenever Pier Giorgio blessed himself in front of a church, the horse bowed its head.[1] His work with the gardener and later their chauffeur allowed him to experience them being part of his extended family because Pier Giorgio interacted with them, and took interest in them and their lives. All contributed to Pier Giorgio's formation, his sensitivity toward others, and respect for God's creation. Pier Giorgio's receptivity not only toward his family, but also nature, reflected God as the source of all that was good

---

1. Frassati, *I giorni*, 66; see Pierazzi, *Così ho visto*, 9.

because what God created "is good," and the creation of man and woman "is very good"; man and woman are created in God's "image and likeness."[2]

Others, therefore, as part of Pier Giorgio's world, played distinct roles in shaping Pier Giorgio's personality and values through his daily interactions. With others, parents, sibling, grandparents, aunts and uncles, Pier Giorgio grew to listen, to observe, to respect, to reach out. Pier Giorgio learned at an early age "other-centeredness" in continuity with what Alfredo taught his children, "love each other."[3]

1. Pier Giorgio's Sister: Luciana

Luciana Teodolinda Maria was born August 18, 1902; Pier Giorgio and his sister were looked after by the governess, Caterina Bianchetti.[4] Luciana wrote in *Calendario di una vita*, August 8, 1902, in Pollone, "That day Pier Giorgio—who gave himself the name 'Dodo'—seeing in his mother's hands his intrusive sister, screams, 'Take her away, now!' He is the same boy who, reproached, perhaps wrongly, opens the medicine cabinet and exclaims, 'I'll take poison and then die.'"[5] Hiding himself between two twin beds, he exclaimed, 'I am not anybody's joy.'" These thoughts are verbalized when Pier Giorgio was still twelve months old.[6]

The first in this infant series of three distinct utterances, "take her away," revealed his feelings toward his sister as intruder, a year younger than he was, another child in his mother's arms. The annoyance suggested the little boy's jealousy, his mother's affection divided, Pier Giorgio ceased to be the exclusive focus of his mother's attention. This description became representative of the early relationship between Pier Giorgio and his sister, from what Pier Giorgio revealed in his letter, of hitting her, teasing her, ultimately, making her cry. This sibling conflict dissipated as Pier Giorgio and Luciana grew up, learning to understand each other, ultimately, to love each other.

At an early age, Pier Giorgio discovered that he was not alone, and not the exclusive focus of his parents' love. He needed to learn to share their attention and love, to share his possessions, to be respectful, and to

2. Gen 1:28.
3. Frassati, *I giorni*, 28; Frassati, *Beatitudes*, 21.
4. Siccardi, *Pier Giorgio Frassati*, 31.
5. Frassati records Pier Giorgio's words phonetically, so the Italian [r] is replaced with the child's [l]. *Pleno il veleno e poi molo*, instead of, *Prendo il veleno e poi muoro*. Frassati, *I giorni*, 29.
6. Cojazzi, *Testimonianze*, 39, puts Pier Giorgio at two and half years old stating this.

be sensitive. The world was made of others who had feelings, desires, and needs. Eventually, Pier Giorgio's sister would not only be his friend but his confidant as they grew up; in Luciana he discovered her maturity, intelligence, and wisdom. His relationship with his sister also helped Pier Giorgio grow in virtue.

The second utterance in Luciana's script represented dramatic language with his passion-driven comments, "I will poison myself . . . and die." One would have to assume that these words were something he had already heard, and as one finds with children, they repeat what they hear, so, Pier Giorgio repeated the frightening drama himself of suggesting he would go to the medicine cabinet to poison himself. Frightened by what he had heard he made the same threat himself to win the attention of others.

"I am nobody's joy," his third expression, was yet another of emotional pain. Perhaps Pier Giorgio heard his mother or father, or some other family member who repeated that his little sister was their "joy," words they would have used for Pier Giorgio also. And feeling excluded from this joy he repeated the words, "I am nobody's joy." In these three utterances, Pier Giorgio expressed his state of hurt, knowing their meanings by what he had heard, associated with what he observed and felt. These utterances demonstrated that already as a child Pier Giorgio was very sensitive.

1.1. Sensitivity

Pier Giorgio's sensitivity moved from what might appear as a self-focused child, to gradually reaching out to others around him. One particular incident in his childhood reflected Pier Giorgio's sensitivity, "Around the time he was five years old he asked his mother, 'Was Jesus an orphan?' She calmed him . . . 'Of course not . . . Jesus was not an orphan . . . he had in fact two fathers: one in heaven and one on the earth!' The boy illuminated with joy and tranquillity went back to bed."[7]

Pier Giorgio would have known about orphanages from the religious institutes in Turin and perhaps seeing orphans in the streets of the rapidly urbanizing city. Significant in the mind of the five-year-old whom Don Cojazzi described, was his troubled conscience in the sight of orphans, knowing they were without parents, begging in the streets if they had not been admitted into one of the religious houses in Turin, Cottolengo or one of the Salesian or Vincentian houses.[8] Pier Giorgio observed and reflected, these

---

7. Frassati, *Calendario*, "Turin, May 27, 1905."

8. St. Giuseppe Benedetto Cottolengo (1786–1842) founder of the "Little House of Divine Providence," *Piccola casa della Divina Providenza*; St Giovanni Bosco

two characteristics went together, concluding that being an orphan was not a good thing; for the mind of the five-year-old being an orphan was a kind of injustice, not having a mother and father, or at least a parent, as women would have lost their husbands most often at war, or a husband would have lost his wife while she was giving birth, or due to an incurable disease. Then, thinking about Jesus, it crossed Pier Giorgio's mind, if Jesus was born in a stable, who was his mother and father? Not a very simple explanation for a five-year-old who might have heard about the Immaculate Conception and Joseph being the foster father of Jesus. Pier Giorgio's mother answered in a way that he could be reassured that Jesus was not an abandoned or neglected orphan—not even an orphan.

The sensitivity Pier Giorgio showed in this case was not only his awareness of the poverty around him and its implications, but he made connections in his head, and then, he began to wonder about Jesus to whom he prayed every night—if he might have been an orphan.

1.1.1. Flowers and the Garden

The appreciation Pier Giorgio had conveyed for flowers, his knowledge of flora, especially observing and helping in the garden, he described in his letters. His mother also painted flowers and he knew which flowers she preferred. He expressed his love with beautiful flowers. Of course, Pier Giorgio would also want to give flowers to Jesus. Arriving from the nursery, the sister had come to pick up flowers for the chapel. Pier Giorgio waited for her outside of the garden and offered her a scarlet rose. He addressed the woman as "Sister"; she replied, "I am not a Sister," but Pier Giorgio with his enthusiasm continued, "Sister, take this rose to Jesus for me."[9] Having seen the sister leave the nursery, meant that already Pier Giorgio was making religious associations between a female worker picking up flowers for the chapel and a religious duty; hence, he addressed her as "Sister," which seemed to him her appropriate title. For Pier Giorgio, this sister going to a chapel with flowers could also bring his scarlet rose to Jesus.

Gardening in Pollone, with the good summer weather and taking a break from his studies meant that Pier Giorgio learned about flowers and

---

(1815–1888) founder of the Society of Don Bosco and educator; Vincentians also known as Lazarists officially Congregation of the Missions was founded by St. Vincent de Paul (1581–1660) its origins dating back to 1624 and present in Turin since 1655. See also below, chapter 7, n52.

9. In fact, the sister was a *conversa*, "lay sister." Frassati, *I giorni*, 21; Frassati, *Beatitudes*, 18.

vegetables, the flowers he associated with his mother's paintings, and the vegetables with his father's own interest in the garden. The garden placed Pier Giorgio in contact with nature already as a child, the experience of seeding and cultivating, the relationship between working diligently, and fruitful results.

Pier Giorgio studied, he observed, he listened; his inquisitive nature, as that of any child, he would ask questions, names, and his vocabulary of flowers increased; "roses," "poppies" "geraniums," and "vanilla" were described in a letter when he was seven years old.[10] Pier Giorgio wrote his mother detailed letters to describe what was blooming in the garden or the work he had done with the gardener. He could also report to his father the vegetables that had been growing in Pier Giorgio's own little garden. The contact with nature: the real world, the hoe, soil, seeds, water, his little hands penetrating the earth, sun and rain which were the most powerful natural components that determined whether the crop would grow healthy and in abundance or wither and die.

1.2. Pier Giorgio's Upbringing and Family Life

Based on Pier Giorgio's childhood letters in chapter 1, the relational dynamics between Pier Giorgio and his father and his mother become apparent. Pier Giorgio and Luciana's upbringing was highly disciplined, perhaps austere, especially with the moral rectitude of their mother; and as already noted, the moral education of the children was left with Adelaide Frassati.[11] As children their lives were "strictly controlled," and in fact, even "isolated."[12] The winters were spent at their home in Turin and their summers at the Ametis home in Pollone. The experience of home Luciana described as, "days during which we were unable to get away from the same faces, the same rooms and the monotonous streets."[13] Besides the isolation that was experienced, they had a series of restrictions, being prohibited from, "walking about the city, stand in front of windows, give way to little stirrings of

---

10. *Letters*, "To His parents, 1908," 2.
11. Cojazzi, *Testimonianze*, 44; Frassati, *I giorni*, 53.
12. Frassati, *Beatitudes*, 18. One needs to bear in mind these accounts were based on Luciana's experiences, those of a sister writing after the death of her brother, and the relationship Luciana had with her mother which was not the same as the relationship she had with her father.
13. Frassati, *Beatitudes*, 18–19.

curiosity."[14] These prohibitions of sorts were extended to their actual conduct which meant, "we had to walk briskly, without turning our heads."

Pier Giorgio and Luciana both learned the meaning of "discipline and obedience, and acceptance of continual sacrifices."[15] These sacrifices extended to "real hunger" which was considered to be healthy for the children.[16] As a result, they grew to be virtuous by overcoming pain with courage.[17] Experiencing fatigue climbing mountains, feeling thirsty, and wanting to drink water, the mother responded, "Spit in your mouth," *Sputati in bocca*.[18] R. M. Pierazzi comments that her cousin Adelaide was admirable instilling in Pier Giorgio the courage not to fear anything or anyone.[19] When Pier Giorgio was eight years old playing one day in front of his house, he suddenly began coughing, and his great-aunt who was with him offered a candy to help him, but Pier Giorgio refused, "Mamma doesn't allow it."[20] This reply, "Mamma doesn't allow it," *mamma non vuole*, would continue through his adolescence and adulthood to express something that was not in accordance with his mother's wishes, reflecting Pier Giorgio's obedience to his mother. Since they could not converse with adults, as it was also forbidden, and with the numerous restrictions and prohibitions, Pier Giorgio and his sister spent considerable time "in each other's company."[21] Eventually, the exceptions to this obedience were Pier Giorgio's frequent confessions and daily communion.[22]

Pier Giorgio and his sister were up at seven in the morning and washed themselves with cold water, and the day ended at eight thirty in the evening. Lunch was at twelve thirty in the afternoon and then supper was eaten at eight thirty in the evening.[23] They were well-mannered, sitting with their

14. Frassati, *Beatitudes*, 19.
15. Frassati, *Beatitudes*, 19.
16. Frassati, *Beatitudes*, 19.
17. Casalegno, *Pier Giorgio Frassati*, 32; Siccardi, *Pier Giorgio Frassati*, 45.
18. Wanda Gawronska, personal communication, December 2015. Frassati, *I giorni*, 22. Luciana Frassati, in describing the family dynamics in her childhood years, appears severe in some instances toward her parents. This reflected Luciana's response to Don Antonio Cojazzi, who appeared to have distorted the relationship Pier Giorgio experienced with his parents as if to suggest Pier Giorgio's spiritual and moral values were entirely transmitted to Pier Giorgio by his parents. Don Cojazzi, who first collected the "testimonies" on Pier Giorgio, wanted to educate the youth in family values.
19. Pierazzi, *Così ho visto*, 63.
20. Siccardi, *Pier Giorgio Frassati*, 75.
21. Frassati, *Beatitudes*, 19.
22. Pier Giorgio's sacraments will be taken up in chapter 3.
23. Siccardi, *Pier Giorgio Frassati*, 45. The Italian main meal, *pranzo*, "lunch," is in the afternoon, around 1 p.m. The light "supper" is later in the evening, around 8 p.m.

backs straight, their wrists at the edge of the table, and their arms to the sides of their breast.[24] The tension between the parents was especially felt at the dinner table when the entire family was present; the family meals were not a time when comfort or joy was felt, "it was not easy, however, to chase away those heavy clouds at mealtimes."[25] Pier Giorgio even reacted to the tense atmosphere, "Enough!"—*Basta!*[26] Despite the tension in the home between the parents, manifested especially at lunch and supper, Alfredo and Adelaide did not neglect to instill virtues in their children, whether present or absent from home.

Yet, the home environment was not only tension or the absence of Alfredo Frassati preoccupied with *La Stampa*, or their mother's absence from home while in Pollone, Venice, Berlin, or elsewhere. Pier Giorgio's correspondence and Luciana Frassati's writings made it very clear that both parents took an active interest in the lives of their children.[27] Pier Giorgio's father, in spite of his commitment to *La Stampa* in Turin, after meals during his free time, played games with Pier Giorgio and Luciana, filling the house with excitement as they played and raced.[28] Because the Pollone household belonged to Adelaide's family, Turin for Alfredo meant he could be in his own "kingdom"—at the office of *La Stampa*. In the summer when Alfredo Frassati returned to Pollone for the weekend, Pier Giorgio and Luciana would meet their father in Turin at *La Stampa* newspaper office, receiving their father's hugs and kisses. As they returned home all together, they ran in the streets, through the garden, they hid behind trees and doors, and after meals, they bolted through the rooms. "Their mother would send them out of one room from the next, to save the furniture and windows from ruin."[29] While their mother may have been emotionally distant, their father was clearly, playful and affectionate, during his free time.

When the entire family came together daily during mealtimes, Pier Giorgio's surroundings were rooms furnished in baroque pieces from Piedmont. Two windows in the dining room looked onto Corso Siccardi, and another onto Piazza d'Armi where the Victor Emanuel II monument stood.[30] Alfredo's punctual arrival home meant interruption from studies

24. Siccardi, *Pier Giorgio Frassati*, 45.
25. Frassati, *Beatitudes*, 51.
26. Frassati, *Beatitudes*, 51.
27. See chapter 1 above, sections 4–5.
28. Frassati, *Beatitudes*, 21.
29. Cojazzi, *Testimonianze*, 39.
30. At the time via Corso Siccardi which later changed names to Corso Galileo Ferraris. In 1917, the family moved once again on via Corso Galileo Ferraris. See above, chapter 1, section 3, n61.

for Pier Giorgio and Luciana. Impatience appeared to characterize Alfredo as well as irritation with the smallest thing. A climate of joy with the presence of the father home, but no doubt, also anxiety brought upon an impatient and irritable temperament. Their father's dinner conversations focused on wine, cattle and gardening, and a disappointment was visible when their dinner salad was not from Pollone where Alfredo spent time gardening on Saturdays.[31] The table discussions also included justice between men and women, equal rights, and death.[32]

According to one of the domestic workers, Carolina Masoero, Adelaide seemed to be often absent from the home, although present at meals, "Pier Giorgio as well as Luciana helped each other, but they lived somewhat a little scared. I remember the little girl, with the demands of the mother, to stop crying because the father was about to return home, the little girl continued in a manner that was even more obvious. Once I heard the Senator say to Madame, 'You are always away, at least treat these children well.' And Madame Frassati truly was always away: she only returned at seven in the evening, and one might say, she was only present to yell at them."[33] Masoero's testimony conveys the image of an almost indifferent woman toward her children if not unjustifiably severe. Yet, Masoero's testimony, just as Luciana's after Pier Giorgio's death, needs to be read and understood in the light of Pier Giorgio's own relationship with his mother.

The table conversations were significant for the children; Pier Giorgio and Luciana discovered the values of their home. Indirectly, the table simply by talking and listening became a place of education. At the table the children heard stories of their families. The fundamental values were reflected in the meal discussions—a point of reference in terms of what was true, good and just, even though discrepancies might have arisen between what was taught and what was practiced. Given the respect shown toward both their parents, the discipline they received especially from their mother, and the information transmitted to them by their father in terms of politics and society, Alfredo Frassati had the fundamental role in shaping Pier Giorgio's and Luciana's values in terms of "honesty" and "justice," while it was from their mother whom they learned discipline and sacrifice.

The various witnesses offer different perspectives on the family environment and their relations. Emerging with clarity is the close relationship that developed between Pier Giorgio and Luciana as they grew up together.

31. Frassati, *Beatitudes*, 50.

32. Frassati, *Beatitudes*, 50. It should be noted that Luciana described her father with a certain irony because on each of these points she suggested an inconsistency between what he believed and the actual practices in the home.

33. Siccardi, *Pier Giorgio Frassati*, 45–46.

Luciana also showed a certain bond with her father, while Pier Giorgio throughout his life, though he expressed an unquestionable respect and love for both his parents, he manifested a particular attachment toward his mother. The absence of childhood letters between Pier Giorgio and his sister was due to the obvious fact that they lived in the same home, thereby, making it difficult to ascertain their relationship from Pier Giorgio's perspective. Nevertheless, surfacing in later years, as Pier Giorgio's letters reveal when writing to his sister, was the tremendous love Pier Giorgio had for Luciana—sister and trusted friend. In fact, one of the most emotionally intense letters that Pier Giorgio wrote to Luciana was after she had married and left home, when Pier Giorgio accompanied her to the train station.[34] In his extended family, Pier Giorgio also maintained a close relationship with his maternal grandmother, Linda Ametis.

2. Letter to His Grandmother Linda Ametis—Turin, December 1908[35]

One of Pier Giorgio's earliest letters was addressed to his maternal grandmother, *nonna* Linda Ametis, when he was only seven years old.[36] Pier Giorgio wrote to his grandmother from Turin while she was in Pollone, informing her of his activities, including gymnastics and dance. But then, he immediately enquired about what she was doing and invited her to spend Christmas with the family in Turin. The letter showed Pier Giorgio's attachment to his different family members. He talked to his grandmother about the weather and even their Angora cat Scimbo's poor health, sharing his different thoughts with his grandmother. His sign-off was once again *tanti baci*, "many kisses" not just from him, but also on behalf of his parents, and his aunt.

He wrote in December, focused on the winter weather, wondering what it must be like in Pollone where he and his family spent their vacations. A sense of "nostalgia" was conveyed to be with his grandmother in Pollone. Pier Giorgio sent his grandmother a beautiful invitation: he would like his *nonna* to spend Christmas with them in Turin; it would be "good" *buone* Christmas holidays.

Bearing in mind the letter was written by a seven-year-old, one cannot ignore the details in the last part of his letter: his sign-off transmitting

---

34. Pier Giorgio's relationship with Luciana is taken up in chapter 9.
35. *Letters*, 3–4; Ital. ed., 5.
36. I have retained Italian *nonna*. The English, "grandmother," is not a term of address; rather, "grandma" or "nanna," or some other affectionate variation.

affectionate kisses and greetings, in this case to his grandmother, and not only his kisses, but on behalf of the family. Such details are indicative above all the value Pier Giorgio attached to his family relations.

2.1. Pollone Residence

Pier Giorgio's maternal grandmother, Linda Copello, a woman from Genoa, married Francesco Ametis, and moved with him to his native Pollone where he built a magnificent residence with a view of the mountain, Mount Mucrone, and a panoramic view of Pollone. The value of Pier Giorgio's relationship with his grandmother developed at a young age. She taught Pier Giorgio the wisdom of listening and spending time with someone who could instruct him through her experiences, her history, and her story. The rich relational dynamic between a seven-year-old boy and his grandmother, "a religious woman in her own way," was evident.[37] Pier Giorgio's experience with his grandmother and her religious observance offered Pier Giorgio early in his childhood a valuable influence.[38]

Children not only learn from their grandparents' experiences, they discover the history of their grandmother and grandfather as part of their own story; they trace and build their own narrative through mother and father, grandmother and grandfather. The home where Pier Giorgio spent his vacation time and summers was in Pollone, and he could see the sequoia his grandfather planted after working in Peru, a tree he brought back with him while journeying from California, and America.[39] This tree, its roots, relate a story of Pier Giorgio's grandparents, the site where Francesco asked Linda Copello to marry him; a tree under which Pier Giorgio and Luciana played; a tree that stood spreading its branches and producing shade in front of the Ametis home; and a tree where the grandfather who first planted the sequoia could watch Pier Giorgio and Luciana play.[40]

As children spend time with their grandparents, and they become close—like friends—but more than friends, as Pier Giorgio indicated wishing to have his *nonna* in Turin with him: it would be "happy" for her and for him. While this thought to have his grandmother in Turin may reflect something of Pier Giorgio's attachment to his family members, it also revealed the disposition of a child who wished to spend time with those who found time for him, told him stories, and took interest in him. Pier Giorgio

37. Frassati, *I giorni*, 24.
38. Pierazzi, *Così ho visto*, 13–14.
39. Frassati, *I gorni*, 16; Siccardi, *Pier Giorgio Frassati*, 86.
40. Frassati, *I gorni*, 16.

learned the meaning not only of having a sister almost his age with whom he played and fought, with whom he shared his parents and his possessions. But he also discovered the interaction, the meaning and value of someone older than him; that *nonna* Ametis was not only part of his life, but she was an integral part of the family.

The horizontal axis of "Do to others as you would have them do to you," extended significantly in Pier Giorgio's childhood world: his world was not only made of people his own age, namely his sister, with whom he learned to share and to play, but Pier Giorgio also discovered at an early age that family members within a home were also to be respected because of the very nature of their relationship: grandmother-grandson. The role of grandparents, however, was not just to play with grandchildren and teach them, but also to instill a sense of discipline, and in this regard, *nonna* Linda Ametis kept the grandchildren in order when they visited the Pollone home. Pier Giorgio and Luciana had more freedom to move about and play games in Pollone than they would have had in Turin; a small town was less worrisome than a big city. *Nonna* Ametis, however, taught the grandchildren that they needed to be respectful and orderly; they could not jump on beds nor could they run through the sitting room between the antique furniture of Louis XV layered with doilies and furniture covers.[41]

In the attic, Pier Giorgio and Luciana were only allowed to enter after having knocked; an attic adapted to their mother's workshop, where apple and lavender were in a mixed perfume.[42] The Pollone home displayed Adelaide's paintings which Pier Giorgio could admire and appreciate as his mother's artistic achievements. The paintings also included those of Giuseppe Falchetti, Giaccomo Faretto, Lorenzo Delleani, Francesco Michetti and Giovanni Segantini.[43] The home with seventeenth- and eighteenth-century tapestries and canvases created the atmosphere of an art gallery which refined Pier Giorgio's sense of art and the beautiful.

2.2. Nature and the Senses

In the December 1908 letter to his grandmother, Pier Giorgio made reference to the weather, "Yesterday the weather was bad in Turin and today it is fine." This may appear like the little boy wished to engage in some conversation and found the weather as a point of reference—to talk about something which might be of interest to his grandmother. This was hardly the case.

---

41. Frassati, *I giorni*, 17; Siccardi, *Pier Giorgio Frassati*, 83.

42. Siccardi, *Pier Giorgio Frassati*, 83.

43. Siccardi, *Pier Giorgio Frassati*, 87.

GROWING UP—LUCIANA AND THE EXTENDED FAMILY 41

Pier Giorgio took great interest in the weather. While his life might have been especially indoors with rules he was expected to follow, the weather in Turin had relevance: cloudy and rainy, a "bad" December day, but a "fine" day as he wrote. These contrasts Pier Giorgio noticed and mentioned suggest he wondered about the possibility of December snow in Pollone along with the snow on the mountains. Pier Giorgio also remembered in Pollone the garden of flowers and vegetables, having helped with the gardening and picking flowers for the chapel or arranging flower bouquets with his maternal grandmother.[44] The weather, in other words, contained a formative role: it was nature, God's creation that served to produce colorful and beautiful flowers, as well as food for the table.[45] One might say nature belonged to the "real world" of senses and creation, "And God said, 'Behold, I have given you every plant yielding seed which is upon the face of all the earth, and every tree with seed in its fruit; you shall have them for food.'"[46]

He worked with the gardener, Giuseppe Gola, *gnere*, as Pier Giorgio called him, and with whom Pier Giorgio became close friends: he observed, listened and followed Gola's instructions to learn about gardening.[47] He helped Gola as a child to hoe and dig the soil; he learned about enriching the soil with manure and helped Gola manure the ground; the different seeds belonging to different kinds of vegetables, Pier Giorgio learned to sow in rows, and hoeing around the germinating plants to protect them from access water; he discovered the principle of pruning to improve the quality and fruitfulness of plants; he harvested grapes and then learned about crushing them; he gathered crops, including the salads they would eat at home in Pollone and Turin.[48] Giuseppe Gola had arrived at Pollone for Easter 1911, when Pier Giorgio was ten years old. The gardener was a source of ongoing conversation allowing Pier Giorgio to express his "passion" for everything associated with the soil. Pier Giorgio was finally given his own little plot of land for gardening.[49] Working with the gardener, Pier Giorgio developed a "true friendship"; not a relationship with a laborer working for the family—even with gardener's children who were his same age Pier

---

44. Pierazzi, *Così ho visto*, 57.

45. Pierazzi, *Così ho visto*, 61.

46. Gen 1:29.

47. Frassati, *I giorni*, 37. *Gnere* is short for *giardiniere*, "gardener."

48. The value of sensory experience as knowledge-formation is treated by Aquinas in *ST*, I, q. 84, a. 6.

49. Frassati, *Beatitudes*, 21; Siccardi, *Pier Giorgio Frassati*, 83.

Giorgio developed a friendship.[50] Pier Giorgio related to others with goodness and trust, at this young age, developing a sense of friendship with ease.

Reference to their cat, "the cat is sick," referred to Scimbo, their Angora cat in Turin, one of their pets. Pier Giorgio and Luciana took care of their pets besides playing with them as members of the family. Pier Giorgio made reference to this second pet. In his earlier letter Pier Giorgio mentioned that their pet dog, Jor, was "fine."[51] So, greeting the cats and dogs, stating or asking how they were doing became customary for Pier Giorgio preceded by his farewell greetings to the family.

2.3. Relations and Spiritual Growth

"Whatever you wish that men would do to you, do so to them," began with the horizontal relations at home, discovering that the world was not meant to be self-focused creating narcissistic expectations and demands. Instead, in other-centerdness one moves outward. Pier Giorgio throughout his life revealed that he was not preoccupied with himself, but rather people and issues around him that required his attention, and this was manifested in his relationship with his mother. Adelaide Frassati was in every sense protected by her son, already at a young age, and she became the focus of Pier Giorgio's concerns. When his grandfather Francesco Ametis died on May 26, 1909, five months after he wrote the letter above to his grandmother, Pier Giorgio noticed that everyone turned to his mother's sister, *zia* Elena; and very worried about his own mother, the eight-year-old exclaimed, "Nobody asks about mamma!" Pier Giorgio's mother needed to explain to him that "it is not an honor," although an honor to take care of certain matters, and all the practical concerns in the home were taken care of by Pier Giorgio's *zia* Elena.[52]

Although concerned about his mother, Pier Giorgio also learned about other relationships and responsibilities. In this regard he discovered family dynamics which would serve in his friendships. These family ties with a sense of responsibility, seeking the good of others, disposed Pier Giorgio to deepen his relationship with God.

---

50. Siccardi, *Pier Giorgio Frassati*, 83.
51. See chapter 1, section 2.
52. Frassati, *Calendario*, "Pollone, May 26, 1909."

3. Letter to Aunt Elena Ametis, April 1912[53]

Adelaide Frassati traveled to Venice with her sister for the 1912 Venice Biennale. The two sisters journeying together reflected their close relationship, a bond already acknowledged by Alfredo when he had written to his future wife.[54] Adelaide remained tied to Elena even after her marriage, and was her most intimate confidant; in fact, Elena was the administrator of the Pollone household. Alfredo, already aware of their bond, never attempted to break the sisters apart. Instead, he appreciated the good qualities of house governance on the part of his sister-in-law, who also assumed the role of a surrogate mother toward Pier Giorgio.[55]

Pier Giorgio acknowledged with excitement that his mother's painting was admitted to the International Exhibition of Venice in April 1912.[56] After greeting his aunt, Pier Giorgio's question was immediately directed toward his mother and her painting. The question might come as a surprise; he asked whether the painting was displayed in a well-lit place—the visibility of the painting. This must have been the result of discussions at home and how the "lighting" of art clearly makes a difference in its noticeability, detail and ultimately, appreciation. The question did not focus on the reaction to the work on the part of visitors, but the importance that his mother's art should be well-lit. The question further suggested that a "well-lit" place was also not in a dark hidden corner, so that its visibility, and therefore, detail, should not go unnoticed. The question conveyed a sense of Pier Giorgio's awareness of his mother's artistic skill, but also the pride Pier Giorgio took in his mother's work as an artist. Inevitably, his mother's artistic sensitivity would shape Pier Giorgio's own sense of aesthetic in terms of knowledge and appreciation.[57] Pier Giorgio expressed his desire to be at the Venice Biennale and to experience the regal pageantry of King Victor Emmanuel III making his presence on April 25; the historic event included the king's inauguration of Saint Mark's bell tower.

Pier Giorgio's mother had previously informed him of the regal event, opening of the exhibition, and inauguration of the bell tower, and Pier Giorgio repeated these details to his aunt. Attentiveness to detail became another characteristic of Pier Giorgio's personality. The eleven-year-old boy was not dismissive with information, treating it as supplementary and unnecessary,

---

53. *Letters*, 9; Ital. ed., 9.
54. See chapter 1, section 2.1.2.
55. Frassati, *I giorni*, 18; Siccardi, *Pier Giorgio Frassati*, 42.
56. Frassati, *Calendario*, "Turin, April 1912, to his zia Elena."
57. On the subject of beauty see chapter 5, section 4.1.

but rather, each piece of information was recognized as valuable which he remembered and would repeat in his letters, and one could assume in his conversations. The attentiveness to detail, whether as a listener or an observer, served to build character: Pier Giorgio showed receptivity to the world around him.

Pier Giorgio did not focus on his desire to be with his mother and aunt in Venice; obviously he would have liked to be with them in Venice at such a magnificent event—king, bell tower inauguration, exhibition opening, his mother's art. Instead, Pier Giorgio admitted his desire to be there in terms of, "I would like to have been with you to see mamma's painting." Even though he saw his mother every day, and he was exposed to her art work, Pier Giorgio still placed his mother and her art over the king's presence and all the other pageantry associated with the exhibition and inauguration. Pier Giorgio not only showed more interest in his mother's art than the king's presence, but he inverted the hierarchical order: instead of hoping his mother had the opportunity to greet the king of Italy, Pier Giorgio hoped the king of Italy congratulated his mother for her painting, *Sole sul ghiacciaio*, "Sun over the glacier." In fact, not only did King Victor Emmanuel III congratulate Adelaide Frassati for her art, the king purchased the oil painting.[58]

His short letter provided enough details to convey the significance of the Venice Biennale, starting with his mother's painting. The attentiveness, the "being" in Venice with them although he was absent, the news of the event pulsated within him, creating a sense of "oneness" with his mother and aunt. Pier Giorgio expressed early in his letters this "oneness" with people's lives, and this began with those closest to him, his family members.

Pier Giorgio treated others with respect which extended to expressing affection. This respect transformed into something greater, an increasing sense of responsibility toward the underprivileged and marginalized, for those who materially suffered. The "other" in whom he recognized the presence of Christ moved from a childhood ego to a mature Christian who was other-centered.

4. Letter to His Aunt Elena Ametis—Alassio, August 3, 1914[59]

On August 2, Pier Giorgio had already written to his grandmother Linda Ametis expressing the sentiment, "I'm sorry that you couldn't also be here with us." The letter to his aunt reflects a similar attachment to her. Pier

---

58. Frassati, *Un uomo*, 30n82.
59. *Letters*, 13; Ital. ed., 14.

Giorgio's relations with his grandmother and aunt communicated not only the time spent with them in Pollone, but also Pier Giorgio's thoughts about them when he was away: he desired their presence—if only to enjoy their company.

In this August postcard-size letter, Pier Giorgio expressed similar sentiments of longing for his *zia* Elena's company; namely, that he was "sorry" she could not join them to go swimming.[60] The thirteen-year-old Pier Giorgio swimming in the waters of the Ligurian coast wished to share his excitement and joy, thinking about his aunt whom he knew also liked swimming. Pier Giorgio informed his aunt, who had a great passion for sailboats, that the wind was ideal for sailing. The letter sounded like Pier Giorgio was sharing his thoughts with his aunt since Pier Giorgio planned on going sailing himself, *Io forse*, "I perhaps . . ." giving his aunt the name of the island where he intended to sail, "Gallinaria Island." As an adolescent Pier Giorgio continued to share his activities with his family members, even if only in writing. He continued to show an interest in the activity of others, "Write to me all of your news." Pier Giorgio's life was one about sharing, hearing the news of his aunt; he took an interest in her, the "other," who was part of his life.

One would expect to hear about the weather at the Ligurian beach resort, and Pier Giorgio, being receptive to his surroundings, also told his aunt that the "weather is beautiful." With the swimming and sailing, one could imagine the sunlight over the blue waters of the Italian Riviera. In fact, Pier Giorgio was greeted by an acquaintance, "Hi, black of the cod," an allusion to his tanned skin, and time spent in the water swimming.[61]

Pier Giorgio closed his letter with a kiss to his aunt. These postcard and letter closures represented faithfully greetings and kisses sent to other members of the family. As he signed off, Pier Giorgio asked for her news to ensure the correspondence continued, and still made further reference to the beautiful beach weather.

4.1. Outdoor Activities

Living along the Italian Alps, Pier Giorgio throughout his life showed a definite preference for winter sports, namely, skiing and mountain and glacier climbing. But his summers in Alassio were summers spent swimming and sailing, enjoying himself in aquatic activities, too, where Pier Giorgio

---

60. I have retained the Italian, *zia*, which is phonetically closer to the endearing, "auntie," rather than "aunt."

61. "Ciau Moro del Baccalà," Frassati, *Calendario*, "Alassio, August 3, 1914."

became "friends with the sea."[62] Throughout his childhood, adolescence and adulthood, Pier Giorgio exercised a "rigorous and Spartan lifestyle." His world was not only of swimming in streams and alpine lakes, he would jump into cold water with his sister repeatedly warming up by running as fast as he could in the meadows.[63]

Nature characterized these experiences whether in the mountains, meadows, streams, sea, exercising his physical capacities within the framework of the natural world, the stamina, endurance, and strength of the body. Not only did this reflect Pier Giorgio's physical endurance, but the spiritual dimension where the body's submission to the will is absolutely necessary. Pier Giorgio grew up with this Stoic spirit, and he developed this first playfully with his sister, then, with his friends, and finally, at a spiritual level, he learned the value of self-denial and sacrifice. These physical activities spiritually contributed to shape Pier Giorgio, teaching him especially endurance, but also bringing him in proximity with nature, the created world that was an imprint of the Divine.

The spiritual dimension of these outdoor activities kept Pier Giorgio in contact with nature, cold water, ice, snow, glaciers, mountains, as he continued to grow, bringing him closer to God. At the same time, Pier Giorgio's love for his family, his close ties at home, opened him to the love of true friendship, and a deepening love for God.

Questions

(Note: *ST* refers to *Summa Theologiae* of Saint Thomas Aquinas—part [I/II/III], question, article, response)

1. Describe Pier Giorgio's relationship with his sister, Luciana, as little brother and sister (§1).

2. How does Pier Giorgio respond to nature (1.1.1; 2.2)?

3. What do Pier Giorgio's letters reveal about him in his relation to his grandmother Linda Ametis (§2; December 1908)? And his aunt, Elena Ametis (§3; §4)?

4. What kind of outdoor activities does Pier Giorgio pursue as a child (§4)? What time of year does Pier Giorgio normally engage in these outdoor activities (4.1)?

---

62. Frassati, *I giorni*, 28.
63. Siccardi, *Pier Giorgio Frassati*, 81.

5. Pier Giorgio expresses an immense desire to share his experiences of enjoyment with others. How is this conveyed in his letters (§2; §4)?

6. What is the relationship between the senses and knowledge according to Saint Thomas Aquinas? (See note 48 above; *ST*, I, q. 84, a. 6, *resp.*)

3

Sacramental Life

> 55. Q. How often may we go to Holy Communion?
> A. We may go to Holy Communion as often as we are advised to do so by a pious and learned confessor.
>
> CATECHISM OF SAINT PIUS X (1908)

The focus of this chapter will be Pier Giorgio's sacramental life, especially his initial contact with the Jesuits. His relationship with his family reflects his deep love for each member, clearly conveyed in his letters, his respect and his sense of responsibility. His sacramental life develops within the framework of these family relations, but quickly, Pier Giorgio's spiritual life intensifies with frequent confession, communion, the sacrament of confirmation and devotion to the Blessed Virgin Mary.

1. Letter to Parents, 1908[1]

The seven-year-old Pier Giorgio expressed his guilt for doing "two bad things": he made his parents cry and his teacher was upset with him. Pier Giorgio's recognition of guilt represented more than subjective feelings: he stated precisely why he was guilty. Should he have simply relied on feelings, he might never have felt guilty. Instead, Pier Giorgio received an education

---

1. *Letters*, 3; Ital. ed., 4–5. Neither the month nor the location is given. He may have been seven years old.

at home, by his parents, grandmother, aunt, homeschool teacher and priests, who all guided Pier Giorgio to develop a sense of responsibility.

Pier Giorgio wrote to his parents when he was only seven years old. Two years before the sacrament of confession, Pier Giorgio already displayed a remarkable sense of conscience: "I did wrong, I beg you to forgive me." In fact, he ends his letter by repeating, "forgive me." A year after his first confession, a requirement for Holy Communion, Pier Giorgio received first communion. The spiritual preparation for communion was shaped by one's conscience adhering to the teachings of Christ and his church and for the seven-year-old his parents played a fundamental role in the formation of his conscience. Pier Giorgio already manifested a clear sense of right and wrong, good and bad. His conscience told him that he was guilty.

1.1. Repentance

Christianity is fundamentally a response to the call of Jesus Christ to follow him, the way, the truth, and the life.[2] To adhere to the teachings of Christ entails repentance and conversion: the reward promised for one's fidelity to Christ is eternal life.[3] John the Baptist prepared those who believed in the coming of the Messiah by repentance of their sins, an expression of conversion; "and they were baptized by him in the Jordan River they confessed their sins."[4] John the Baptist opened the way for the Promised One by calling men, women and children, to repentance and conversion. To love Jesus meant to obey his commandments, "If you love me you will keep my commandments."[5] Violations of Jesus' teachings requires the forgiveness of sins, presented dramatically in the story of the Prodigal Son, where the son claimed his inheritance, departed from home and lived a life of debauchery; then, after exhausting himself and his funds, returned to his father seeking forgiveness. The father not only forgave his son, but he even celebrated his conversion.[6] With a converted heart, reconciled with God, with one's mother, father, brother, sister, family, friends, neighbors; in other words, with God and his church, one may receive the body and blood of Christ.[7] Crucial, therefore, is the formation of conscience. Christ's teachings, the magisterium of the Church, are the objective criteria employed in

- 2. John 14:6.
- 3. John 3:16.
- 4. Matt 3:1–6, at v. 6.
- 5. John 14:15.
- 6. Luke 15:11–24.
- 7. 1 Cor 11:27–29.

conscience-formation.[8] God already offers both the believer and the non-baptized assistance through natural law.[9]

This seven-year-old Catholic expressed his interior state, the state of his soul, as "bad," *cattivo*. Pier Giorgio related how he felt: he could see the consequences of his actions because he made his mother and father cry. Causing his parents to suffer, violating the fourth commandment, Pier Giorgio knew that he was guilty. Pier Giorgio further recognized the contradiction of his actions: his parents who loved him, he made them cry. In other words, he did not only consider their crying, but the reason why he should not be the cause of their crying: they loved him. The relationship is not only one of cause-effect: bad child-crying parents; but, the qualifier Pier Giorgio attributes to his parents, "loving," suggest the case should be the opposite causal relationship: loving parents-good child. So, Pier Giorgio was guilty on two accounts: first, he made his parents cry; and second, his parents were loving parents, so, he had no reason to make them cry.

In the second sentence, he explained he did two things that made his parents cry—conveying Pier Giorgio's sensitivity to the feelings of others: their reaction to his wrongdoing; and then, he observed his teacher's expression: "stern and sad face." The teacher's face was a visible sign that Pier Giorgio had done something wrong. In other words, Pier Giorgio's actions caused an effect on others, and this noticeable effect was indicative of his wrongdoing: Pier Giorgio's conscience was in response to the negative reaction of others.

Pier Giorgio's letter makes it evident that the seven-year-old was not indifferent to how others felt about him when he knew very well these people cared about him. Parents love their children, and teachers want their students to learn what is true and good. Pier Giorgio did not even state that his teacher told him that she was not happy with him; but he observed her "stern and sad face" that conveyed how she felt. Such facial indicators were sufficient for Pier Giorgio to know that he had done wrong.

With his parents crying and his teacher sad, Pier Giorgio believed he "hurt everyone," and as a result, he had reason to be "upset." Pier Giorgio revealed his deep sense of responsibility, his conscience that guided him based on objective facts to which he was not indifferent. Remarkable in Pier

---

8. The reliance on subjective feelings or thoughts to inform the conscience is deficient if one's conscience violates Christ's commandments, magisterial teachings or natural law principles. Catholics, of course, are also guided by the lives of the saints. The error "man is the measure of all things" can be traced to Protagoras, the fifth-century BC Greek philosopher. Aquinas shows that objectively error is the result of violating right reason—rooted in natural law—or divine law, *ST*, Ia–IIae, q. 91, a. 4.

9. *ST* Ia–IIae, q. 96, a. 6, resp; Rom 2:15.

Giorgio's letter is the absence of any attempt to justify himself; instead, he assumed full responsibility: he was upset because he hurt everyone. Having hurt others meant some correction, some way of rectifying the situation, was needed.

1.2. Conscience-Formation

Even though Pier Giorgio had not yet received the sacrament of reconciliation when he wrote the above letter, he developed the letter along the lines of sacramental reconciliation: he began by the visible effects of father, mother, teacher; he then turned to the cause: he was responsible for their pain; and concluded, he did "wrong." This was the motive for seeking forgiveness, "I beg you to forgive me." But, recognizing guilt with a contrite heart, and seeking forgiveness, left one element: the promise to make changes; this was conversion, and Pier Giorgio expressed this desire to change, "I promise you that I will become good."

How did a seven-year-old have such a refined conscience? Childhood experiences, especially in terms of values, are inseparable from what parents have taught in the home—what Pier Giorgio learned and observed. Although Alfredo Frassati had been referred to as an "agnostic," he held humanist values which he transmitted to Pier Giorgio. He conveyed to his son a strong sense of truth, justice and coherency reflecting his social concerns, channeled into his political views. In the case of Pier Giorgio's mother, Adelaide Ametis, even though described as a "formal," Catholic, Pier Giorgio learned from her the value of diligence and sacrifice, learning respect and responsibility.[10] Adelaide was also a woman who suffered because of her personal problems, and Pier Giorgio would have been sensitive to this.

Pier Giorgio's teacher, Rosina Busatto was hired based on her suitability to teach the Frassati children. Certainly, she reflected the family's values. Finally, and most important, as a baptized infant, Pier Giorgio experienced God's grace at work in him, grace with which Pier Giorgio actively collaborated.

---

10. Calling Alfredo Frassati an "agnostic" and Adelaide Ametis a "formal" Catholic is not really justified. Both of Pier Giorgio's parents show values that suggest they not only respected the teachings of the Catholic Church, but the practices, and morals of Catholicism were transmitted to their children. This is especially evident in the formation of Pier Giorgio's conscience.

1.3. Sacrament of Penance

Pier Giorgio received the sacrament of penance when he was nine years old, but the letter of 1908 written to his parents when he was seven, reflects a letter of a boy who was already prepared for confession. On June 11, 1910, Pier Giorgio confessed his sins for the first time in the Church of Corpus Domini in Turin. He confessed to Canon Giovanni Grossi, and his mother helped Pier Giorgio to list his "gravest" sins.[11] The involvement of Pier Giorgio's mother meant practicing confessing his sins to his mother, highlighting the sacrament's value.[12]

The purpose of the sacrament is to purify the soul of the sinner of venial sins, or cleanse the soul and restore God's grace in the case of mortal sins reestablishing communion with God and his church. The contrite heart recognized faults, seeks pardon, promises to make changes by avoiding occasions of sins, and makes satisfaction through an act of penance. Even before the sacrament, Pier Giorgio had already recognized the state of his heart and the need to make change. He begged pardon. But now, Pier Giorgio sought through the sacrament, reconciliation not only with God, but his church, being in harmony with the community that he had hurt by his sins. The failure to adhere to Christ's two principal commandments of love leads the believer to confession, "You shall love the Lord your God with all your heart, with all your soul, with all your strength, and with all your mind: and your neighbor as yourself."[13]

Advancing toward the baroque confessional and its purple curtain, Pier Giorgio's eyes were illuminated with his extended time in prayers afterwards. Although Pier Giorgio followed the precepts of the church regarding confession, this would soon change; Pier Giorgio began confessing himself frequently, at times even on consecutive days in the morning. He believed that a slightest mark on the soul of a venial sin could weigh as much as that of a grave sin, so, he needed to confess even the quick outbursts of impatience or anger.[14]

---

11. Frassati, *Calendario*, "Turin, June 11, 1910." The Church of Corpus Domini in Turin is associated with a eucharistic miracle which Pier Giorgio will later write about in detail to his friend Miss Maria Fischer when he is twenty years old. The miracle which took place June 6, 1453, became the sight of the present day baroque basilica. Construction was completed in 1671 located in Piazza Corpus Domini.

12. Frassati, *La fede*, 28.

13. Luke 10:27. Cf. Deut 6:5; Lev 19:18. "Neighbor" is literally the one close/next to you, which may be family, friends, acquaintances, colleagues.

14. Frassati, *La fede*, 29.

Pier Giorgio sought a more intense encounter, a sublime union with him, a desire that continued to intensify. A fundamental trait of Pier Giorgio was his sensitivity, his refined conscience, and at seven years old he experienced for the first time purification in the sacrament of confession. Don Felice Cane, a Salesian priest, was Pier Giorgio's regular confessor from the time he was fourteen years old until his death. In fact, Pier Giorgio was more concerned about confessing his sins than having a regular confessor and because of his changing locations, and limited time, he would go to any priest for confession rather than miss Holy Communion.[15] But the advantage of having a regular confessor was that the person could be helped to make improvements in areas of repeated sins that caused difficulty for the penitent. Pier Giorgio was so indifferent to what people thought of him frequently confessing, and so pure in heart, that he did not bother with what people were thinking even if he could be overheard. Pier Giorgio's sensitive conscience seeking to overcome his smallest defects, led him regularly to the sacrament and kept him in a state of grace.[16]

2. Letter to His Mother, December 20, 1910[17]

Pier Giorgio was about six months away from his first communion and receiving the sacrament of penance when he wrote to his mother in December 1910. At nine years old he acknowledged his mother's nameday. The activities with his sister mentioned in his letter included a poem they wrote together in German for their mother. When Alfredo Frassati had studied in Germany he developed a great admiration for the German culture and people. His Germanophile values were transmitted to his children who learned German, and the language became part of Pier Giorgio and his sister's cultural formation.

In his letter, the poem along with the bouquet of flowers had one objective: to please his mother. Pier Giorgio knew his mother's love for flowers as they were often the object of her paintings. Going to the garden with his grandmother, Linda Ametis, then, growing his own flowers, and picking them, he could offer them as a gift to his mother. The love for flowers refined Pier Giorgio's sense of beauty, offering his mother a beautiful bouquet.

Besides the bouquet, Pier Giorgio made his mother a threefold promise: to pass his exams, to please his mother, to be good. A sense that Pier Giorgio truly desired to please his mother, to make her happy, emerged in

15. Frassati, *La fede*, 29.
16. Frassati, *La fede*, "Testimony of Father Mario Zabelli, SJ," 31.
17. *Letters*, 7; Ital. ed., 8.

his letters. The significance of this "making happy" was the other-centeredness of his wish. His focus was not on what he wanted, but on what made the "other" happy, and at this young age, the focus was on his mother.

To show the truthfulness of this desire, Pier Giorgio "prayed for this." He did not stop with praying for his own needs, passing exams; in his letter the coordinating conjunction, "and," unified praying for himself with praying for his mother, "that he always makes you happy." A second coordinating conjunction extended his prayers to his father, although he was writing on his mother's namesday, but he also prayed that God would keep his father in good health. Pier Giorgio's prayers included his exams, his mother's happiness, and both his father and mother's health.

As he closed his letter Pier Giorgio conveyed best wishes on behalf of others, and in this instance, the "Salesian priest," since he was taking his exams at a Salesian institute, Don Bosco College, in the month of July in Alassio, in preparation for secondary school in Turin at Massimo D'Azeglio.[18]

2.1. First Communion

In June 1911, a few days before Pier Giorgio received his first communion, he and his sister, Luciana, were with Mère Sainte Catherine, who belonged to the institute of the Helpers of the Souls in Purgatory, walking on corso Duca d'Aosta in Turin. They were present when the Viaticum was brought past them with the bell ringing. Mère Sainte Catherine had observed the indifference among the people; in fact, she commented that the people should have been kneeling just as when a king walks past. She told them, "Let us kneel. It is right for a King."[19] This was precisely what Pier Giorgio did, he knelt in the street and exclaimed, "He is the King of Kings!"[20]

Pier Giorgio clearly received a Roman Catholic formation in the sacraments: he knew that the Blessed Sacrament, the Viaticum being brought, is Jesus Christ, the King of kings, and if one kneels for a king, then one should be kneeling for the King of kings all the more. Pier Giorgio was ten years old with remarkable attentiveness to the presence of Christ, transforming his posture for the Lord's presence. Sensitivity, conscience, education all contributed to Pier Giorgio's understanding of the Real Presence, but especially his faith prompted by God's grace. Per Giorgio was prepared to receive his first communion.

---

18. *Letters*, 8n3; see Siccardi, *Pier Giorgio Frassati*, 79.
19. Casalegno, *Pier Giorgio Frassati*, 42.
20. Frassati, *Calendario*, "Turin, June, 1911."

On June 19, in the Chapel of the Auxiliary Sisters of the Holy Souls of Purgatory, Pier Giorgio and Luciana received their first communion, and their mother commented how the two looked like "two newlyweds."[21] Pier Giorgio received both sacraments with his sister, Luciana, confession and two years later communion. These intense spiritual occasions also reflected the bond the two developed as brother and sister. So, the brother and sister not only grew up playing together, learning how to get along, but most important, they shared key moments in their spiritual journey.

Pier Giorgio and his sister received their first communion from the same priest who heard their first confession, Canon Grossi. When Pier Giorgio was signalled by the Sister to approach the altar rail to receive the Consecrated Host, Pier Giorgio turned around to his mother before getting up from the pew, waiting for her nod, which she gave more than once, so that he could step forward to receive communion.[22] Did Pier Giorgio turn to his mother because he was uncertain of his actions, seeking his mother's approval? Pier Giorgio grew up to become a self-confident individual and with leadership qualities; but, at this stage, Pier Giorgio sought his mother's reassurance as he rose to approach the altar. Undoubtedly, focused on the Holy Eucharist, having knelt in the streets of Turin only a few days previously when the Viaticum was brought past him, Pier Giorgio approached the Altar of God in awe as he received the Sacred Host for the first time. His religious sensitivity made him wonder whether he could, or could not approach—even with the approval of the religious Sister, and even with his own sister ready to go ahead.[23] Pier Giorgio needed in this exceptional moment of receiving Christ's body the reassurance of his mother that he may do so, as Pier Giorgio had trusted his mother as his moral teacher and guide who sought what was best for him. It was not a sign of uncertainty, or insecurity, but rather, complete trust.

Adelaide Ametis, an artist, visually sensitive and receptive to harmony and symmetry, recognized the value of form and appreciated the reverence in the sacred liturgical rite, as part of an experience where one's soul is raised to the Transcendent. Now, her children could partake in this most intimate union with God, through the body and blood of his Son, Jesus Christ. The

---

21. Frassati, *Calendario*, "Turin, June, 1911." *Suore Ausiliatrici delle Anime del Purgatorio*, "Auxiliary Sisters of the Souls in Purgatory." The female religious institute was formally erected in Paris, January 19, 1856, by Eugene Smet (1825–1871) under the recommendation of Jean-Marie Vianney. Mère Marie de la Providence (religious name) was beatified by Pope Pius XII in 1957.

22. Frassati, *La fede*, 39.

23. Luciana describes herself as, "rebellious in nature, and above all certain of my actions." Frassati, *La fede*, 39.

Latin chant, the fragrance of incense, clear ring of bells, flicker of candles in the Baroque chapel of the Helpers of the Souls in Purgatory, celebrating the sacrament Jesus himself commanded. "'Take, eat, this is my body.' And he took a cup, and when he had given thanks he gave it to them saying, 'Drink of it, all of you; for this is my blood of the covenant which is poured out for many for the forgiveness of sins.'"[24] For the first time, Pier Giorgio received the Sacred Host; the altar boy holding the gold paten under his chin, Pier Giorgio in his communion suit and Luciana in her white communion dress, in the chapel the brother and sister looked like a "beautiful picture," receiving their first communion.[25]

The morning liturgy was followed by another in the afternoon with the theologian Don Borla preaching on the Eucharist, in addition to their preparation by Emilia Giuliano.[26] Both Pier Giorgio and Luciana received a catechetical preparation for the reception of the sacrament with the catechesis followed by renewing their baptismal promises in the afternoon.[27]

When the nine-year-old Pier Giorgio received first communion, he grasped with the help of Mère Sainte Catherine that Jesus in the Holy Eucharist is the King of kings. In the providential occurrence only a few days previously, Pier Giorgio had knelt in the streets of Turin as the Viaticum went passed. Together the sacramental and eschatological marked Pier Giorgio's first communion—and his spirituality: the realism of Jesus Christ, King—past, present and future—before whom he knelt, indifferent to the presence of others, meant a lived faith. Even this indifference toward others became a spiritual trait of Pier Giorgio's. He knew who the eucharistic Jesus was and having grasped the realism of Christ's body and blood, Pier Giorgio's heart, mind and body responded; accordingly, his posture expressed adoration.

Don Cojazzi had been tutoring Pier Giorgio and Luciana with their studies at Massimo D'Azeglio Secondary School, and so, when the two received their first communion, the Salesian gave them each a book as a gift, to Pier Giorgio, *Christopher Columbus*, and to Luciana, *Fabiola*. Don Cojazzi's

24. Matt 26:26–28.

25. Frassati, *La fede*, 39. It should be noted that Luciana Frassati's tone tends to be critical in describing the events surrounding their first communion, especially strong is her criticism of their mother who was more preoccupied with outward "appearance," *apparato*, 39. Besides Pier Giorgio's obedience to his mother, Luciana questioned their preparation for the sacrament, and even their upbringing. See nn27, 29 below.

26. Frassati, *La fede*, 38.

27. Frassati maintains that the catechesis she and Pier Giorgio received from the Canon Grossi, Don Cojazzi, and Eimilia Giuliano was inadequate to explain Pier Giorgio's spiritual life. Pier Giorgio's spiritual intensity already as a child can only be accounted for by his interior disposition toward God. See Frassati, *I giorni*, 34.

dedication written to Pier Giorgio, was signed, "To you, dear Pier Giorgio, on the memorable day of your First Communion, the book in which the undertakings of *Christopher Columbus* is written, glory of Italy and pride of religion. Imitate him in his greatness, and you too, be like him, *bearer of Christ* in your life. This I wish you with affection of a friend and the blessing of a Priest, your tutor, Turin, June 19, 1911."[28] Don Cojazzi wrote in his biography of Pier Giorgio that his words were "providential." Certainly, for the nine-year-old Pier Giorgio he did not only receive Christ, he would, in fact, bear Christ in his own life and also bring Christ to others.[29]

2.2. Frequent Communion

In the Catechism of Pius X of 1908, the practice of receiving the Holy Eucharist was extended to "frequent" reception with the counsel of a spiritual director. This change came about only three years before Pier Giorgio received his first communion. In Pier Giorgio's sacramental life, frequent confession and frequent communion quickly developed with the guidance and counsel of a good Jesuit while he pursued his secondary school studies at the Social Institute.[30] In other words, an unplanned spiritual rerouting had occurred when his planned studies at Massimo D'Azeglio were interrupted, leading Pier Giorgio to the Jesuit Social Institute in 1913.[31]

Father Pietro Lombardi, Pier Giorgio's Jesuit spiritual director while he was studying at the Social Institute, soon discovered who Pier Giorgio's mother was, and Father Lombardi would have to confront her while he spiritually directed the twelve-year-old. Two testimonies serve well, expressing Pier Giorgio's determination with matters involving his mother, and both involved sacraments, confession and communion. These issues pertaining to the sacraments reflected Pier Giorgio's intuitive understanding of sacramental theology, knowing confession and communion belonged together.

---

28. Cojazzi, *Testimonianze*, 34.

29. Don Cojazzi's acquaintance with Pier Giorgio and the Frassati family led to the first biography on Pier Giorgio based entirely on Cojazzi's collected testimonies. Luciana Frassati's tone and comments with regards to her parents in *I giorni* are often a reaction to Cojazzi's exaggeration or over-emphasis of harmonious relations between Pier Giorgio and his parents.

30. Details on Pier Giorgio's studies will be given in chapter 4.

31. This interruption is due to having to repeat Latin; Pier Giorgio's shock and confusion with his Latin results was expressed in his letter to his father, October 1913. See chapter 1, section 5, and also chapter 4, sections 3 and 4. See Frassati, *Calendario*, "Torino, November, 1913."

Having left the secular environment of Massimo D'Azeglio, Pier Giorgio was surrounded by Christian symbols, values and instruction.

The first issue was when Pier Giorgio had returned home one day after confessing to his spiritual director; his mother was frightened because Pier Giorgio had a very pure and innocent soul. So, Adelaide Frassati confronted Father Lombardi on matters of purity, knowing this subject was often examined with a good intention. But she also knew that an innocent soul such as Pier Giorgio's could only be shocked with the wrong questions; for Pier Giorgio, there was no such thing as impurity. So, she told the Jesuit spiritual director, "You cannot confess my child without my permission!"[32] However, Father Lombardi reassured Pier Giorgio's mother that he had plenty experience spiritually directing boys and hearing their confession.[33]

The second matter concerned communion which in fact became a "battle." Father Lombardi also had the reputation for preaching on the Holy Eucharist and had invited the pupils of the Social Institute to frequent communion.[34] The frequency of confession with his confessor meant that Pier Giorgio could also go to frequent communion; his confessor, who at this time was also Pier Giorgio's spiritual director, had recommended frequent confession. Pier Giorgio's desire to receive frequent communion also impressed Father Lombardi. Pier Giorgio began attending Mass several times a week, eventually, every day.[35] However, Pier Giorgio's mother was concerned that the practice would become "habitual" in a way that communion would lose meaning and Pier Giorgio would not be reflecting on the significance of the Eucharist, the practice would become a mere habit. Pier Giorgio's mother was opposed to Pier Giorgio's frequent communion. It took four days of insistence on Pier Giorgio's part, returning once again to Father Lombardi, and with great joy exclaimed, "Father, I won." Father Lombardi asked Pier Giorgio what he had won to be so happy, and Pier Giorgio replied, "You know very well, Father, I can receive Communion every day I insisted so much."[36] Father Lombardi stated, "Adelaide Frassati did not know her son."[37] But what did Pier Giorgio's mother not know? She certainly knew that her son was sensitive, that he was very pure, he respected his parents and family

---

32. Frassati, *La fede*, 32; *I giorni*, 45.
33. Frassati, *Beatitudes*, 24.
34. Casalegno, *Pier Giorgio Frassati*, 60.
35. Cojazzi, *Testimoniananze*, 34–35.
36. Frassati, *Beatitudes*, 24–25; *I giorni*, 45.
37. Siccardi, *Pier Giorgio Frassati*, 99.

members, God and the church. But, Adelaide sensed that her son might be gravitating toward the priesthood.[38]

Pier Giorgio's mother knew him very well and especially because his parents originally sent Pier Giorgio to Massimo D'Azeglio, they expected a more secular development in his studies, thinking in terms of a professional career. Alfredo Frassati considered a future for Pier Giorgio with his son as successor of *La Stampa*.[39] Pier Giorgio's spiritual life manifested those cardinal virtues acquired at home and cherished by his parents: prudence, justice, fortitude, temperance. These humanist virtues contain nothing distinctly Christian about them until they are elevated and perfected by divine grace and the sacramental life.[40]

Frequent communion and confession began at the Social Institute and this is where Pier Giorgio intensified his religious practices. The virtues he acquired at home were being perfected through the sacramental life. Pier Giorgio was becoming the person God meant him to be. Adelaide Frassati's fear was that Pier Giorgio's sensitivity and his desire to be virtuous would lead her son to religious life or the priesthood, something that would ultimately go against her wishes.[41] Pier Giorgio's spiritual life deepened. Seeds that had been planted in his soul received the nourishment needed to grow in abundance: confession, communion, eucharistic adoration, and the preaching on the Blessed Sacrament. When Pier Giorgio attended the Social Institute, he began listening to Father Lombardi's preaching on the Eucharist penetrating his soul. Moved by the Word, being moved by grace, created an ardent desire in Pier Giorgio to receive the Eucharist—with frequent confession; hence, Pier Giorgio desired to be in a state of grace each time he went to communion. A boy with a refined conscience, values instilled by his parents, illuminated by the teachings of Christ and his church, would only want to be in a state of grace each time he received communion.

Pier Giorgio desired to remain in a state of grace, and to persevere in sanctity, but whether he was on the path to the priesthood he could not know. All signs would appear that his sacramental life was leading him in the direction of ordination. Could these deep desires in Pier Giorgio germinating toward religious life and Holy Orders have been thwarted out of obedience to his mother? Pier Giorgio's sister seems to raise this possibility with regards to their mother, "but she did not realize that in the name of

38. Frassati, *I giorni*, 49.
39. Frassati, *I giorni*, 179.
40. *ST*, Ia–IIae, q. 62, a. 1.
41. In discussing the matter of Pier Giorgio's priestly vocation with Signora Wanda Gawronska, she asked me, rhetorically, "Do you think any mother who has only one son would want him to be a Priest?" Personal communication, December, 2015.

strict obedience a certain spiritual 'yeast' did not rise in us, especially in Pier Giorgio, who already most certainly held aspirations towards religious life and very beautiful moral ambitions."[42]

3. Letter to His Father—Pollone, October 1913[43]

Pier Giorgio's letters to his father were significantly fewer than those written to his mother; moreover, in his letters to his father, one does not find Pier Giorgio express the same depth of affection as in Pier Giorgio's letters to his mother. Even if the tone in this letter to his father was primarily informative, very matter-of-fact, Pier Giorgio still felt an intense desire to see his father. Pier Giorgio unquestionably manifested great love and respect for both his parents.

In his letter of October 1913, Pier Giorgio conveyed his desire to be with his father, then, wrote about his mother, then, the weather. For Pier Giorgio, these categories of discourse do not suggest attempts at "making" conversation. The statements contained relevant pieces of information. Then, he updated his father with his own activities which he gave in detail, specifically in reference to helping the gardener "carry" flower pots, reporting that the upper garden was being entirely "spaded," and finally, if it stopped raining, he would be able to "spread" the manure. The gardening reflected the importance of discussing the weather, especially in Pollone. Pier Giorgio made it clear he was working hard and not wasting any time. Even though school was approaching, and he was at their vacation home, this did not mean taking an extended break. The family had a strong work ethic and this was reflected in Pier Giorgio's responsibilities.

Based on the previous letter, plans had been changed.[44] In his September letter, Pier Giorgio had written to his mother on what was supposed to be his "last day" in Pollone, happy knowing he would soon be seeing her. But, Pier Giorgio's mother went to Pollone, instead. A significant piece of information that Pier Giorgio transmitted to his father was his mother's visit to Felicina. After telling his father that his mother went to visit one of the farmers who worked for them, Pier Giorgio pointed out that his mother promised to pay Paolino's tuition because the farmer could not afford to send her child, Paolino, to school. This awareness of poverty, which radically contrasted with Pier Giorgio's own secure lifestyle, made Pier Giorgio sensitive not only to the misery around him, but also to how his mother

---

42. Frassati, *La fede*, 39.
43. *Letters*, 12; Ital. ed., 12–13.
44. See *Letters*, "To mamma, Pollone, September 1913," (second letter), 11.

offered assistance to a poor worker's child. Adelaide Frassati paid for the boy's tuition, and thereby, secured his enrollment at school. Pier Giorgio was exposed not only to the charity offered to the poor through his father's newspaper, but also the kindness of his own mother's charitable acts.

3.1. Sacramental Life and Christian Responsibility

Pier Giorgio was not yet Confirmed; he had not yet made a transition to the Social Institute that would intensify his spiritual life, but at twelve years old, however, his letters reveal a strong sense of duty and responsibility, besides qualities of sensitivity and respect. His parents' receptivity to the needs of the poor, and Pier Giorgio who observed and reflected on his parents' actions, indirectly educated him in being attentive to the needy. His parents whom he admired, respected and loved served as role models of Christian charity. Pier Giorgio experienced the reception of the sacraments not only in terms of the value the spiritual value of the sacraments in one's vertical relationship with Christ, but also the horizontal relationship with Christ's church. The sacramental life reached outward to the needs of others, the value of helping others, the "common good," that one could not be content with one's own privileged lifestyle, but an awareness of the "other" by living and sharing gospel values.

Pier Giorgio attended to the garden in Pollone, cultivating rich crops. He sowed seeds and watered them. Pier Giorgio's soul was also a rich soil that he nurtured with the help of grace to grow and bear good fruit. "A sower went out to sow. And as he sowed, some seeds fell along the path, and the birds came and devoured them. Other seeds fell on rocky ground, where they had not much soil, and immediately they sprang up, since they had no depth of soil, but when the sun rose they were scorched; and since they had no root they withered away. Other seeds fell upon thorns, and the thorns grew up and choked them. Other seeds fell on good soil and brought forth grain, some a hundred-fold, some sixty, some thirty."[45]

The exam results from Massimo D'Azeglio at first appeared like a tragedy, but instead, unveiled the work of Providence: repeating Latin led him out of a public school, Massimo D'Azeglio, to the Roman Catholic Jesuit-run Social Institute.

---

45. Matt 13:3–8.

3.2. Start of Catholic Associations

Once at the Social Institute, under the spiritual direction of his Jesuit confessor, Father Pietro Lombardi, only three months after having started his studies, he registered in the Apostolate of Prayer and the Association of the Blessed Sacrament.[46] The membership for the Apostolate of Prayer was dated February 12, 1914, and signed by the local director, Father Lombardi. Pier Giorgio always kept his membership identity card of these associations in his pocket suggesting his religious identity was his true identity. This spiritual membership corresponded to Pier Giorgio's practice of daily communion. The associations themselves expressed Christian principles in two axes, prayer and service, Christ and one's neighbor.

During this time, early 1900s, with the presence of the Sacramentine Fathers at Santa Maria in Piazza in Turin, eucharistic adoration was promoted based on the teaching of their founder, Saint Peter Julian Eymard.[47] Among the registered members of eucharistic adoration was Father Pietro Lombardi.[48] In February 1914, Pier Giorgio also registered himself in the Association of the Blessed Sacrament.[49]

4. Letter to His Aunt Elena Ametis—Alassio, August 16, 1916[50]

Pier Giorgio just turned fifteen years old. His letter to his aunt appears as though he was writing to a friend; the closeness in the relationship between the two is evident, but also the capacity and desire to share his experiences with his aunt. Pier Giorgio believed his aunt would enjoy herself knowing she liked sailboats and sailing. His detailed description reflected the desire to be with others, as he thought about their presence, those whom he loved, as he referenced them in his letters, whether mother, father, sister, grandmother or aunt. The letter conveyed the genuine closeness Pier Giorgio had with his family members.[51]

---

46. Frassati, *Beatitudes*, 25.

47. The history of the Sacramentine Fathers goes back to the early 1800s with their founder, Peter Julian Eymard.

48. For details on the presence of the Sacramentine Fathers in Turin at Santa Maria in Piazza, their influence on the spiritual life of Turin, and the origins of the Sacramentine Fathers, see Casalegno, *Fra Terra e Cielo*, 2011.

49. Frassati, *Calendario*, "Turin, February, 1914." See also, Casalegno, *Fra Terra e Cielo*, 28.

50. *Letters*, 14–15; Ital. ed., 16.

51. The first friend Pier Giorgio wrote to after this letter to his aunt was his good

Pier Giorgio wrote to his aunt Elena from Alassio where he spent his summer vacations on the Italian Riviera, the Ligurian coast. His letter served to acknowledge and send his best wishes to his aunt on her namesday, and he found time to write and post his letter, hoping his letter arrived on time.

The description Pier Giorgio provided referring to his father's lunch with the Salesians was suggestive of the Salesian presence in Alassio. With the Salesian Don Bosco Institute where Pier Giorgio had written his exams, the family's ties with Don Cojazzi, and the presence of the Salesians in Turin, Saint John Bosco's native city, it should not be surprising that Alfredo had lunch with the Salesians. Pier Giorgio wrote about this detail rather naturally.

The visit with Father Besnate, a beekeeper, represented an educational encounter to learn about bees, and taste of the honey they produce. This was the first instance that Pier Giorgio commented on "taste," referring to something he had eaten. Tasting the honey Father Besnate offered them, Pier Giorgio described it as the "best honey." Pier Giorgio's appreciation for nature was further reflected in this early adolescent experience of honey which he related to his aunt, and felt that the "best taste" was worth mentioning—to share the experience as if his aunt Elena were there with him.

The value of nature and Pier Giorgio's surroundings continued with the subject of weather; in this instance the weather changed, "the last two weeks of August," becoming cloudier. The weather, of course, related to Pier Giorgio's outdoor activities, what could be enjoyed under the sun, on the beach, sailing and swimming. Axerio, a friend of Pier Giorgio's from secondary school, invited him to go swimming, a visit to his home or to go elsewhere, indicating the activities Pier Giorgio shared with his friends, and so, his aunt was also informed not only how he spent his time, but even with whom he interacted.

Sailing in Mascardi's Jole, Pier Giorgio described the adventure being in the "speeding" boat and the water splashing into the boat. But Pier Giorgio's real desire was to have enjoyed the boating day with his aunt, seeing her happy sailing in Mascardi's Jole. Just as Pier Giorgio had given his father's departure day and time, he also let his aunt know the precise date of his arrival in Pollone, the twenty-third, a week from the day he wrote his letter, mentioning that he would be home, seeing his aunt and grandmother. Although enjoying himself at the beach, Pier Giorgio sounded homesick, longing to be with his family in Pollone.

---

friend Carlo Bellingeri, the following month in September.

Pier Giorgio's sign-off was not only a farewell to his aunt, but he repeated his best wishes for her namesday, sending his grandmother a kiss, as well as a kiss to his aunt.

4.1. Confirmation

About a month before his fourteenth birthday, on June 10, 1915, in his parish church of *La Crocetta*, Pier Giorgio was confirmed by Monsignor Costanzo Castrale, the Auxiliary Bishop of Turin, along with many other children.[52] In spite of the favorable outcome with the Jesuits, Pier Giorgio's mother, not expecting him to separate himself from his sister, sent Pier Giorgio to a "common confessor," thus, removing him from Father Lombardi, and directing Pier Giorgio to the Salesian, Don Felice Cane, spiritual disciple of Don John Bosco.[53] From his godfather as a gift for his confirmation Pier Giorgio received *The Mass in History and Art, in the Soul of Saints and in Our Life*, with the dedication, "A gift as a modest remembrance of Holy Confirmation ... what a blessing if from the readings of these pages you will feel your devotion to the Sacrifice of the Altar increase, and will remember to say a prayer, from your most affectionate, godfather."[54]

Confirmed in the Holy Spirit, Pier Giorgio was visibly overjoyed having prepared for four years since his first communion, already receiving frequent communion, an active prayer life in his Apostolate of Payer and Association of the Holy Eucharist, the preparation and desire for the sealing of the Holy Spirit was reflected in Pier Giorgio's joyful smile.[55] With the celebration over, and outside of the church, Pier Giorgio could not stop smiling out of excitement, a smile that could only be defined as "angelic."[56] His delightful smile was so bright, that his mother, in order to take pictures of him, ordered him to keep his mouth closed.[57] Adelaide observed that Pier Giorgio most certainly received from the Holy Spirit the gift of joy.[58]

---

52. Frassati gives two different dates published for Pier Giorgio's confirmation: "June 10," *Calendario*, and "June 19," *La fede*, 58; also, Cojazzi, "June 21," *Testimonianze*, 81. The *Positio* records the date as June 10, 1915, *Positio*, X.

53. Frassati, *Calendario*, "June 10, 1915."

54. Frassati, *Calendario*, "June 10, 1915." Pier Giorgio's godfather was Count Enrico Luigi Balbo di Vinadio and his godmother was his aunt Elena. *Positio*, p. X.

55. Pier Giorgio's Confirmation photo shows him with a big smile of a thirteen-year-old confirmed in the Holy Spirit.

56. Frassati, *La fede*, 59.

57. Frassati, *La fede*, 59.

58. Pierazzi, *Così ho visto*, 53.

The cook for the Frassati family, Carolina Masoero, asked Pier Giorgio a question relating to his confirmation, "What Grace did you ask from the Lord, today that you made your Confirmation?" Pier Giorgio replied, "I asked him a Grace for me and one for Luciana," but the cook insisted on knowing the grace, but Pier Giorgio replied, "Graces are not meant to be revealed."[59]

5. Virgin Mary

Pier Giorgio was blessed to grow up in the vicinity of two major Marian shrines, in Turin, *La Consolata*, "Saint Mary the Consoler," and the other shrine near Pollone, *Madonna di Oropa*, "Our Lady of Oropa." Both shrines date back to the fourth century with centuries of devotion, processions and pilgrimage, and both shrines have the status of "basilica." Pier Giorgio was not only accustomed to praying in both shrines, he had a devotion to both Marian titles, "Consolata" and "Oropa." Pier Giorgio's eucharistic-centered life also meant he united himself with the Mother of God, especially through praying the Rosary.

5.1 Rosary

Pier Giorgio's practice of praying the Rosary each day developed the same time as he began going to daily communion. Pier Giorgio preferred a "rough" Rosary, one that he could feel praying with his fingers, and he made by his own hands by cultivating the "tears of Job," grey hard berries, which he brought to the sisters to make his Rosary. More than once Pier Giorgio's mother found him late in the evening, asleep on his knees.[60] Sister Angelica used to say, "If Pier Giorgio cannot be found, he must be in his room praying his Rosary."[61]

5.2 Our Lady of Oropa

When Pier Giorgio was studying at the Social Institute and nourishing his spiritual life through the sacraments, his love for Our Lady also increased. At thirteen years old, while on vacation in Pollone, Pier Giorgio made the

---

59. Pierazzi, *Così ho visto*, 55.

60. Frassati, *La fede*, 182. A Rosary from the "tears of Job" which Pier Giorgio would give to the sisters is visible on his bed in his Pollone room.

61. Frassati, *La fede*, "Testimony of Sister Prassede Barbero delle Rosminiane," 186.

five-mile walk to the "Black Virgin."⁶² In order for Pier Giorgio to be back home by exactly eight in the morning, before his absence could be noticed, he would ask the gardener, Giuseppe, to wake him before dawn by having a cord tied to his wrist and letting it hang from the window on the second floor.⁶³ Then, the gardener only needed to pull on the cord to wake Pier Giorgio before sunrise, who would then make his five mile walk to Oropa, praying the Rosary on the way, attending Mass, paying homage to Our Lady, and returning home by eight in the morning.⁶⁴

Situated in a valley surrounded by rocks and mountains, the Latin words are inscribed over the arch entering the ancient basilica, *O quam beatus, o beata, quem viderint oculi tui*, "Oh, how blessed the one, who will have set his eyes on you." The devotion to the Virgin Mary, attributed to Bishop Eusebius of Vercelli, began in the fourth century.⁶⁵ The devotion to the Black Madonna loved by the people of Biella was felt early in Pier Giorgio's life. Our Lady of Oropa was "his" Madonna.⁶⁶ Pier Giorgio loved the Black Madonna intensely; at eleven or twelve years old, his eyes were so fixed on her that at times it seemed as if he wanted to "devour" the Madonna with his eyes, as if in a state of rapture. Even the Mass celebrant, Don Felice Paschetto, would have to remind him that Mass was about to begin.⁶⁷

---

62. The title "Black Virgin," Italian, *Madonna Bruna*, comes from the dark wood used to give the three-dimensional presentation to Mary. The wood is of *pinus cimbra* which is hard but easy to work of a red-black color; it does not appear to collect dust, and remains a dark color. The face and hands of the Madonna and Child are varnished in black. Catella, *La Vergine bruna*, 18.

63. Frassati, *Calendario*, "Pollone, 1914"; Frassati, *I giorni*, 43.

64. Walking uphill early in the morning would have still been cool; a beautiful walk northeast toward the Sanctuary of Oropa. On April 6, 2017, I walked from Favaro to Blessed Pier Giorgio's family home in Pollone to celebrate a private Mass in the Blessed's room on the occasion of his birthday. The spring scenery on the road from Favaro was displayed in exquisite beauty: snow-capped mountains, fir and pine descending the hills, jingle of cattle bells and songs of sparrow, water splashing through a brook, and homes quietly at a distance. Pier Giorgio's walks since his childhood through such breathtaking scenes brought him this sense of contemplative beauty in nature leading him to the Madonna of Oropa—and ultimately to the majestic Creator God.

65. Catella, *La Vergine bruna*, 13–14.

66. Frassati, *La fede*, 168.

67. Frassati, *La fede*, "Testimony of Don Felice Paschetto, rector of Cossato," 171. In the ancient basilica, in the northeast transept, a painting is displayed of Blessed Pier Giorgio Frassati.

5.3. Saint Mary the Consoler

The celebrated Marian shrine in the heart of Turin was built over a Roman temple of what had been the entrance to the city. The sanctuary was elevated to Papal Basilica by Pope Pius X in 1906, when Pier Giorgio was five years old. Honor of *La Consolata*, Saint Mary the Consoler, dates back to the fourth century. The sanctuary of *La Consolata* with the picture of Our Lady represents "everything for the Turin people."[68] The extraordinary Baroque artwork reflected the devotion of the people and their spiritual life. The Marian sanctuary in the heart of an industrial city such as Turin meant a spiritual point of reference for the Catholics to strengthen their faith.

Pier Giorgio, being devoted to the Virgin Mary, had the custom of going to *La Consolata* for prayers, often heard saying, he was "going to Mass at *La Consolata* . . . ," "going for Communion at *La Consolata* . . . ," "accompany his sister to *La Consolata*. . . ."[69] The presence of Saint Mary the Consoler to whom Pier Giorgio turned in prayer, pointed to the sacramental life: the devotion to Mary and the Eucharist are united: the heart of Mary leads to the heart of Christ.

Questions

(Note: *ST* refers to *Summa Theologiae* of Saint Thomas Aquinas—part [I/II/III], question, article, response)

1. How was Pier Giorgio prepared for the sacrament of penance (1.2; 1.3)?
2. What motivated Pier Giorgio's frequent communion (2.2)? What was Pier Giorgio's mother's concern, and how was the matter resolved (2.2)?
3. In which Catholic Associations did Pier Giorgio enrol (3.2)? How old was he at this time (3.2)?
4. What are the details of Pier Giorgio's confirmation (4.1)?
5. Which three ways does Pier Giorgio express his devotion to the Blessed Virgin Mary (§5)?
6. How is the conscience aided by the natural law, "the good is to be pursued and evil is to be avoided?" (See note 9; *ST*, Ia–IIae, q. 96, a. 6, *resp*;

---

68. Pope Pius X, 1906, elevating the Sanctuary to status of Papal Basilica.
69. Frassati, *La fede*, "Testimony of Luciana Frassati," 176.

Rom 2:15.) How is the conscience enlightened by the divine law? (See note 8; *ST*, Ia–IIae, q. 91, a. 4, *resp.*)

4

Studies

Anyone who wishes to understand Christ's words and to savor them fully should strive to be like him in every way.

IMITATION OF CHRIST 1:1

This chapter treats five of Pier Giorgio's letters, all pertaining to the development of his studies: home tutoring, Massimo D'Azeglio, Social Institute, Bonafous Institute, and finally, the Turin Polytechnic. Pier Giorgio's institutional studies providentially change when he is registered at the Jesuit-run *Istituto Sociale* in Turin; from a public school to Catholic education. Although Pier Giorgio spent only two years at the Social Institute, they were sufficient to produce spiritual fruit that had been germinating in him since childhood.

1. Rosina Busatto: Home Tutor

Pier Giorgio started his formal studies when he was five years old with his sister, Luciana, who was a year younger. They were home tutored by Rosina Busatto from 1906–1909.[1] Having moved from via Legnano N. 33, to corso Siccardi N. 55, Alfredo and Adelaide employed a private teacher, the common practice among the middle- and upper-middle-class families. This also meant that while Pier Giorgio and Luciana were being taught, they

---

1. Casalegno, *Pier Giorgio Frassati*, 33.

continued to receive the values their parents wanted for their children. Alfredo and Adelaide knew very well the significance of their children's initial education; these early childhood years would be most formative, not only in the subjects entrusted to Rosina Busatto, but also preserving the coherency of values which the two children received at home. Pier Giorgio and Luciana, therefore, were home tutored for three years, until they sat for their exams in July 1910, which they took at the Salesian College in Alassio.

Besides Italian and Latin, Pier Giorgio and his sister already as children knew some German; as his letters indicate, Pier Giorgio was already writing poems and letters in German. Pier Giorgio's letter of December 20, 1910, included a poem written in German to his mother by him and Luciana.[2] Even before Pier Giorgio had gone to Massimo D'Azeglio, signs were, however, already present that he might have difficulty with studies. The year before Pier Giorgio sat for his exams for Massimo D'Azeglio, both Pier Giorgio and his sister had to repeat their state exams taken in Alassio. Alfredo wrote to his wife, "I received today the news of the complete failure. In time we shall have to absolutely look into this because if they accustom themselves as children in this way, I don't know what we could expect when they're adults. . . . I'm really very disappointed. Let them know that I will be late to come to Alassio because I am heart-broken with their failure."[3] With their parents visibly upset and worried, both Pier Giorgio and Luciana made efforts to improve, and by October, the exams showed favorable results with grades obtained in the 80s.

Rosina Busatto was entrusted with the elementary school education of the Frassati children for three years, but the teacher was also expected to prepare Pier Giorgio and Luciana for their entrance exams to Massimo D'Azeglio where they planned to attend in the autumn of 1909. Concern over Pier Giorgio's progress in particular was an issue since he was a boy and he would have to earn a living.[4] Having sat for exams and passed at the Salesian College, in Alassio, Pier Giorgio and his sister were prepared to attend the first years of middle school.[5]

2. Chapter 1, section 2, above.
3. Frassati, *Calendario*, "Turin, July, 1909, Alfredo to his wife."
4. Frassati, *Calendario*, "Turin, July, 1909, Alfredo to his wife."
5. Corresponding to grades 6 and 7 in North American schools; or what is technically referred to in Italian as *prima e secondo ginnasiale*. See below, nn15 and 22.

2. Don Cojazzi and the Salesians

The Frassati connection with the Salesians should not come as a surprise given that Turin was the home of the congregation founded by Don John Bosco in 1859. The new but politically controversial congregation was devoted especially to Turin's homeless boys, although to the education of boys in general. Drawing their spirituality from Saint Francis de Sales, they became known as "Salesians." Working with the youth made the Salesians successful educators of young boys, following Don John Bosco's principle of "reason, religion and kindness."

Don Cojazzi's interaction with Pier Giorgio and his sister drew from the Salesian tradition of education.[6] Don Cojazzi spent two years with Pier Giorgio and Luciana, tutoring them in Latin after they had been removed from their first year of secondary school by their mother. Don Cojazzi's own testimony revealed that Pier Giorgio, even as a child, preferred to have instruction on Jesus rather than on schoolwork, "I remember at the first lesson, when after having hurried up with his schoolwork chores, he got up from his chair, standing upright in his black apron, with his arms folded, and, staring straight at me with his two dark eyes, saying, 'And now tell me a story about Jesus.'"[7] This passage suggests that Don Cojazzi focused on studies in Latin rather than spiritual content. In fact, Don Cojazzi's influence on Pier Giorgio was minimal, *praticamente nulla*, "almost nothing."[8] Over a two-year period, from the spring of 1911 to the autumn of 1913, before entering the Social Institute, Don Cojazzi's presence was that of a Latin tutor.

The Salesians rejected the secular ideals of revolutionary France being exported to Italy, namely, atheist philosophers such as Rousseau and Voltaire.[9] In fact, Don Bosco supported political views recognizing the supreme authority of the pope. Don Cojazzi promoted a Christian and anti-positivistic culture against philosophical texts introduced into the secondary schools, rejecting atheists, idealists and pantheists, such as G. Berkeley, G. Bruno, G. Hegel, D. Hume, E. Kant, J. Locke, J.-J. Rousseau, A. Schopenhauer and B. Spinoza. These philosophers, radical empiricists, idealists and pantheists,

---

6. John Bosco was born in Casatelnuovo d'Asti, Piedmont, on August 16, 1815, and died in Turin, in January 31, 1888. He was beatified in June 2, 1929, by Pope Pius XI, and canonized by the same pope five years later, April 1, 1934.

7. Cojazzi, *Testimonianze*, 31. Aprons were traditionally worn by children in Italian schools.

8. *Positio*, 50.

9. Bosco, "Storia ecclesiastica, 496.

were studied in many of Turin's state schools, leading to disagreements and confusion reinforcing philosophical errors.[10]

Pier Giorgio and his sister began their studies at Massimo D'Azeglio in October 1910, the same year that anticlerical forces began a persecution of religious congregations and orders across Italy. During these attacks slander was also used to diminish the credibility of the church and thereby weaken its influence. The Salesians were also target of these offensive accusations, claims that the "corruption" of minors had occurred at their Salesian college in Varazze.[11]

Alfredo Frassati, who was respectful of the Catholic Church, made his chief editor responsible, and followed the Varazze matter. Alfredo printed its final developments to make sure the public was presented with the outcome of an enquiry. Frassati's newspaper published the results of the Varazze accusations noting that the vice prefect was removed from his position by the Italian government and from his seat in Savona to one of lesser influence, being accused of spreading false rumors to discredit the Salesians.[12] With the outcome of the affair and Alfredo Frassati having defended the Salesians, Alfredo was approached by Don Bosco's congregation in gratitude, offering their assistance to him in any way. As a result, Don Cojazzi entered into the Frassati residence as a Latin tutor in the spring of 1911.[13]

3. Letter to Carlo Bellingeri—Pollone, September 23, 1916[14]

The letter to Carlo Bellingeri is the first letter available among Pier Giorgio's letters that was not addressed to a family member. Pier Giorgio was fifteen years old when he wrote to Bellingeri, and his writing style remains in continuity with his earlier letters, the structure of the letter, and the subject matter. Examining the letter Pier Giorgio's dominant thought concerns his studies, the issue of his exams, in particular his French exam. The tone was friendly, sensitive and respectful, and in only a few lines of his writing, Pier Giorgio communicated the constancy of goodness in his personality.

Pier Giorgio began by thanking Bellingeri for his thoughtful card, suggestive of Pier Giorgio's ongoing desire to engage in dialogue with his

---

10. Siccardi, *Pier Giorgio Frassati*, 79.
11. Siccardi, *Pier Giorgio Frassati*, 80.
12. Details on the Italian government and politics will be taken up in chapter 7.
13. Siccardi maintains Don Cojazzi's entry into the Frassati resident as Latin tutor was in December 1910, *Pier Giorgio Frassati*, 93.
14. *Letters*, 15; Ital. ed., 16.

addressee. Pier Giorgio responded with words of gratitude to Bellingeri, for the "kind postcard," and he added, the "pleasure" the card brought him. Pier Giorgio expressed indirectly the value he attached to his friend.

Only after acknowledging the card did Pier Giorgio proceed to talk about himself. A relational structure emerges in his letters present since childhood. His studies almost always had a place of central importance, earlier when he wrote to his parents and family members, and in this letter, writing to his friend. Pier Giorgio invited Bellingeri to his home for a visit. They were classmates and Pier Giorgio asked for practical information regarding which professor would be giving the exam.

In his respectful style, Pier Giorgio closed his letter by asking Bellingeri to greet his mother as well as his brothers, Nanni and Alberto, on his behalf. The politeness the fifteen-year-old expressed in his closure to his friend, reflected Pier Giorgio's thoughtfulness: he included all of Bellingeri's family members in his farewell, besides his handshake to his good friend. These farewell wishes to others were not only extended when writing to his family, but they reflected Pier Giorgio's sensitivity toward others, as these affectionate farewells characterized Pier Giorgio's letters to his friends.

3.1. Massimo D'Azeglio Middle-Secondary School[15]

Massimo D'Azeglio was a reputable secondary school for the formation of future intellectuals.[16] Pier Giorgio first started studies at Massimo D'Azeglio when he was nine years old, October 1910. At the beginning of their secondary school studies, Pier Giorgio and his sister sat together at the same desk. One of their classmates, Guido Bonous, commented on how similar they were to each other, and how he, Guido, also helped both of them reorganize their books at the end of each class.[17] Adelaide withdrew them from Massimo D'Azeglio before the end of the school year.

In October 1911, after a six-month absence from secondary school, Pier Giorgio and his sister were registered once again to study, "seriously," in their first year.[18] He and Luciana sat side by side possibly to offer each other help.[19] But two years later, as Pier Giorgio advanced from his second

---

15. Officially, *Regio Ginnasio Liceo Massimo D'Azeglio*. Middle and secondary school meant technically eight years of studies. Details on the school system below, n22.

16. Siccardi, *Pier Giorgio Frasati*, 93.

17. Guido Bonous was two years older than Pier Giorgio. See Frassati, *Calendario*, "Turin, October 1910, Regio Ginnasio Liceo Massimo D'Azeglio."

18. Frassati, *Calendario*, "Turin, October 1911."

19. Frassati, *I giorni*, 36.

to third year of secondary school, he would have to repeat Latin, a required course, and he would have to repeat his second year of secondary school.[20] The news came to Pier Giorgio as a shock, especially knowing the reaction of his parents.[21] Pier Giorgio was removed from Massimo D'Azeglio and sent to the Jesuit, Social Institute. Pier Giorgio, however, would be required to repeat Latin a second time: this meant he would return to the Social Institute a second time.

3.1.1. Years in Public Middle-Secondary School

Pier Giorgio's years at Massimo D'Azeglio appear as follows: October 1910 to April 1911 (the two Frassati children were withdrawn by their mother); they were re-registered in October 1911 at Massimo D'Azeglio. In his second year of secondary school Pier Giorgio was required to repeat Latin, and so he was removed from the public school and his parents sent him to the Catholic Jesuit-run Social Institute beginning November 1913. Having completed his second and third year of secondary school in one year at the Social Institute, in October 1914 Pier Giorgio was readmitted to Massimo D'Azeglio where he joined his friends all in the fourth year.[22] He completed the two remaining years of secondary school, fourth and fifth years, and in October 1916 he was admitted to the *liceo* which lasted three years.[23] But, Pier Giorgio was required to repeat Latin, and in the second occurrence he was in the company of his sister who also had to repeat Latin. Pier Giorgio returned to the Social Institute where he registered in October 1917, and completed his last year of senior secondary school.[24]

It would appear strange that while Pier Giorgio had an excellent memory, he seemed to have difficulty as a student, not only in terms of the material studied, but even his classroom discipline. The following comment is

20. In the Italian system of education this would be the second year *ginnesiale* advancing to his third year.

21. The matter of "failing" is addressed in Pier Giorgio's letter dated "October, 1913, Pollone" and developed in chapter 1, section 5.

22. The *ginnesiale* system in Italy goes from years 1–5 of middle-secondary school. Once the fifth year is completed students have two years of *liceo* required for admission to polytechnic or university. Students normally begin polytechnic or university, if their studies begin early, and are not interrupted or repeated, at seventeen years old. "Middle" school studies began around nine or ten years old depending on the preparation of the child. Pier Giorgio began at nine and Luciana at eight years old.

23. The *liceo* corresponds to senior secondary school years.

24. Pier Giorgio was seventeen years old when he finished; because of World War I, the last year of *liceo* in 1918 was suppressed.

revelatory when he first began studies at Massimo D'Azeglio, "He was not a model student in the first years of secondary school. Often distracted, talker, he did not understand collective discipline. Homework was always his terror. Mathematics, geography, history were easy subjects because he really had an impressive memory. Even the grammatical rules he knew well and remembered. Only that he did not apply them. But even in these subjects he did not always show brilliant results. Many things he understood, he did not know how to present them; this is why he made a poor impression if he was asked questions."[25] These contrasts were present in Pier Giorgio's letters. He related events in minute details, such as in his appointments, travels dates, and keeping records. While his writing revealed syntactic errors, incorrect punctuation, and misspelled words, the events being related Pier Giorgio often described beautifully and precisely. In spite of the difficulties, Pier Giorgio with prayer and determination advanced in his studies, especially with his desire to please his parents and to do what was pleasing to God.

3.1.2. Public Secondary School Activities

Pier Giorgio's extra-curricular activities were numerous during this time. During his studies, Pier Giorgio not only developed an intense spirituality, he also became more aware of his responsibility toward the poor around him and became actively involved in works of charity, the influence of his Catholic formation at the Jesuit institute. The public school setting was also a venue where Pier Giorgio further developed a network of friends and social activities. These all had a common source which was his spiritual life and religious principles.[26] Interesting, however, was that while studying at Massimo D'Azeglio, Pier Giorgio did not register in any associations or memberships of any kind. His memberships from spiritual and outdoor to charitable activities all occurred during his studies at the Social Institute, and after he was seventeen, at the Turin Polytechnic.

3.2. Student Population

The students who attended Massimo D'Azeglio came from a variety of backgrounds although belonging to families with high expectations. The *liceo classico* which focused on the humanities and social sciences, not unlike a

---

25. *Positio*, 50–51. Testimony based on Adelaide Frassati, 62n34.

26. I will cover each of these in detail in the relevant chapters, "friendship," "politics," and "spiritual life," chapters 6, 7, and 8.

liberal arts college, had demanding requirements, especially language skills, Latin and Greek, and modern languages; hence, Massimo D'Azeglio was also associated with a "prestigious" education. Massimo D'Azeglio reflected the class stratification of early twentieth-century Italy: "It was that which society at that time could give . . . a place where the wealthy upper middle-class could offer their children, morally and physically healthy, shoulder to shoulder with a smaller middle and lower middle class student population, less stable, more restless, and unequal, envious of their neighbors of a more elevated class and only eager to be able to equal or overcome the difference."[27] In other words, class consciousness was evident among the students, the upper middle class wishing to maintain their status or advance the social echelons following the expectations of their parents. The envious middle and lower middle classes somehow agitating and restless, sought at least equality. Pier Giorgio, although belonging to an upper-middle-class family, sympathized with those whom he felt were excluded or marginalized on the basis of class status. He was not someone to choose a friend on the basis of social level, or use his own family status to his advantage. Having received a profound Christian formation at the Social Institute, Pier Giorgio's values were to see Christ in the other, and to bring others to Christ. His values were emptied of any kind of desire for social status, and instead, he offered Christ's love.

4. Letter to Carlo Bellingeri—Pollone, October 26, 1917[28]

Pier Giorgio moved directly into the bad news, writing Bellingeri, "I failed." With the information circulating among friends, he thought Bellingeri might already have known. He even explained why he failed: he was more focused on composition when he should have spent more time working on Latin. One might say a typical student's dilemma: where to focus one's energy. He continued to provide Bellingeri with his latest news: he would be going to the Social Institute proceeding with the second year, while also taking exams for the first year. In spite of his unfortunate situation, Pier Giorgio concealed nothing from his friend and he even wished to hear Bellingeri's news. His own disappointment did not diminish the importance of hearing the news Bellingeri might have to share with him.

---

27. Levi, "Al D'Azeglio Insieme," 52.
28. *Letters*, 19; Ital. ed., 20.

4.1. Social Institute and the Jesuits

The decision made by Alfredo and Adelaide Frassati to send Pier Giorgio to the Jesuit Institute reflected the tendency among families "not particularly religious" to send their children to Roman Catholic schools when there were academic problems.[29] Pier Giorgio received three years of public education and two years of Catholic education; the Social Institute took Catholic spiritual formation seriously. The parents' interest in the Social Institute was only to keep Pier Giorgio from falling behind in his year of study.[30] His two first years of secondary school from the time he was ten to twelve, were in a public institution; then, at the beginning of his adolescence, Pier Giorgio attended the Catholic school where the practice of frequent confessions and communion began with spiritual direction. Spiritually, the Social Institute was the beginning of intense religious experience.

The Jesuits had been in Turin since 1567. Duke Emanuel Filiberto had ensured the opening of a Jesuit college nearby the Church of the Holy Martyrs. But with the reorganization of education in 1729 by Victor Amadeus, followed by ecclesial sanctions placed on the Jesuits in 1773, the Jesuit teaching presence in Turin was interrupted and even threatened for almost a century. Only in 1814 with the invitation of Pope Pius VII were the Jesuits reestablished in Turin under both the protection of King Victor Emmanuel and Charles Felice.[31] Again by the order of Charles Albert, the Jesuits were forced to leave Piedmont until 1881, returning to their teaching mission at the Social Institute in 1883.[32]

4.2. Spirituality of the Institute

The fact that the students came typically from upper-class families should not come as a surprise given that secondary education was not widespread in the early 1900s until the end of WWI. In 1889 the Jesuits established the Marian Congregation, attaching increasing value to the Christian formation of students. The Jesuits sought to form those whom they understood would have a major positive influence on society.[33] Having recognized that

---

29. Armini, *Pier Giorigo Frassati*, 13.

30. Casalegno, *Pier Giorgio Frassati*, 59.

31. Charles Felice, brother of King Victor Emmanuel succeeded his brother on the throne. Charles Felice's cousin, Charles Albert, was appointed regent.

32. Casalegno, *Pier Giorgio Frassati*, 60. The society kept the name of the previous teachers who owned the property, *soci*, and operated the private "institute."

33. *Positio*, 51.

it was the influence of the upper class who had been exposed to "liberal, anticlerical and masonic theories," the Jesuits taught with the objective of "Catholicizing" them.[34]

Father Pietro Lombardi was posted to the Social Institute from 1913–1920 during the same years that Pier Giorgio had been a student there. Being the spiritual director for the students, Father Lombardi particularly focused on the development of their interior life. The spiritual formation of the students was published after Fr. Lombardi's death, "His solid spiritual direction, substantial with a powerful Eucharistic thrust, he was of a clear and definite direction for so many of the youth."[35] Given Father Lombardi's influence on Pier Giorgio as his spiritual director and confessor, further comments concerning Father Lombardi may be considered reflecting Father Lombardi's eucharistic spirituality: "It seemed so natural to him [Fr. Lombardi] that all should aspire towards perfection, that it should even exclude certain concessions, and to being rigid. But everything was surpassed through the apostolic character of a pioneer in the Eucharistic movement towards daily communion. This was the fixed point of his preaching."[36] With such a confessor and spiritual director for someone with the sensitivity and conscience of Pier Giorgio, an intense spiritual life reflected the period of Pier Giorgio's studies at the Social Institute.

The movements at the *Sociale* were numerous, enriched with Father Lombardi's preaching and in harmony with the eucharistic spirituality. In other words, a coherency between what the institute stood for in spiritual terms, what the students experienced in their activities, and the spiritual direction that was offered, presented a unified lifestyle developing toward both human and spiritual excellence. A trait in Pier Giorgio's personality that reflected his values since childhood was the sense of coherency: to live a life that was reflected in his beliefs and values.

4.3. Associations and Membership

By February 1914, Pier Giorgio joined two associations at the Social Institute, the Association of the Blessed Sacrament and the Apostleship of Prayer. The Apostolate was founded by the Jesuits in France in 1844 by Father Francis Xavier Gautrelet.[37] At this same time Pier Giorgio joined as an

---

34. *Positio*, 51
35. *Positio*, 52.
36. *Positio*, 52.
37. Casalegno, *Pier Giorgio Frassati*, 60. On October 15, 1885, the twelve-year-old Thérèse-Martin (Thérèse of Lisieux) joined the apostolate.

escort the Society of the Most Holy Sacrament, accompanying the Blessed Sacrament in processions. When Pier Giorgio returned to the Social Institute in October 1917, to complete his *liceo*, he registered in the Eucharistic League. In January 1918, Pier Giorgio registered in his first nonreligious club: the Italian Alpine Club.[38] A few months later, in May, the month of Mary, Pier Giorgio joined a fifth spiritual association, the Marian Confraternity, which Father Lombardi had promoted along with frequent communion and eucharistic devotion.[39] It was daily communion that shaped the Christian life of Pier Giorgio, as observed by one of the Jesuits at the Social Institute, Father Leandro Ballario, "I always thought that when he began to receive daily Communion, a practise that I believe he never left until his death. And it was under the powerful action of the Eucharist, as far as I can judge, that he began to shape his Christian character, pious, convinced and truly strong, which succeeded in being a splendid example to so many."[40]

At sixteen years old, Pier Giorgio was a secondary school student, but the spiritual extension of his activities reflected his ardent desire to grow in sanctity participating in the sacramental life of the church and to live in grace of God. At the end of September of 1918 just before the month devoted to the Holy Rosary, Pier Giorgio joined his sixth spiritual association, Confraternity of the Rosary. Pier Giorgio enrolled in this last Marian confraternity during his remaining months at the Social Institute. The Confraternity of the Holy Rosary associated with the Social Institute dates back to Jesuit origins in Messina, Sicily, 1550. Contemporaneously in Rome in the 1550s, a group of students and pious individuals turned to the Jesuit Fathers to develop a devotion to Mary as well as perform charitable works. This Marian Confraternity developed quickly in the Italian and European colleges administered by Jesuits. When Pier Giorgio joined the confraternity, his spiritual activities reflected a confraternity that was spiritually rigorous: daily prayer, spiritual exercises of Saint Ignatius, participation in weekly meetings where the Holy Spirt was invoked with the *Veni Creator*, spiritual readings, prayers and hymns of the Office to the Virgin Mary were recited, and finally, the Litany to the Blessed Virgin Mary. In addition to

---

38. Club Alpino Italiano (CAI). Pier Giorgio was a member until his death. CAI's head office is in Turin.

39. Casalegno, *Pier Giorgio Frassati*, 66. The certificate on display in Pier Giorgio's Pollone bedroom reads: *Solidatis Beatae Virginis Mariae, Petrus Giorgius Frassati, 30 Maii, 1918, Taurini*. Pier Giorgio's bedroom balcony faces a northerly direction with a superb view of Mount Mucrone.

40. Frassati, *La fede*, "Testimony of the Jesuit Father, Leandro Ballario," 44–45.

these prayers and spiritual exercises were works of charity, visiting the sick, the imprisoned and helping the poor.[41]

When Pier Giorgio turned seventeen years old his academic life at the Social Institute was inseparable from his spiritual life. He did not assume a student life on weekdays, then, a Catholic one on Sundays; rather, Pier Giorgio's spiritual impulses permeated his daily activities—while he remained committed to fulfilling his duties as a student and his *proponimento*, the promise made to his parents when he first had to repeat Latin.[42] His academic responsibilities did not keep him from taking part in six different Catholic Associations focused on Marian devotion and the Holy Eucharist. Pier Giorgio subordinated his academic life to his spiritual goals.

It should be noted that when Pier Giorgio joined the three additional prayer groups at the Social Institute, it occurred after repeating Latin a second time when he left Massimo D'Azeglio. Pier Giorgio never returned to the public secondary school. He finished his two remaining senior years of *liceo* in one year due to the First World War, completing his studies "with a brilliant licentiate" at the Social Institute.[43] Pier Giorgio then enrolled in the Turin Polytechnic in November 1918.

4.4. Imitation of Christ

Although Pier Giorgio's mother had been described as "formal" in her approach to Catholicism, she would have good reason to believe that her only son gravitated toward religious life.[44] On Christmas 1917, when Pier Giorgio was sixteen years, she gave her son as a Christmas gift *The Imitation of Christ*. Hardly the gift that a formal Catholic would give to her deeply spiritual son; Adelaide desired to see her son on the right path, and of course, to be a good student. The dedication in *The Imitation of Christ* reads, "Christmas, 1917, Giorgio my dearest, may this book, also in the coming years, be a guide and comfort, on the way of honesty, of charity and of purity, with the help of God and the blessing of your mother."[45] *The Imitation of Christ*

---

41. Casalegno, *Pier Giorgio Frassati*, 67. The confraternity was established and promoted in Jesuits institutes. This form of Marian spirituality would serve to prepare and strengthen Pier Giorgio's discernment as a Dominican. See chapter 8 below on Pier Giorgio's spirituality.

42. See chapter, 1 section 5.

43. Frassati, *Calendario*, "Turn Polytechnic, November, 1918," and Testimony of Domenico Bulferetti.

44. Frassati, *I giorni*, 49; Pierazzi, *Così ho visto*, 33.

45. Personal Communication, Wanda Gawronska, December 2015. The Italian reads, *Natale 1917 Giorgio mio carissimo, ti sia questo libro, anche negli anni venturi,*

was not light spiritual reading, either. For a son to receive such writings from his mother reflected the value attached to the Christian spiritual life, to become a true disciple of Christ. A sixteen-year-old student in the middle of adolescence, Pier Giorgio recognized through the direction of his mother the core message of the Christian life: following Christ was lived, and not just a formality taught.

The opening lines of the *Imitation of Christ* are taken from Saint John's Gospel, "He who follows me will not walk in darkness."[46] Pier Giorgio was given the light he needed to keep him out of darkness and to remain in the light: Jesus Christ. The first and second paragraphs of the *Imitation* continue,

> This is the highest wisdom: to see the world as it truly is, fallen and fleeting; to love the world not for its own sake, but for God's; and to direct all your effort toward achieving the kingdom of heaven. So, it is vanity to seek material wealth that cannot last and to place your trust in it. It is also vanity to seek recognition and status. It is vanity to chase after what the world says you should want and not to long for things you should not have, things that you will pay a high price for later on if you get them. It is vanity to wish for a long life and to care little about a good life. It is vanity to focus only on your present life and not to look ahead to your future life. It is vanity to live for the joy of the moment and not to seek eagerly the lasting joys that await you.[47]

A student at the Social Institute, Pier Giorgio's love for his family, his sensitive nature, delicate conscience, Father Lombardi's preaching and his mother's gift of the *Imitation of Christ*, set Pier Giorgio on an ever deeper spiritual journey. His beliefs were not compromised either by his commitment to his studies or the greater challenge for a sixteen-year-old, his friends.

The first chapter and first paragraph in the *Imitation of Christ* chart the path to which Pier Giorgio would commit himself in following Jesus Christ. The serious danger of "vanity": seeking more riches which lead to pride, when riches, in fact, perish; "vanity," that leads to a body that lusts and desires for which one was severely punished; "vanity" when one seeks the riches of the world that do not endure, honors that lead to pride; "vanity" which is preoccupied with a long life rather than leading a moral life; "vanity" that seeks to satisfy one's present needs rather than prepare one's soul for eternity; "vanity" which is fixed on a world and things that do not

---

guida e conforto sulla via dell'onestà, della carità e della purezza, con l'aiuto di Dio e la benedizione della mamma.

46. John 8:12; Thomas à Kempis, *Imitation of Christ*, ch. 1, para. 1.

47. *Imitation of Christ*, ch. 1, paras. 1 and 2.

last, rather than preparing oneself for eternal life. These six elements attaching oneself to the vanity of life, contrasted radically with the direction of Pier Giorgio's spiritual life. Pier Giorgio lived with a spirit of detachment, and always seeking the good in God's creation. Joy became an identifiable trait of Pier Giorgio's personality: the joy that prepared the individual for something far greater: "Eternal Joy" awaiting in paradise. This joy Pier Giorgio already experienced in his spirit of freedom and detachment following the gospel of Jesus Christ. Pier Giorgio showed prudence in his relations to keep lust far from his thoughts; the good things he experienced he wished not for himself but for others; he distanced himself from acquiring possessions which he considered an obstacle to humility; hence, Pier Giorgio understood a spiritual life resembling Saint John's Letter, "For all that is in the world, the lust of the flesh and the lust of the eyes and the pride of life, is not of the Father but is of the world."[48] Pier Giorgio's life became focused on bringing Christ's love to others; his decisions meant "preparing" his soul for final judgment.

5. Letter to Carlo Bellingeri—Pollone, August 15, 1917[49]

Pier Giorgio's letters were often short—postcard-type letters, his writing was precise in terms of details and facts. One would say he did not waste words, nor did Pier Giorgio waste time. August 15, 1917, Pier Giorgio decided to write a long letter to his good friend Bellingeri. One can recognize in Pier Giorgio's letter the child who matured into an adolescent: Pier Giorgio's respectful tone and his sensitivity, "thank you for the kind remembrance." The value Pier Giorgio attached to his studies and activities with his family and friends is further reflected in this letter, and Pier Giorgio's receptivity to the beauty of nature.

5.1. Further Characteristics of Pier Giorgio's Personality

Pier Giorgio's education is transmitted in his letter to Bellingeri, "Tusculanae" and "Horace," authors he cites in reference to translation exercises from Latin to Italian and Italian to Latin.[50] Giving details on the excursion to Oropa, the "tram from Favaro," "we ate a good plate of polenta concia,"

---

48. 1 John 2:16.

49. *Letters*, 17–18; Ital. ed., 19–20.

50. It should be noted that these studies were part of *Massimo D'Azeglio Liceo Classico* a specialized humanities program.

also becomes a hallmark of his descriptive style.[51] Although Pier Giorgio's syntax was faulty at times, he had a remarkable sense of poetic narrative, "cool breeze was blowing overhead, and the sun was hot." The overlap of sensitivity and details brought out the artistic side to Pier Giorgio and the appreciation of the beautiful.

Pier Giorgio's affectionate side also remained present from the time he used to write to his aunt and grandmother; in this case, he tells Bellingeri, "I think of the beautiful hours spent at the Bonafous with you, and the beautiful walk I took with you and Camillo," *belle passeggiate*, indicative of Pier Giorgio's frequent reminiscing. The sensitive/affectionate characteristics remained with him, looking back at times spent with friends whom he treasured. His diligence not only studying during the summer months since his childhood but also shown working in the garden picking potatoes. His spiritual disposition as he conveyed to Bellingeri during the Oropa excursion walking with family and friends Pier Giorgio fulfilled with "Holy Mass at the main altar of the Madonna." Pier Giorgio's love for nature continued to grow with his desire to climb Mt. Mucrone, "from the steep side." His polite closure always included greetings to the addressee's family, and in this case he transmitted *saluti*, "hellos," from his sister, ending in a hug. This beautiful letter written to one of his first close friends reflected a person who grew in virtue which did not begin when Pier Giorgio was sixteen years old; rather this letter expressed a continuity with his childhood. Pier Giorgio became richer, through the sacraments, perfecting his virtues as his letter reveals.

The Marchisios, husband wife, and two daughters, visiting Pollone, with whom Pier Giorgio spent time playing billiards in the evening, were friends of the Frassati family. Together they took the trip to Oropa and Mt. Mucrone making the outing one of family and friends, Pier Giorgio with his father, sister, and the Marchisios. The stop at Favaro enabled them to take the tram to Oropa.[52] Pier Giorgio would have been just born when this new tram service started, and for the sixteen-year-old this represented an exciting mode of transport to the sanctuary.

---

51. *Polenta concia* is a speciality of Biella in this part of Piedmont and can be ordered in any of the restaurants of the Oropa sanctuary. *Polenta concia* consists of corn meal mush cooked in butter and fontina cheese.

52. In fact, the tram service began in 1901 and continued until 1961. The original tram and tracks can still be seen on the southeast side of the entrance of the Oropa Sanctuary.

5.2. Bonafous Institute

Pier Giorgio attended Bonafous in the summer of 1917 due to the First World War, when his help was needed at home.[53] The gardener, Giuseppe Gola, left the Frassati-Ametis residence, being called to war as Italy got embroiled in the First World War; Pier Giorgio helped the gardener's wife with the gardening. During this period, Pier Giorgio obtained an Agricultural Certificate from Bonafous.[54] The program at the Agricultural Institute created some thoughts and the vague possibility of pursuing a degree program at the Agricultural University of Perugia.[55] Although perhaps a passing thought, it reflected the extent to which Pier Giorgio was drawn by nature to help others and even acquire the necessary skills.

The motivation, however, to pursue agricultural studies was fundamentally practical. Pier Giorgio had since his childhood the impulse to help where and when help was needed, *dimostrare coi fatti*, "show with deeds," and not just discuss matters. Whether a poor child at the door or his mother lying sick in bed, the need to respond—his childhood sensitivity—continued; Pier Giorgio understood he had a duty to assume in the garden. The gardener had been called to serve in the war, and so, Pier Giorgio helped the gardener's wife. These two dimensions remained present in Pier Giorgio's life: the need to help others, and the response to God who prompted him to act with goodness. Pier Giorgio's desire to assist others in ways that were "validly constructive" led him to pursue a program of study at the agricultural institute.[56]

Pier Giorgio's interaction with nature also represented more than working in the garden. Nature became for him empirically formative: the beauty and value of the created world—feelings experienced since his childhood—nature penetrated deeper than the seeds in the ground, nature moved higher than the mountain peaks. The richness, the harmony, the awe of nature, pointed toward the goodness of the Divine Creator.

5.3. Secondary School to University

Having received a solid Christian formation with the Jesuits at the Social Institute, Pier Giorgio put into practice the fundamentals of the Christian

---

53. The context of World War I will be given in chapter 7.
54. The certificate is displayed in Pier Giorgio's original Pollone bedroom and reads: *(Corso Libero) Istituto Bonafous, Studenti Volontari Agricoltari, 15 agosto, 1917, Torino.*
55. Frassati, *Calendario*, "Turin, July 15, 1917."
56. Casalegno, *Pier Giorgio Frassati*, 64.

spiritual life; frequent communion which presupposed regular confession, as well as his Marian prayer life. Having the Eucharist as the pillar of his spiritual life, sustained by confession and devotion to Mary, the activities Pier Giorgio joined during his time with the Jesuits emphasized good works. Christian deeds constituted an integral part of Pier Giorgio's Christian journey. Since his childhood Pier Giorgio expressed a sense of *dimostrare i fatti*, "performing deeds," as he would say, and if he neglected his duties, there was his *proponimento*, "resolution" to make changes. One can say that Pier Giorgio entered the Social Institute providentially, with a good ethical foundation, but with the help of the Jesuits, Pier Giorgio's armor was strengthened, equipping him to move into the secular environment of the Turin Polytechnic. "Stand therefore, having girded your loins with truth, and having put on the breastplate of righteousness, and having shod your feet with the equipment of the gospel of peace; above all taking the shield of faith, with which you can quench all the flaming darts of the evil one. And take the helmet of salvation, and the sword of the Spirit, which is the word of God."[57] Pier Giorgio was known to be fearless about expressing his Catholic faith.[58] In November 1918, Pier Giorgio was registered at the Royal Turin Polytechnic in the Faculty of Mechanical Engineering.

6. Letter to His Parents—Turin, February 28, 1922[59]

Pier Giorgio was twenty years old when he wrote a short letter to his parents, February 28; but the contents contained plenty of information. In the few sentences he wrote, Pier Giorgio conveyed his numerous activities without going into detail. He limited the content of the letter due to his studies. The letter presents the constancy of structure in Pier Giorgio's correspondence: salutation with acknowledgment, in this case, "thanks for your letter," indicating he was replying to an earlier letter he had received; he provided valuable information to his parents in the body of the letter, regarding his studies and social activities; and then, he closed with greetings and kisses to the family.

Since January 1921, Alfredo Frassati took up residence as the Italian ambassador to Germany in Berlin.[60] Pier Giorgio's mother, sister, and aunt were in Berlin for Christmas where they would be with Alfredo, and where they would remain for the winter. Pier Giorgio, after having visited Central

---

57. Eph 6:14–17.
58. Frassati, *Calendario*, "Turin, Polytech, November, 1918."
59. *Letters*, 80–81; Ital. ed., 108.
60. Frassati, *Calendario*, "Turin, January, 1921."

Europe and Germany the previous year between September and December, remained home to study for his exams.[61]

6.1. Recreation with Family Friends

Pier Giorgio related his social activities, in this letter, having dinner with the Axerios. The family developed a friendship with the Axerios since Signore Axerio worked at *La Stampa*. Pier Giorgio kept his family informed of his friends and his activities with them, so, his parents knew how, and with whom, he was spending his time. Nor was it in Pier Giorgio's nature to keep hidden his friendships or activities from his parents. An item of detail that Pier Giorgio provided was the absence of Tonino and Mrs. Axerio's husband visiting San Maurizio, and so, Mrs. Axerio apologized "profusely." What was the relevance of such information? Even though Pier Giorgio would like to have visited his friend Tonino, the apology that Mrs. Axerio offered showed that her son's absence, as well as that of her husband, was felt with regret, and not indifference. Sensitivity with regards to Pier Giorgio was expressed, and Pier Giorgio acknowledged this.

Pier Giorgio continued with another invitation he had received from Mrs. Micheli, although not certain whether this was for dinner. Pier Giorgio reassured his parents that he remained in the company of family friends, that he was not alone, while his parents resided in Berlin. These friends shared between Pier Giorgio and his family in Turin showed the close ties that existed in these relations: Pier Giorgio wrote to his parents about his time spent at home so they knew the people whom he was visiting, either for dinner, or through some invitations that he had received. It suggested the openness that the twenty-one-year-old maintained with his family; Pier Giorgio had nothing to hide, and his parents in turn, showed their complete trust in their son.

The Axerio family and the Micheli family were related: the Axerios had two children, Tonino and Giulio, and it was Giulio who studied with Pier Giorgio at Massimo D'Azelgio and later at the Turin Polytechnic. Giulio attended classes for several years with Pier Giorgio and Giulio's beautiful testimony reaffirmed Pier Giorgio's exquisite personality during all the years that Giulio had known him, "Yet, I will not ever forget something, and something quite important for which I am indebted to Pier Giorgio: this continuous caring affection, attention that is superior to that of a brother. Without words, without loud messages, he knew how to set an example,

---

61. Details on Pier Giorgio's travels with special attention given to Germany will be discussed in chapter 5.

to give the most authentic and effective advice. I will always consider him one of those exceptional creatures sent by God to earth, to reassure humanity the existence of angels, because all his friends—all—received from him at least some kindness and a smile."[62] While a student with rigorous studies during his Turin Polytechnic years, committed to his engineering work, and the demands of his program, Pier Giorgio was not self-absorbed, preoccupied with himself and his career; he was still able to smile seeing his friends, and express some kindness simply because Pier Giorgio was more concerned about others than himself.

6.2. Royal Polytechnic of Turin

In his letter, Pier Giorgio immediately discussed the most important matter for his parents, and so, also of significance for him: his studies. His years at the Turin Polytechnic began in November 1918, right after completing his secondary school at the Social Institute. Since childhood, his initial studies at Massimo D'Azeglio, Pier Giorgio clearly did not find the academic life an easy one. However, being a determined student, in spite of the distractions, in spite of the numerous extracurricular activities, Pier Giorgio never abandoned his childhood *proponimento* he had made to his parents. He did not diminish his sacramental observances, either, or his numerous religious activities. He never reduced his charitable works, as time-consuming as they were. Pier Giorgio was an example of a Christian who grew: a tiny mustard seed that blossomed into a massive tree; at the Polytechnic, his activities transformed into an active political life.

The Turin Polytechnic had only been erected in 1906.[63] The specialized studies of the polytechnic were in architecture and engineering as well as industrial and commercial studies. As indicated by Giulio Axerio's testimony, Pier Giorgio registered at the polytechnic and immediately developed a reputation among both professors and students for his exceptional goodness which became one of his distinguishing traits.[64]

---

62. Frassati, *La carità*, "Testimony of Giulio Axerio," 114. The testimony is in the third person; I have put this into the first person.

63. The polytechnic recognized as a university institution was a merger of two previously existing institutes: Royal School of Applied Engineering and the Royal Museum of Italian Industry, instituted in 1860 and 1862, respectively. See Casalegno, *Pier Giorgio Frassati*, 88–89 for details.

64. Casalegno, *Pier Giorgio Frassati*, 90.

6.3. Industrial Mechanical Engineering

Although Pier Giorgio was registered in the industrial mechanical engineering program, he took a specialization in mining engineering. Pier Giorgio, drawn by nature, was fascinated by the origins of minerals and how they connected to the mystery of the universe. He even put together his own mineral collection during his university studies, classifying the individual rocks with their Latin names.[65]

Pier Giorgio's only motivation to study mining engineering was to work and serve Christ among the miners. His visit to the mines, especially after his visit to the Silesian mines in Germany and Poland, reaffirmed his commitment to work among miners.[66] The mining career formed part of Pier Giorgio's desire to work with the poor: "his great passion for the poor, pushed to the point of studying mining engineering was shaped by his desire to embrace a profession which guaranteed an ongoing closeness to the most humble, and most sacrificed among the workers."[67]

6.4. Religious and Social Activities[68]

In his letter, Pier Giorgio informed his parents that "Msgr. Pini arrived and so we will have a cosy little evening at our club." The little details Pier Giorgio provided for the evening, most likely his attempt to de-emphasize his involvement with the "Club," served to update his parents without telling them more than they needed to know about his charitable activities. But this modest sentence, in fact, did not reveal the richness of Pier Giorgio's life of charity. Msgr. Giandomenico Pini was the ecclesiastical assistant of the Federation of Italian Catholic Universities (FUCI).[69] When Pier Giorgio referred to "Club," reference was being made to the Cesare Balbo Club which held the Turin university seat of the FUCI. Pier Giorgio joined FUCI in November 1919, his second year as a student at university. Observing Pier Giorgio as a member of the club, Msgr. Pini stated, "I always admired his faith, his charity towards the poor: a perfect Christian youth."[70]

65. Casalegno, *Pier Giorgio Frassati*, 93.

66. Mines will be discussed during his travels in chapter 5. The experience of Germany and working among the poor will be taken up in chapter 8.

67. Frassati, *Calendario*, "Turin, November 29, 1918. Testimony of Rodolfo Venditti." *Positio*, 67; Pierazzi, *Così ho visto*, 79.

68. Details on these various spiritual, social and political clubs will be taken up in chapter 8.

69. Federazione Universitaria Cattolica Italiana.

70. Frassati, *La fede*, "Testimony of Msgr. Giandomenico Pini," 260.

The same month that Pier Giorgio became a member of the FUCI he also faithfully attended and contributed to the anti-Communist meetings at the Savonarola Club. This club, however, served as a worker's club. Even at this club Pier Giorgio was described as "bold," *sfacciato*, because "he was not afraid of anyone."[71] The attendance at this club was significant in two respects: first, Pier Giorgio while a university student clearly wished to identify with the difficult conditions of the Catholic workers; and second, this club provided the connection Pier Giorgio made with the historical Dominican figure Girolamo Savonarola. This Ferrarese Dominican played a significant influence on Pier Giorgio's social and political views inseparable from the gospel of Christ.[72] By June 1920, Pier Giorgio received from Father Filippo Robotti, the Dominican chaplain of the Cesare Balbo club, a booklet entitled "The Dominican Rule."[73]

7. Letter to His Parents—Turin, April 6, 1922[74]

Pier Giorgio wrote on his twenty-first birthday to his parents a moving letter expressing his deep respect and love toward them. His polite format started off his letter in gratitude, acknowledging them for their kindness, in this instance, their letters and gift. Pier Giorgio even qualified his appreciation for the gift which his parents "shouldn't have bought" because he recognized already they had "done too much" for him. These expressed the words of someone who reflected on the goodness of others, and what he recognized in his parents: that they were sending him a gift when they had already done so much. The gift might be a small article of little value, but Pier Giorgio was touched by the "thought" the "gesture" of the act.[75] Pier Giorgio did not take relationships for granted, whether family or friends. Given his sensitive disposition to write that he would "always treasure" the gift, Pier Giorgio meant those very words.

Studying on his birthday, Pier Giorgio showed the commitment he had made to his engineering program and the time the exams required for preparation. His time was organized between religious duties, helping the poor, and studying for exams—identifying the subjects which were the most

---

71. Frassati, *Calendario*, "Turin, November, 1919."

72. Savonarola was born in Ferrara, Italy, in 1452. The influence of Savonarola's life on Pier Giorgio will be taken up in chapter 8.

73. Robotti, essay, in *Beato Pier Giorigo*, 97.

74. *Letters*, 82–83; Ital. ed., 112.

75. Luciana Frassati points out, "these gifts which Pier Giorgio received from his family were always few and of little value." *Letters*, 83n2; Ital. ed., 112n1.

difficult and required for his fourth year. Pier Giorgio also hoped that he could spend some time in Pollone to relax.

Fluent in German, with his father working in Berlin, Pier Giorgio planned to continue his studies in Germany. Correspondence with his sister expressed Pier Giorgio's intention to complete his fourth year of mechanical engineering at the Berlin Polytechnic. His father concerned that he could be inhibited by the language, told Luciana, "He shouldn't be frightened with the difficulties one of which is the language."[76] The following year Pier Giorgio's mother questioned such a move; writing from Berlin, she advised him, "So, you're project would be to do Year IV in Berlin? Think carefully—in the case where papa should return to Turin—could you still pursue Year V? Are the exams done here valid?"[77] In fact, on October 18, 1922, with Benito Mussolini's March on Rome, Alfredo Frassati resigned as the Italian ambassador to Germany.

Having informed his parents about his exam preparation and leisure time, Pier Giorgio proceeded to discuss the weather, the topic of his letters since his childhood. Sitting in his room where his family had moved on corso Galileo Ferraris, N. 70, Pier Giorgio thought of the summer and seeing the "summer sun." He had been away from their summer home in Pollone, although it was only 45 and half miles away from Turin. This conveyed the sense of discipline and determination: Pier Giorgio needed to focus on his studies, though the beautiful weather and the summer home might have been a temptation—even distraction. But, Pier Giorgio did not submit: he had exams and he was committed to his program regardless of the gruelling requirements, even if his interests might have been elsewhere. The virtue of "force" certainly characterized the personality of this twenty-one-year-old.

The last lines of his letter were represented as an afterthought. Pier Giorgio truly wished to respond to his parents' kindness, and the most precious gift he could offer them was to pray that God would "reward" his mother and father for all they had done for him, and asked for God's blessings upon them.

7.1. Memberships: Religious, Social, and Political[78]

Pier Giorgio studied at the Turin Polytechnic from November 1918, to June/July 1925, when he was registered for his last exam of the thirty-three

---

76. Frassati, *Calendario*, "Berlin, February 1, 1921, father to Luciana."
77. Frassati, *Calendario*, "Berlin, January, 1922, mother to Pier Giorgio."
78. Details on these memberships will be treated in chapter 7.

exam requirements for his program—extending across seven years.[79] At the Polytechnic, Pier Giorgio joined the anti-Communist FIAT club, Girolamo Savonarola, in 1919, a year after starting his studies. The Savonarola Club's objective was to unite Catholics and workers. In December 1920, he became a member of the newly formed Italian Popular Party (PPI), founded in 1919 by Don Luigi Sturzo, an Italian priest.[80] In 1921, Pier Giorgio also became a member of two eucharistic groups associated with Santa Maria in Piazza where the Sacramentine Fathers were established, All Night Youth Adoration and Young Workers Adoration. Also in 1921, Pier Giorgio became a member of the international federation of Catholics promoting peace, *Pax Romana*. At his home parish of *La Crocetta*, with other youth Pier Giorgio founded the Catholic Action (AC) club, *Milites Mariae*.[81] In 1923, Pier Giorgio was among the first members of the Friends of Catholic University of the Sacred Heart and in the same year he also became a member of excursion section of Young Mountaineers (GM).[82] By May 1924, Pier Giorgio and his friends created their own club, spiritual and social, *Tipi Loschi*, "Shady Ones."[83]

Questions

1. Who was Pier Giorgio's tutor as a child (§1)?

2. What role did the Salesian, Don Antonio Cojazzi, have in Pier Giorgio's education (§2)?

3. What was the difference between Massimo D'Azeglio and the Jesuit Istituto Sociale in terms of education (3.1; 4.1)?

4. How did l'Istituto Sociale impact Pier Giorgio spiritually (4.2)? Which were some of the spiritual associations that Pier Giorgio joined (4.3)?

5. Where did Pier Giorgio complete his *liceo* before entering the Turin Polytechnic (5.3)?

6. What did Pier Giorgio study at the Turin Polytechnic (5.3)? What were the religious, social and political activities that occupied Pier Giorgio's time besides university studies (6.4; 7.1)?

79. *Positio*, 73, 87–88.

80. PPI = Partito Populare Italiano. Servant of God, Luigi Sturzo, Cause for His Canonization was opened by John Paul II, March 23, 2002.

81. AC = Azione Cattolica; *Milites Mariae*, "Soldiers of Mary."

82. GM = Giovane Montagna, "Young Mountaineers."

83. *Tipi Loschi* are covered in detail in chapter 6.

5

Pier Giorgio's Culture and Travels

> Virgin Mother, daughter of your Son,
> more humble and sublime than any creature,
> fixed goal decreed from all eternity...
>
> DANTE, *PARADISO*, CANTO XXXIII

Pier Giorgio's childhood letters reveal that he had been studying languages at an early age, German, French, and Latin. He and his sister even composed poems together in German. With the early exposure to language, especially in the Germanophile home, Pier Giorgio's world opened to cultural diversity. Benefiting from a mother who also painted, an artist whose paintings were on exhibition at the Venice Biennale, Pier Giorgio developed a refined artistic taste of the beautiful. His natural surroundings, especially Mount Mucrone, the Italian Alps, mountains he climbed first with his mother, Pier Giorgio discovered the majesty of nature. Then, his summer holidays on the Italian Riviera, at Alassio where he swam and sailed, offered Pier Giorgio the natural settings that signaled the Divine.

The letters describe Pier Giorgio's first travel experiences outside his family excursions to the Alps and Riviera, beginning with Pier Giorgio's visit to Rome with his mother. By the time Pier Giorgio turned twenty years old, his travels took him to Berlin where his father worked as ambassador, stopping in Central Europe during his train journeys. His love for literature, especially Dante Alighieri, memorizing passages of the *Divina Commedia*, and William Shakespeare's *Hamlet*, scenes which he also recited from memory, reflected the depth of culture that Pier Giorgio had acquired. Pier Giorgio's cultural development was not only the result of opportunities his parents gave him, and the privileged home environment in which he grew up, but he also learned the value of time. He was brought up with a sense of accountability with how he spent his day, even if his mother and father were not home. His letters show that if Pier Giorgio was not studying, he was working or writing, or engaged in an apostolate or with his friends. Pier Giorgio also learned to balance his activities, the value of work, and time for leisure.

1. Letter to His Father—Rome, October 10, 1915[1]

The fourteen-year-old Pier Giorgio related to his father his first travel experience in the Italian capital, also the ancient capital of the Roman Empire, and the seat of the Roman Catholic Church. All historical, political and religious elements were expressed in his letter, besides the cultural relevance of Rome.

A reader familiar with Pier Giorgio's letters would immediately identify his opening lines, acknowledging the telegram he had received with the implied appreciation. In this instance, his aunt's news brought Pier Giorgio disappointment: hoping his father could join him, his mother and sister in Rome, Pier Giorgio found out from his aunt that such a reunion was not going to happen.

1.1. Rome

After his introductory lines, a clear response to the telegram he received, Pier Giorgio entered the second part of his letter, the body of the text, which narrated his visit to Rome. Pier Giorgio provided his father with tremendous details of his experiences which could be divided into three cultural components, historical, religious, and culinary.

The Roman forum, the Coliseum, and the Castle of Constantine represent the historical part of his morning visit to Rome. In the afternoon, they proceeded to the baths of Caracalla. Pier Giorgio did not simply state he visited the baths, but provided his father with details of what impressed him, suggestive of Pier Giorgio's careful observation of the sites and attentive

---

1. *Letters*, 14; Ital. ed., 15.

listening to the explanations given, "the furnaces which had two clay pipes which sent the hot air into a room, where the Romans took the so-called Turkish baths." Pier Giorgio was neither bored nor distracted. He made full use of his visit to Rome to learn about Roman culture, and what he had learned he conveyed in a letter to his father.

Relating the activities of the following day, Pier Giorgio moved from the historical and discussed the religious component of his tour which still carried cultural relevance, in this case, the Vatican museums. At the Vatican, Pier Giorgio discovered the museums of sculpture and painting. Pier Giorgio was skilled in providing details and informed his father that the visit lasted for three and a half hours, from 10 a.m. to 1:30 p.m. Besides the visit to the Vatican, the other piece of religious exploration was Saint Paul Outside the Walls, a short distance outside of the walled city of Rome.

After their visit to the Coliseum, they ate their lunch at the castle of Constantine from where they had a wonderful view of the city of Rome. On the following day, after their visit to the Vatican museum, they dined at *Scarpone's* just outside the Porta San Pancrazio.[2]

Pier Giorgio ended the letter in his recognizable closure which meant sending greetings and kisses to his father.

1.2. Literature

Having developed as a child the value of language, by the time Pier Giorgio completed home tutoring and started secondary school at ten years old, he reasonably comprehended three languages besides his knowledge of Italian. Already writing poetry, as Pier Giorgio's childhood letters testify, he developed a value for literature. Memorizing verses from the Canti of Dante's *Divina Commedia*, his favorite poet remained unquestionably Dante Alighieri. Pier Giorgio also memorized and dramatized parts of Shakespeare's *Hamlet*, "enthusiastic about theatre, as far as reciting in a loud voice in the garden verses from *Hamlet*."[3]

Many of Dante's political and religious insights became a source of reflection for Pier Giorgio, and suggested the basis of his comments from Italian politics to Dominican saints. The words honoring the Blessed Virgin which Dante put on the lips of Saint Bernard of Clairvaux, Pier Giorgio wrote on a sheet of paper, placing it on his bedroom door so to always have

---

2. *Ristorante Il Scarpone* still stands just outside of Porta San Pancrazio in Rome.

3. Frassati, "Pollone, September 22, 1920." Alfredo Frassati even wrote on Hamlet, *La volontà di Amleto*, "The Will of Hamlet," dedicated to Pier Giorgio in a series of six articles written in 1949. See, Frassati, *Un uomo*, 24 and n69.

the verses within his vision.⁴ Pier Giorgio's poetic taste moved toward his religious passion, and so, his literary expression became increasingly a manifestation of his faith. Pier Giorgio was often heard by his neighbors reciting Dante's *Paradiso* in his Pollone garden. On a feast day, Pier Giorgio appeared at 5:30 a.m. to climb the sequoia in their garden reciting the *Divine Comedy*.⁵ The literary works extended to the religious which Pier Giorgio also assimilated in his heart and mind, especially, Saint Augustine's *Confessions* and Saint Paul's Hymn to Charity.⁶ The poetic experience for Pier Giorgio clearly touched his soul and his receptivity to the divine meant he could interpret this inspiration as leading him to a deeper religious experience which he also recognized in Saint Catherine of Siena and Saint Thomas Aquinas.⁷

The authors which Pier Giorgio read included Alessandro Manzoni, considered a master of Italian literature, as well as Giovanni Papini, Heinrich Heine, Niccolò Foscolo, Ludovico Ariosto.⁸ Manzoni's writings included *Comments on Catholic Morality*. Pier Giorgio's interest in German writers such as Johann Goethe and Heinrich Heine reflected especially the Germanophile inclinations of his father that had been transmitted to Pier Giorgio.⁹

2. Letter to His Father—Perugia, September 6, 1919[10]

Pier Giorgio visited the regions of Le Marche, Abruzzo and Umbria between August and September of 1919. In his correspondence Pier Giorgio faithfully wrote letters to his father, mother, grandmother, Linda Ametis, and his friend, Carlo with greetings always sent to family members. His September letters made reference to Perugia, but he also visited Aquila, Assisi, and Foligno. The Marian pilgrim city of Loreto in Le Marche (not far from the capital, Ancona) was part of their excursion.[11]

---

4. Casalegno, *Pier Giorgio Frassati*, 74.

5. Casalegno, *Pier Giorgio Frassati*, 73.

6. 1 Cor 13:1–13. See "Notes for a Speech about Charity," *Letters*, 239–41, Ital. ed., 353–55.

7. Reference to St. Thomas appears in his letter to Beltramo. See chapter 8, below for further details on Dominican Saints.

8. *Positio*, 75.

9. Frassati, *I giorni*, 167.

10. *Letters*, 25; Ital. ed., 26.

11. Casalegno, *Pier Giorgio Frassati*, 97.

2.1. Perugia/Assisi/Loreto

If one considers the September 6 letter as a continuation of the letter Pier Giorgio had written to his father two days previously, September 4, Pier Giorgio's epistolary format remained present in both letters from Assisi and Perugia: greetings and thank you, brief body of his message, and farewell and kisses.

With Pier Giorgio writing two consecutive letters to his father from Assisi and Perugia in early September, one is left with the view that Pier Giorgio may have seriously considered pursing agricultural studies in Perugia, especially having studied agriculture at the Bonafous Institute where he obtained a certificate in agriculture.[12] Pier Giorgio's love for nature, his work in the garden in Pollone since his early childhood, may have been reasons that he gravitated toward an agricultural path of studies as a future career. He also reported in his letter that the studies were completed in the fourth year at a convent, certainly appropriate, in keeping with his deeply religious lifestyle. Pier Giorgio appeared to have every reason to consider such a program in Perugia given his interests, the program of studies, and the residency requirements. He thoroughly researched the program for the School of Agriculture, assuring his father, it looked "very fine." Even the agricultural museum which he explored he commented on, reflecting Pier Giorgio's continued interest in agriculture. The letter from Perugia sounded like he wished to inform his father of the program, waiting for his father's response. Pier Giorgio's desires were implied, but he expected to receive further guidance from his parents. Pier Giorgio did not go into details of his Umbrian visit; the focus appeared to be updating his father with his travels, and providing information in particular on the School of Agriculture.

Although Pier Giorgio described Assisi as a "real wonder," he did not convey any kind of impression on Saint Francis or Franciscan spirituality. At eighteen years old, Pier Giorgio had already developed an intense spiritual life with religious convictions that were lived, especially, with regards to reaching out to the poor. Yet, Pier Giorgio wrote little in regards to Assisi, the birthplace of Saint Francis, and he remained silent on the *Poverello*. Pier Giorgio appeared to be focused on the prospect of his future studies. Nevertheless, his visit to Assisi reflected popular devotion to Italy's patron Saint.

His devotion to Mary he expressed in his pilgrimage to the ancient pilgrim route to Our Lady of Loreto.[13] Pilgrims had been traveling to Loreto, praying before the Blessed Virgin Mary since the thirteenth century,

12. Frassati, *Calendario*, "Turin, July 15, 1917."

13. Loreto is on the Adriatic pilgrim route that connects with Monte Sant'Angelo further south in the Region of Puglia.

asking for her intercession, or in thanksgiving with their *ex voto*.[14] The eighteen-year-old's Marian piety had been witnessed at Loreto when Pier Giorgio disappeared: "We could not find him in the hotel. We began to look for him everywhere and we ended up finding him alone in the Church kneeling on the cold steps of the altar. He had felt such a strong attraction to the house of the Virgin that he could no longer resist staying in bed."[15] The love Pier Giorgio had for the Blessed Virgin, and knowing her home stood in the vicinity of his hotel, Pier Giorgio preferred to pray alone in the profound and stirring silence of the Loreto shrine than sleep in his hotel bed.

2.2. Pier Giorgio's Personal Poverty

Did Saint Francis's life of austere poverty have an impact on Pier Giorgio?[16] The parallel between Pier Giorgio and Saint Francis requires consideration. While the two share a common concern for the poor, the two personalities are quite distinct. First of all, for Pier Giorgio it would have been inconceivable to rebel against his mother and father the way Saint Francis had done. Pier Giorgio throughout his life displayed a tremendous love and respect for his parents, recognized their goodness without a doubt. It would not be justified to suggest a parallel on the basis of their relationship with their parents. The second difference concerns poverty and wealth. For Pier Giorgio the response to the poverty in the streets of Turin, and the impoverished German students he met in Berlin, never meant rejecting wealth the way Saint Francis had done.[17] While Pier Giorgio wanted to help the poor, he never spoke against any of the middle or upper middle class who possessed wealth. In fact, Pier Giorgio did not even express contempt for his own bourgeois lifestyle or background.

Pier Giorgio enjoyed his time visiting family and friends. He went to musical performances, theatre productions, and art galleries. But, Pier Giorgio was not indifferent toward the poor and the reality of poverty; he made personal choices in how he used the little funds he had, to economize,

14. *Ex-voto* "from a vow" refers to graces requested or in thanksgiving for graces received.

15. Frassati, *La fede*, 176.

16. Pierazzi associates Pier Giorgio's simplicity and love for nature with the figure of St. Francis of Assisi. Pierazzi, *Così ho visto*, 148. Siccardi holds the view that Pier Giorgio, who visited Assisi and Foligno, was fascinated by the *Poverello* who wanted to "live the Gospel to the letter." Siccardi, *Pier Giorgio*, 88–89.

17. On the subject of poverty, see St. Thomas, *ST*, II–IIae, q. 88, a. 7. Also, Torrell, *Saint Thomas Aquinas*, who takes up the Dominican-Franciscan controversy on poverty, *Saint Thomas Aquinas*, 88–89.

to walk instead of taking the tram, or to travel third class on the train when he could go first class. He had nothing against passengers traveling first class, but he realized he could use the money which he had saved to help poor people. In other words, Pier Giorgio recognized that wealth served a purpose: the surplus money he had from his economizing could be used to help the needy. But he did not criticize wealthy people. His criticism was launched against employers, whether factory owners or industries, who showed greed, obsessed with profits, and who failed to take into account the basic needs of workers.

Eventually, Pier Giorgio framed such concerns politically.[18] A year after writing his letter Pier Giorgio politically channeled these social matters and sought a solution to the serious poverty he encountered both in Italy and Germany. Without showing contempt toward wealthy individuals, regardless of their status, Pier Giorgio expressed a sense of personal poverty recognizing that sociopolitical change required interior conversion.[19]

3. Letter to His Mother—Freiburg im Breisgau, October 12, 1921[20]

Dearest,
I received with great pleasure your letter dated the 10th and your card also of the 10th.

Papa is already in Berlin, I phoned him last night, but I almost did not understand anything of what papa was saying.

Today after dinner I will write a card to zia general delivery to Prague; I also already received a card from Venice from the lady travelers.

As far as funds are concerned I still have plenty, that is, 5261 Marks and 4218 Crowns; for the suits, I am doing well: for now I am always wearing the grey summer one, because it is very warm.

The Black Forest is a complex of hills and little mountains all covered in fir, beech, birch, pine, and other trees, but certainly in the winter, when only the fir are green, while everything is dead, the dark note on the white of the snow must cause great sadness. But now it is very beautiful because the colors alternate.

---

18. Sociopolitical and religiopolitical elements of Pier Giorgio's letters are taken up in chapter 7.

19. Girolamo Savonarola is covered in chapter 8.

20. *Lettere*, Ital. ed., 63–64 (my translation; I have retained Pier Giorgio's punctuation).

> I received from Turin your letter with Luciana's from bed the 7th and that of the 5th. All your letters that you sent to Klarastrasse were delivered to me, because I left my address there.
>
> The city is not very big totalling approximately 80,000 inhabitants but it is very beautiful because the houses are all in the midst of trees and flowers. Streets of houses one after another are not seen except in the center, as in Turin, where there is one house after another.
>
> The other evening I went with Prof. Rahner to the concert of a Pole, who played Beethoven and Chopin and I thought about all of you who like music so much.
>
> Here in the evening one can go to the theater, but I prefer to study a little and then go to bed early to be able to get up early in the morning.
>
> Perhaps I will go hear "Die Braut von Messina" but first I would be pleased to read it so I would be able to understand much more.
>
> Today after dinner I will go for a walk with Dr. Eiffler, a friend of Sonnenschein, then this evening I am invited together with the daughter and son of prof. Rahner to a student at the University of Freiburg.
>
> Today I will also write papa.
>
> Thank Sister, Maria and everyone. To nonna a thousand affectionate kisses and to you a big hug and a thousands and thousands of kisses.
>
> Pier Giorgio
>
> I already received a letter from papa.

Pier Giorgio introduced his letter in his epistolary style acknowledging the letters he received and expressing his appreciation. Having first considered the "other" before proceeding to talk about himself, in the penultimate sentence Pier Giorgio referred to his intention to write to his father who was already in Berlin. The value of family ties and friendships were expressed in the information provided in his correspondence with his aunt and "lady travelers," *viaggiatrici*, referring to his aunt Elena and sister, Luciana. Pier Giorgio also provided his mother details of his financial situation, making it clear that she had nothing to worry about, telling her the exact amount of funds in his possession to the last German crown.[21] Pier Giorgio just moved

---

21. In the *Lettere*, 64, Luciana Frassati provides a note in reference to the German marks and crowns Pier Giorgio had in his possession, "This was certainly one of the largest sums he ever possessed. In fact, contrary to the opinion of many, Pier Giorgio never had money in his pocket! The evidence is in the 'plenty' of this letter."

from Klarastrasse where he had temporary room and board until he could find accommodation with a German-speaking family. Through his Catholic network of contacts Pier Giorgio developed in Germany he was led to the Rahner family with the help of Reverend Doctor Sonnenschein; and with the assistance of the latter, Pier Giorgio also became acquainted with Doctor Eiffler.[22]

Pier Giorgio provided his mother a detailed description of the area, Black Forest with the vegetation, and the names of the different trees. He even attempted to imagine what winter would be like in the snow. In the following paragraph, Pier Giorgio described Freiburg with its population, and the city's rows of houses. A sense of Germany's cultural life, and his own taste in music and theater, also reflected his family's cultural values. Pier Giorgio ended his letter sending greetings to the workers, family members, and for his mother, "big hug and thousands and thousands of kisses."

3.1. Germany: Berlin

With his nomination as ambassador to Germany at the end of 1920, Alfredo Frassati moved into his residence in Berlin, creating further excitement for the family by strengthening ties with Germany.[23] Pier Giorgio's letters from Germany expressed fascination with newness and his desire to explore the unfamiliar: cities, museums, Cathedrals and the countryside were visited; urban and natural, cultural and religious, were consistently part of his itinerary; spending time with his German contacts Pier Giorgio deepened his German friendships.

Pier Giorgio's extensive visits to Germany included Munich, and also along the Rhine he traveled from Koblenz to Mannheim. These journeys offered Pier Giorgio the opportunity to spend time in Central Europe's cultural capitals, Vienna, Innsbruck and Prague. Pier Giorgio's love for the German-speaking people was expressed in his letters. His experience in post-WWI Germany is reflected in his letters, revealing both concern and empathy for a people who suffered economic hardships as a result of the Versailles Treaty.[24] The suffering of the German people, their poor living conditions, reinforced Pier Giorgio's desire to respond to their needs, in particular, the German Catholic students.

---

22. Pier Giorgio's ties with Father Sonnenschein will be taken up in chapter 6.

23. Frassati, *Beatitudes*, 61; *Calendario*, "Turin, January, 1921."

24. The political and economic climate of Italy and Germany in the post-WWI period will be taken up in chapter 7.

Pier Giorgio's first visit to Berlin was from March to May 1921. Having already expressed his desire to pursue studies at the Berlin Polytechnic, his project to master the German language was justified. After his May departure from Berlin, he returned to Turin with a stop in Munich. Four months later, Pier Giorgio departed for Germany, his second trip, and again he visited Munich, as well as Stuttgart, then, Freiburg im Breisgau where he resided as a student of German for one month with the Rahner family.[25] In October Pier Giorgio departed for the city of Heidelberg followed by Bonn, Altenbeck, and finally Berlin. In the German capital, Pier Giorgio remained until mid-November of 1921. Returning to Turin, Pier Giorgio visited Prague and Vienna. The following year, in mid-November of 1922, Pier Giorgio returned for his third trip to Germany, with a stop in Innsbruck.

Significant changes had occurred in 1922 since Pier Giorgio had last visited Germany. With Mussolini's claim to power in the March on Rome October 28, and with Mussolini the rise of Fascism, Alfredo Frassati resigned as Italian ambassador to Germany. Alfredo and Adelaide left the Italian Embassy in Berlin in December, but Pier Giorgio remained, spending his first Christmas away from his family. Residing in Berlin, Pier Giorgio took the opportunity to visit other parts of Germany and Poland, stopping in Danzig and exploring the mines of Katowice, in addition to visits again to Munich and Freiburg where he stayed with his friends of German Catholic movements.

3.1.1. Freiburg im Breisgau

Pier Giorgio made three visits to Germany in all. His above letter of October 1921, addressed to his mother expressed his arrangements during his second visit along with his study plans. His main contact was Father Sonnenschein, whom he met in Berlin looking after the Italian community. Although Pier Giorgio could have lived at the ambassador's residence in Berlin to learn German, he preferred to live with a family in Freiburg im Breisgau with whom he had become close friends, and where he learned the language interacting with Germans. Professor Rahner was not only recommended by Father Sonnenschein, but Pier Giorgio also trusted the Father's advice about where he could live. Pier Giorgio had become quite attached to the Rahner family, "sharing their lives and celebrating their birthdays."[26] In Freiburg, Pier Giorgio lived according to his values: a simple life of helping

---

25. Frassati, *Beatitudes*, 62.
26. Frassati, *Beatitudes*, 62.

with housework and carrying vegetables from the garden.[27] Clearly, Pier Giorgio was more inclined toward the simplicity of living in a friend's home, than to the ambassadorial life of Berlin.

Germany offered Pier Giorgio social and cultural opportunities which also enabled him to reflect on his vocation. The twenty-year-old conveyed to Mrs. Rahner that in Germany priests had more contact with lay people than they did in Italy, suggesting that Pier Giorgio would be better suited for the lay life in Italy if he wished to remain in close contact with the people.[28] The twenty-year-old felt compelled to serve the needs of the church, and with his intense sacramental life, the further deepening of his vocation produced the desire to work among the miners. Perhaps in time he would have discovered a missionary vocation, returning to Latin America where his maternal grandfather had worked.

3.2. Music

Pier Giorgio's letter also reflected the extent to which he benefited from the local culture in terms of music, making reference to the concerto he had heard with professor Rahner, and the specific reference to a Pole playing Beethoven and Chopin. Pier Giorgio's thoughts were present to music, as much as they took him back to his family members, reuniting himself with them in his thoughts, and the music he knew they appreciated. These thoughts echoed his experiences which he took pleasure in, the time spent with others, his family, and friends, knowing how much they would also enjoy themselves. From the time he was a child Pier Giorgio reminisced about people whom he cherished; as his presence at the concerto revealed, his thoughts moved to others. He added that he might even be going to hear, *Die Brat von Messina*, "The Bride from Messina," Friedrich Schiller's tragedy. For Pier Giorgio, sharing with others, even at a distance, meant being united.

The central figure for music in the Frassati home was unquestionably Richard Wagner, and this, no doubt, reflected Alfredo Frassati's influence as he had since his days studying in Germany been deeply moved by Wagner's pieces.[29] Alfredo had written to Adelaide in 1893, "I work a lot; I have renounced the world and its pomp, but not theater. I saw the entire Wagner cycle, with the exception of a few pieces, true gems."[30] Pier Giorgio's

27. Frassati, *Beatitudes*, 62.
28. Frassati, *Beatitudes*, 62.
29. Frassati, *Un uomo*, 35.
30. Frassati, *Un uomo*, 35.

musical culture had its source in his home, and so in Germany, he could further appreciate Chopin symphonies and Schiller's dramas. Besides Chopin, Beethoven, and Wagner, Pier Giorgio was also fond of Verdi. Drawn to music and the arts, while in Prague, he saw Bedrich Smetana's *Two Widows*, and in Vienna, Wolfgang Mozart's *Don Giovanni*.

4. Letter to Alberto Falchetti—Freiburg im Breisgau, October 14, 1921[31]

In his letter to Falchetti, Pier Giorgio expressed his relationship with the painter who was not only Adelaide Frassati's art teacher and friend, but Falchetti had also become Pier Giorgio's friend. With his mother a painter, already as a child Pier Giorgio developed a great interest in art.[32] The correspondence clearly reflected Pier Giorgio and Falchetti's shared artistic interests as well as the depth of Pier Giorgio's artistic and literary culture. Pier Giorgio thought of Falchetti in terms of the art which may have interested him and conveyed his artistic experiences to Falchetti. Pier Giorgio's relationship with Falchetti, especially his art piece, *Rhapsodist in Africa*, also contained a degree of humor.[33]

4.1. Art, the Beautiful, and Pleasure

Visiting the cities of Munich, Stuttgart and Karlsruhe, Pier Giorgio made use of his travels to view paintings. A particular interest was the nineteenth-century German artist Hans Thoma, who joined the Karlsruhe Academy. With a Hans Thoma exhibition in Karlsruhe, Pier Giorgio believed the Thoma paintings were the only ones that would have been of interest to Falchetti. Pier Giorgio did not forget Falchetti's *Rhapsodist in Africa*, which the artist had been working on for some time; and so, he inquired about Falchetti's progress while he related his travels.

As Pier Giorgio wrote from Freiburg im Breisgau, he informed Falchetti that the city did not offer any museums, but instead, the city had a magnificent cathedral which Pier Giorgio described in terms of its Gothic and Romanesque architecture. These details communicated to Falchetti were also indicative of Pier Giorgio's knowledge of architectural styles and

---

31. *Letters*, 54–55; Ital. ed., 65–66.

32. See chapter 1, section 2.1.1, when Pier Giorgio had written to his mother while she was participating in the Venice Biennale.

33. *Rhapsodist in Africa* refers to one of Alberto Falchetti's paintings.

periods. He compared Freiburg's cathedral to the one he had visited in Nuremberg and considered them to be among the best he had seen in Germany, offering the critique of what constituted good religious architecture.

Pier Giorgio's attendance at a Dante lecture while in Freiburg related his appreciation for Italian literature, and his remarkable knowledge of the *Divina Comedia*. Pier Giorgio responded with poetic sensitivity to the Italian language. He criticized the German rendering of Count Ugolino, Sordello and Saint Bernard, revealing the extent to which he was familiar with Dante's characters, even Saint Bernard's prayer. He was blunt in his criticism of the German rendition: "But it was no longer Dante's lovely harmonious poetry. Dante can't be translated, no translation can render the same effect as hearing the Divine Comedy in our own beautiful language." These are all sound-related criticisms: "harmonious poetry," "same effect as hearing," "our own beautiful language." Pier Giorgio referred to the sonorous vowels in which most Italian words end, and in poetry, the poet deliberately chooses vocalic sonority to heighten emotions, something that Pier Giorgio could audibly recognize—and feel; sonority that was not possible in German consonantal endings. Pier Giorgio's sensitivity was not only to the artistically visual, but also the musically audible, and the beauty found in both music and art.

His wide literary culture was expressed in his last line where he mentioned *The Kaiser in Exile* written by a "Dutch countess." Pier Giorgio, of course, referred to the German emperor, William II, who was sent to exile in the Netherlands in 1918. Pier Giorgio's familiarity with German artistic and literary culture as well as German history, increasingly created a sense of connectedness with the German people. The diversity of readings and authors not only reflected his literary culture; but, he shared his knowledge, telling Falchetti what he was reading, and that "I'll let you read the translation," so his friend could also appreciate German culture. Only a few months previously, while Pier Giorgio was visiting Berlin in May, he had written to his aunt Elena to tell her that he had gone to see Shakespeare's *Midsummer Night's Dream*.[34]

Pier Giorgio's letter offered details of his German cultural experience through the different cities as well as his travels along the Rhine from Heidelberg to Hamborn. Then, Pier Giorgio proceeded with his train journey to join his father in Berlin, keeping Falchetti updated on his delights of cultural exploration.

One can recognize in Pier Giorgio an appreciation of the aesthetic, values he received from his mother and father. Adelaide, the sensitive artist

---

34. *Letters*, "To his aunt Elena, Berlin, May 5, 1921," 37.

transmitted to her son form and color.³⁵ Alfredo who cried at Wagner's performances conveyed to Pier Giorgio the power of emotion in music. Pier Giorgio embraced the beautiful as an experience of the spiritual. The intensity of artistic beauty reflected the "spiritual experience" that Adelaide and Alfredo shared. Pier Giorgio acquired from his parents the sense of beauty as spiritual, leading to the Transcendent, as Saint Thomas states, "Therefore there must also be something which is to all beings the cause of their being, goodness, and every other perfection; and this we call God."³⁶

4.2. Social Culture and Family Life

Reading his letters during his travels, one might have the impression that Pier Giorgio was simply a "man of the world" enjoying bourgeois culture and lifestyle visiting art galleries, museums, and churches. While working on his German, with his social network between Freiburg and Berlin, and the friends he visited during his stops, might suggest that Pier Giorgio remained attached to the world and pursued its pleasures. Such a reading of Pier Giorgio may be tempting, and almost seem credible, but it is simply false. Pier Giorgio continued to refine his cultural interests and appreciated the beautiful because he desired to know, to discover and to grow, and the German and Central European cultural experiences testify to this. Pier Giorgio was receptive to the world God created and the creativity of the individual. He recognized and acknowledged the "good." Yet, he was not "indulgent": Pier Giorgio did not justify or exploit his family status to degenerate into a hedonistic lifestyle which he could have pursued. He knew that the human being was not a dualism of body and soul but substantially one; he desired, he reflected, and he acted coherently as "unified" person.³⁷

Pier Giorgio was clearly inclined toward discipline, even when he traveled, whether for purposes of his studies, or because of his moral rectitude; ultimately, his connections had a common thread: they were individuals who shared his Catholic faith, and in Germany many of these were priests or Catholic German students. Pier Giorgio never detached himself from the core of what motivated him: his faith—even in his social life.

Pier Giorgio's letters, in this regard, might not always give the full picture of his activities, and in some instances, especially those involving charity, he preferred discretion. Yet, through an exchange of correspondence from other sources, one could detect that during his time in Germany, Pier

---

35. Pierazzi, *Così ho visto*, 135–36.
36. *ST*, Ia, q. 2, a. 3 (fourth way).
37. See *ST*, IIa–IIae, q. 22, a. 1.

Giorgio was detached from the embassy's social life in Berlin.[38] Pier Giorgio's family at the embassy residence engaged in a social life which did not interest Pier Giorgio; in fact, he almost seemed to avoid the social functions associated with Italy's ambassadorial presence in Germany, "displeasure at my brother's absence from a brilliant social life," reflected his sister's observation.[39] Pier Giorgio's disinterest was not surprising, "It was an enterprise to drag him to a little bit of worldly life, 'Pier Giorgio is quite confrontational—but he was at the Embassy dinner—(after his stubborn and capricious ways) and at the dance.' He was obliged by his mother to learn the art of dance, and runs to Fr. Roccati for help. The good pastor asks: 'Does your father know how to dance?' To a definite no, Fr. Roccati replied: 'You see, he made a good career for himself just the same!'"[40]

Monseigneur Alessandro Roccati, the parish priest of *La Crocetta*, and the same priest to baptize Pier Giorgio, knew him well and "rescued" him in this problematic matter—the expectation that Pier Giorgio as part of his social development, and possibly culture, should learn how to dance. The intervention of Mgr. Roccati showed how much Pier Giorgio trusted priests to help him even in nonreligious matters. The incident was significant not so much in Pier Giorgio's refusal to learn to dance, but that when he flatly disagreed with his mother, he sought the help of a priest, believing his mother's expectations were incongruent with his personality. Although he was described as "stubborn" and "capricious" this was nothing more than Pier Giorgio asserting himself feeling strongly about certain matters and having the reassurance of a priest that Pier Giorgio's refusal could not be a violation of the Fourth Commandment.

Pier Giorgio's letters to his mother from Germany were frequent and constant, sometimes even several times a week. When Pier Giorgio found himself in the dilemma of whether to write individual letters to his mother and father, or simply write to one of his parents, writing to one, he maintained he was writing to the entire family, without having to repeat himself in letters. He preferred communication with his mother, so the letters remained personal, and addressed to her. But while his father was working in Germany, Alfredo expressed disappointment with his son's silence, and reproached Pier Giorgio, "Dear Giorgione, I can ask you the same question that I have already asked you other times, do you remember having a father? I remember having a son whose name is Pier Giorgio and who signs his

---

38. Frassati, *I giorni*, 94–95.
39. Frassati, *Beatitudes*, 64.
40. Frassati, *Calendario*, "Berlin, May 16, 1921, Adelaide to Elena."

name Pier Giorgio Frassati, but writes, rarely, very rarely to his father."[41] Pier Giorgio loved his parents and would not do anything to hurt them; he thought of them daily, and they were the point of reference for the serious decisions he had to make. Unquestionably, Pier Giorgio could only be hurt reading such a letter, but this reflected the strain frequently placed on relations due to the absence of family members who were loved and missed. Pier Giorgio left Berlin mid-November 1921, and his father decided to write after three weeks of Pier Giorgio's silence. The interpretation of silence was regarded as indifference or worse, failing to "remember." This could not apply to Pier Giorgio as his parents were always on his mind, but his father was hurt and troubled with his son's silence. Alfredo was not alone in Berlin, as Luciana had remained with him. He loved his son and he wanted to hear from him—to hear his voice. Pier Giorgio replied to his father a few days later explaining that he assumed his mother would write, and once she had left Berlin, he would write to his father himself, "Certainly I remember my dear papa is in Berlin. . . . I was thinking, Mama writes, I will write as soon as she leaves."[42] About one month later, writing from Turin in the New Year, Pier Giorgio responded to his father in the same concerned tone, "It's not that I've forgotten my dear papa who is so far away, but when I write to one of you I am writing to all of you."[43]

5. Letter to Maria Fischer—Katowitz, December 28, 1922[44]

Pier Giorgio wrote to his Austrian friend Maria Fischer, giving her details of his travels since his departure from Berlin. He had written Fischer only the previous week relating to her details of his planned visit to Austria, keeping Fischer updated on his activities, sharing with Fischer his first experience in Poland. He wrote to his mother the same day expressing a rather disappointing account of his interaction with Polish border officials, admitting, "I regret having such trouble with the Poles."[45] Pier Giorgio proceeded with his travel arrangements through Regensburg, Munich, and to Vienna. He closed his letter sending his greetings also to Maria Fischer's parents.

---

41. Frassati, *Calendario*, "Berlin, December 8, 1921, father to Pier Giorgio."
42. *Letters*, "To his father, Turin, December 13, 1921," 68–69.
43. *Letters*, "To his father, Turin, January 10, 1922," 76.
44. *Letters*, 108; Ital. ed., 151–52.
45. *Letters*, 108–9. Pier Giorgio will have a different experience with the Poles when his sister marries a Polish diplomat.

5.1. Polish Experience

Pier Giorgio who displayed the enthusiasm of a twenty-one-year-old traveling, discovering the richness of new cultures, exploring cities he had studied, visiting museums he had read about, praying in cathedrals he had touched in pictures, could express his delight and satisfaction of novel experiences. He conveyed his fascination in his correspondence with his mother, sister and friends. Yet, Poland did not fit into this pleasurable catalogue of experience. One might ask, what went wrong? Pier Giorgio was unusually harsh and critical of his brief travels in Poland. He sounded, in fact, quite irritated with his overall Polish excursion. He wrote to his mother, "I wanted to push on all the way to Krakow, but I decided not to because it just isn't good to travel with the Poles," and described Katowice in his letter to his mother as this "somewhat dirty city."[46] He decided to cancel his visit to Krakow, Poland's cultural and religious capital, due to the extent of his disappointment upon arriving in Poland.

On the same day he wrote to Fischer, Pier Giorgio conveyed his frustration to his mother, "Today the Polish customs agents at the border made me open my bags, which has never happened to me neither in Germany nor in Austria nor in Czechoslovakia until today." Pier Giorgio was unhappy with his treatment and how he perceived the situation in Upper Silesia which had fallen into the hands of a "villainous" people. Such comments seem surprising given Pier Giorgio's generally respectful and understanding disposition. These views serve to help further understand Pier Giorgio's cultural experiences including his expectations.

In 1922, Upper Silesia was part of Poland with its capital at Katowice, while Lower Silesia belonged to Germany, with its capital at Breslau, a city Pier Giorgio also intended to visit. Pier Giorgio found himself traveling across Upper and Lower Silesia, divided between Poland and Germany, respectively. The unstable political boundaries of Silesia shifted from Germany to Poland with Polish agitation seeking a united Silesia.[47] Until his arrival in Poland, Pier Giorgio was able to make use of German in German-speaking countries, but also in Prague where German was widely spoken. This was not the case with Poland, beginning with the upsetting encounter with the Polish customs official who undoubtedly did not appreciate being addressed in German. When Pier Giorgio arrived in Katowice, he was tired, frustrated, and irritated which would explain his comment, "a somewhat dirty city." This might have been true, Katowice being a mining capital, but

---

46. *Letters*, 108–9.

47. Pier Giorgio was visiting Upper Silesia shortly after the Silesian Uprising of 1921.

Pier Giorgio had already been exposed to misery in the streets of Turin and the depressed conditions of Berlin.

5.2. Mining Vocation

Pier Giorgio's primary purpose to visit Poland was the coal mines of Upper Silesia. His interest in minerals and mines can be traced to his childhood, and later adolescence; this interest was more than a hobby-collection of minerals. The mines of the Biella region, Bergamo valleys, Emilian Mountains, later, his German and Polish visits, point towards Pier Giorgio's fascination with mines.[48]

Pier Giorgio's captivation with minerals led him to the mystery of creation. Visiting mines also connected Pier Giorgio with those who worked with the minerals, the miners. For Pier Giorgio the miners represented the workers who lived a "sacrificial life, and he wished to be at their side."[49] Mining engineering was part of his Turin polytechnic program and his interest in mines was leading him to a mining career so he could be close to men working in filthy and risky jobs. While students changed their registered program after visiting the mines, especially given the dangers of going down into the mines, the effect on Pier Giorgio, even after his visits of the Polish and German mines of Silesia, was to reinforce his mining vocation.[50]

Questions

(Note: *ST* refers to *Summa Theologiae* of Saint Thomas Aquinas—part [I/II/III], question, article, response)

1. How old was Pier Giorgio when he traveled to Rome with his mother (§1)? Given the details of Pier Giorgio's letter to his father (§1; 1.1; 1.2), what does the letter reveal about Pier Giorgio?

2. What are the indications that Pier Giorgio was especially fond of Dante Alighieri (1.2)? Which verses of Dante attributed to St. Bernard of Clairvaux did Pier Giorgio learn by heart (1.2)?

3. What is the significance of Pier Giorgio's visit to Assisi (2.1)? What role did poverty have in the life of Pier Giorgio (2.2)? How does St. Thomas

---

48. Casalegno, *Pier Giorgio Frassati*, 93.
49. Frassati, *La carità*, "Testimony of Giuseppe Graziano," 48.
50. Casalegno, *Pier Giorgio Frassati*, 94.

Aquinas approach the question of poverty (See note 17; *ST*, II–IIae, q. 88, a. 7.)?

4. In his letter to his mother from Freiburg im Breisgau, how does Pier Giorgio describe Freiburg (§3; October 1921)? What does Pier Giorgio convey about his musical culture (3.2)?

5. Who was Alberto Falchetti and what role did art have in the Frassati household (§4)? How did Pier Giorgio experience art, beauty and pleasure (4.1)?

6. How did Pier Giorgio spend his time in Poland (5.1; 5.2)? What was the motive of his visit to Katowice (5.2)?

6

Friendship

> Not every love has the character of friendship, but that love which is together with benevolence, when, to wit, we love someone so as to wish good to him.
>
> SAINT THOMAS AQUINAS,
> *SUMMA THEOLOGIAE*, IIA–IIAE, Q. 23, A. 1

This chapter on friendship offers different perspectives on Pier Giorgio's friends, and therefore, his personality: respectful, joyful, compassionate, and coherent. These qualities lead Pier Giorgio to develop an extensive network of friends. Besides his closest friend and confidant, his sister, Luciana, Pier Giorgio creates friendships during his studies at Massimo D'Azeglio. Then, at the Turin Polytech these friends belong to the numerous Catholic Clubs in which Pier Giorgio is involved, spiritual, social, and political. The Polytechnic friends all share a common truth: Jesus Christ. So, one discovers that the core of Pier Giorgio's friends is sharing with them his fundamental values: communion with the church through the sacraments, the spiritual, charitable, and political activities centered on Christ and his gospel. Pier Giorgio's friends were both lay as well as numerous priests, Italians and a wide circle of non-Italians, especially Germans. In Germany Pier Giorgio's main contact was Father Sonnenschein, who opened the way to a network of Roman Catholics in Germany, families, priests, and Italian Catholics. Another group of friends, an intimate circle with whom Pier Giorgio shared his faith and social activities, a "club" which he started with others, "The Shady Ones," *Tipi Loschi*.

1. Letter to Maria Fischer—Turin, May 17, 1922[1]

Pier Giorgio turned twenty-one years old in April when he wrote to Maria Fischer the following month. Although Pier Giorgio's writing had been criticized for its punctuation and grammar, his letters, nevertheless, express remarkable continuity. Pier Giorgio's writing revealed with consistency, stylistically a descriptive narrative, and the depth of being, his beautiful soul. In his correspondence with Fischer, Pier Giorgio employed a highly formal Italian register, never calling Fischer by her first name, but always, *Signorina Fischer*, "Miss Fischer." In the distant and formal Italian, Pier Giorgio employed the third person singular, *Lei*, "she," in addressing Fischer. Pier Giorgio's use of the formal register out of respect characterized his correspondence with his female friends. His skill in adapting his Italian register according to his audience reflected Pier Giorgio's control and knowledge of the language for purposes of social etiquette, formality as well familiarity. With Fischer Pier Giorgio shared his Catholic faith, evident in his description of Turin's eucharistic miracle; and, as active members of *Pax Romana*, both Pier Giorgio and Fischer worked together on the Christian commitment to world peace.

1.1. Eucharistic Miracle

Pier Giorgio's letter began with an apology for the delay in writing Fischer. The body of the letter conveyed to his Austrian friend his love for his Catholic faith, and no doubt, the letter was motivated by his zeal to share with Fischer the spiritual intensity with which he experienced the commemoration of the eucharistic miracle offering her a historical description of the event. Pier Giorgio, delighted with Turin, the city of his birth, stated, "I witnessed a day of triumph of our Faith." He continued in his tone of joy and satisfaction, "My city is called the City of the Blessed Sacrament." Here Pier Giorgio recounted the historical and miraculous event which took place in 1453.[2]

Besides details of the eucharistic miracle, Pier Giorgio wrote Fischer a detailed account of the commemoration of the miracle in Turin where Pier

---

1. *Letters*, 85; Ital. ed., 115.
2. Pier Giorgio writes 1456; the eucharistic miracle occurred three years earlier.

Giorgio was present on the Sunday. A comparison was made with Palm Sunday in Jerusalem in which he considered the biblical parallel between the Eucharist and Christ's entry into Jerusalem. The significance of the procession was the presence of the faithful to testify their faith in an act of worship. Pier Giorgio made himself a witness by his presence, and then, shared these experiences with his friends, bringing the Scriptures into the sensory world of lived experience: sight of the Real Presence, the sound of chants, the fragrance of incense, the eucharistic procession, the prayers, the believers gathered. Pier Giorgio wrote to Fischer to share with her his lived faith, in one Lord and one baptism.[3] Worship that was natural—and supernatural—how Catholics were called to live their communion with God and with each other. Pier Giorgio wrote a letter of spiritual fervor that conveyed his convictions with zeal.

Pier Giorgio provided details, "when the children and the people threw flowers on the streets as Jesus Christ passed by." This was not just his imagination: the entry of Jesus into Jerusalem, in honoring their King, the people waved olive branches, spreading them on the ground with cloaks, and other greenery.[4] In a similar tradition, the people of Turin welcomed their King, their Sovereign. Pier Giorgio's sensitivity to color, to beauty, to the Sacred, left him spiritually overjoyed, needing to express this experience with his Austrian friend.

1.2. Miss Fischer

Fischer lived in Vienna and so Pier Giorgio could not visit her often; yet, they still developed a friendship based on their memberships in Catholic university federations. For Pier Giorgio to be deeply religious came across as something natural, and this faith had been cultivated over the years. He sent Fischer a detailed description of the history of Turin's eucharistic miracle.

When the tenth national FUCI Congress was held in Ravenna, August 29, 1921, the meeting organized two celebrations: the twenty-fifth anniversary since the foundation of FUCI, as well as Dante Alighieri's sixth centenary anniversary of his birth. Among the eight hundred students that participated in the event, about eighty were external delegates from the *Pax Romana* and among the non-Italian delegates was the Austrian Miss Maria Fischer from Vienna.[5]

---

3. Eph 4:5–6.
4. Mark 11:8–9; John 12:12–13.
5. Casalegno, *Pier Giorgio Frassati*, 142.

With Pier Giorgio, who spoke German, his interaction with German speakers came with enthusiasm. The congress was hosted by the Italian city of Ravenna, and Pier Giorgio, as the official delegate for foreign students, offered Fischer his services. Both were committed members of *Pax Romana* which formed the basis of their friendship.[6]

On November 17, Pier Giorgio visited Vienna and had the opportunity to spend time with Fischer, including "spending the Sunday with the Fischer family."[7] The family commented on Pier Giorgio's farewell, "It seemed as if he had left when instead, shortly after, the Fischers see him returning to their house, more worried than before because he had just reached the station and deposited his baggage, he returned in a rush to leave that family of friends all the remaining money he had so that they could give it to the poor people of Vienna."[8] The greetings Pier Giorgio conveyed in letters to family members were physically expressed when he was present with handshakes or Italian *baci*, "kisses." Certainly, the Fischer family became fond of Pier Giorgio's warmth and politeness, and edified by his generosity. Pier Giorgio also replied to Fischer's request for the ingredients and cooking instructions for *tagliatelle*. The wonderful letter showed how in the midst of his studies, Pier Giorgio could find the time to sit down to write a pasta recipe for his friend with all the details, and then requested that the friend keep him informed on the results of a *maccheroni* dish.[9]

In November 1922, Pier Giorgio arrived in Innsbruck with two gifts for Fischer but she had already left for Munich. One of the gifts was a novel by a prominent Italian author and devout Catholic, Alessandro Manzoni's *Promessi Sposi*, "The Betrothed"—the most widely read novel in the Italian language.[10] In his dedication Pier Giorgio wrote, "Remembering the days full of faith and enthusiasm spent together in Italy, to the dear Miss Fischer, I offer this book, Pier Giorgio Frassati."[11] Along with the novel, Pier Giorgio left Fischer a Rosary made from seeds from his garden known as *Lacrimae Jobi*, "Job's Tears." He also informed Fischer that the Rosary was already blessed and had all the "indulgences"—gifts from a deeply religious twenty-one-year-old. For Pier Giorgio he saw in Fischer a wonderful friend

---

6. *Letters*, "To Maria Fischer, Pollone, August 29, 1922," 88–89. This represented the first meeting of *Pax Romana*.

7. *Lettere*, Ital. ed., "To Gian Maria Bertini, Vienna, November 17, 1921," 85; and "Mother, Vienna, November 18, 1921," 85.

8. Frassati, *La carità*, 49.

9. *Letters*, "To Maria Fischer, Turin, December 20, 1921," 70–71.

10. *Letters*, "To Maria Fischer, Innsbruck, November 13, 1922," 100.

11. Casalegno, *Pier Giorgio Frassati*, 143.

with whom he could share his Catholic faith and the concerns of Catholic university students through *Pax Romana*.

From Turin Pier Giorgio wrote a long letter repeating the words of the pope calling for peace as well as expressing his own admiration for the German people.[12] He sent Fischer his remaining funds from his trip to be used as she desired, so long as his name remained anonymous. His following letter, written in March, Pier Giorgio discussed both his active social life in Catholic Clubs, skiing, and the Lenten season. Pier Giorgio's letters to Fischer take on an increasingly political tone; he responded to the severe economic conditions of the Germans who were suffering due to the Versailles Treaty, especially France's politics regarding Germany. Identifying with the suffering Germans, Pier Giorgio admired their strength.[13]

The last letter to Fischer in Pier Giorgio's *Lettere*, was written on Good Friday, April 10, 1925.[14] He enquired whether Fischer would be at the *Pax Romana* congress in Bologna that summer, the annual convention meeting in 1925. He related his plans hoping to go to the Netherlands to visit his sister, and on the way back, he wanted to stop in Germany to join the German delegates for the *Pax Romana* convention. Pier Giorgio's friendship with Fischer showed that Pier Giorgio was capable of maintaining a pure friendship with a young lady. For Pier Giorgio who grew up with a sister only a year younger, he was accustomed to female companionship; he knew how to interact, play, socialize, and joke with a young lady, being as usual himself, respectful and sensitive.

1.3. Pax Romana

Pier Giorgio joined the international student organization, *Pax Romana*, in August of 1921, one month after its foundation, in July 1921, in Freiburg, Switzerland. The organization represented delegates from the different Catholic university associations in Europe, Switzerland, Germany, France, Austria, Hungary, Belgium, Czechoslovakia, Great Britain, and Italy. He identified with the objectives of the organization of peaceful coexistence among the nations that had been destabilized by the First World War. Being a member himself of the Federation of the Italian Catholic Universities, *Pax Romana* was a mechanism by which Pier Giorgio channeled his Christian commitment to peaceful coexistence at an international level. The name

---

12. *Letters*, "To Maria Fischer, Turin, January 23, 1923," 116.

13. The political climate of the period starting with WWI and the following years will be taken up in chapter 7.

14. *Lettere*, Ital. ed., "To Maria Fischer, Turin, April 10, 1925," 329.

Pax Romana itself reflected the organization's trust that the Roman Catholic Church could offer the world. Besides the 1921 convention in Ravenna where he became friends with Miss Maria Fischer, Pier Giorgio had planned to participate in the August 1925 convention, in Florence, writing to his friend Willibald Leitgebel, "The Pax Romana convention will take place in August in Florence. Would you be able to come? I will probably go and I hope to meet you with the new and old friends of 1921."[15]

2. Letter to Willibald Leitgebel—Turin, January 28, 1923[16]

Dear Willibald,

Please forgive me if I hadn't written to you anymore, but unfortunately I always have a lot to do.

Although I write little to the Germans, I think of them a lot.

The days spent in Germany are for me amongst the most wonderful of my youth and it is with profound sadness that I observe, unfortunately helplessly, your Country's harsh and difficult situation.

We too have lost the most beautiful and best thing that God has given to all men, namely, freedom, without which life becomes difficult.

The Governments, above all that of France, don't want to recognize the Pope's warnings: "True peace is more a fruit of Christian love for one's neighbor than it is a fruit of justice," and so hatred is sown in the world today instead of Charity.

War has annihilated moral sensibility in all Nations and we become helpless witnesses of France's brutality, while our Catholic conscience trembles in the face of this infamy.

But we can do nothing about foreign policy, since Catholics in Italy have unfortunately lost their freedom; with a bleeding heart we watch our Government help France and we cannot stop it. But we are sure that God will reward Germany for her harsh sufferings.

A friend of mine has finished University and would like to enroll at Rentlingen near Stuttgart in the school of textile arts. He asked me to inquire in Germany whether the school is still open *and if they cause difficulties for foreigners.*

---

15. *Lettere*, Ital. ed., "To Willibald Leitgebel, October 11, 1924," 257–58.

16. *Lettere*, Ital. ed., 162–63 (my translation). The European political context of this letter will be taken up in chapter 7.

> Please, when you have time, ask for the professors in Charlottenburg for some information. My friend being from Merano, speaks better German than he does Italian.
> When you have a reply, please write to me.
> Many greetings to your brother and your sister and my regards to your parents and a cordial greeting to you from
> Pier Giorgio Frassati

Pier Giorgio opened his letter with an apology for not having written "anymore," and gave his reasons, as he did with his other friends—"lot to do." In the body of his letter he admitted to not having a frequent correspondence with the Germans, but they were on his mind and he acknowledged the value of his time spent in Germany, "the most wonderful of my youth." Pier Giorgio was afflicted by Germany's suffering; misery always had a tremendous effect on Pier Giorgio. He acknowledged that Italy was going through the same difficulty having lost that which was most valuable: "freedom." The loss of freedom became the point of transition in his letter bringing the discussion to a political level.

The harsh criticism directed toward "France's brutality" was in reference to France's occupation of the Ruhr region, and the socioeconomic collapse of Germany due to the Versailles Treaty. Pier Giorgio, disturbed by the suffering of a people, described their cruel treatment and an unjust war treaty. The pope's message of "peace" had previously been mentioned in his letter to Fischer, showing the constancy of Pier Giorgio's thoughts on the pope's message of "Christian love."

Pier Giorgio maintained that when people unjustly suffer, whether these were the poor in Italy, or the oppressed in Germany, the people would still be rewarded by God. This thought of God rewarding the poor, that their suffering does not go unheard or unnoticed by God, is contained in a biblical source,

> The poor man died and was carried by the angels to Abraham's bosom. The rich man also died and was buried; and in Hades, being in torment, lifted up his yes, and saw Abraham far off and Lazarus in his bosom. And he called out, "Father Abraham, have mercy upon me, and send Lazarus to dip the end of his finger in water and cool my tongue; for I am in anguish in this flame." But Abraham said, "Son, remember that you in your lifetime received your good things, and Lazarus in like manner evil things, but now he is comforted here, and your are in anguish."[17]

---

17. Luke 16:22–26.

Luke's Gospel captured the justice of Christianity in relation to misery and suffering on earth; those who received "bad things" on earth will be recompensed in heaven. Pier Giorgio understood this to be part of his Christian faith: the poor were close to God—through their suffering they participated in the cross of Christ.[18] He expressed this, however, without showing hostility toward the wealthy or the upper social classes. Pier Giorgio rejected, however, a political system that deliberately sought to privilege the wealthy, to the detriment of the poor which prolonged their misery and suffering.

With his different connections Pier Giorgio found ways to find help for his friends, as indicated in this letter, help for a friend who wished to study at Rentlingen. Pier Giorgio made a point of asking Leitgebel to obtain the information sought through the professors in Charlottenburg; Pier Giorgio believed it was his Christian duty to help his friends however possible.

2.1. Leitgebel Friendship

Pier Giorgio wrote his postcard letter to Leitgebel in May 1921, when Pier Giorgio made his first trip to Germany. While visiting his father in Berlin, Pier Giorgio met Leitgebel through Father Sonnenschein, and he became friends with Leitgebel and his family who lived in Hamborn, in Westphalia.[19] Members of the Leitgebel family were included in his farewell, extending his greetings to Leitgebel's brother, sister, and parents.

Few details are available on the Leitgebel family apart from Pier Giorgio's friendship with the entire family. However, while Luciana was in Berlin, Pier Giorgio insisted that she visit the Leitgebel family to give them his regards since they had expressed kindness toward him. Luciana found the family "anything but German" in terms of their affection and hospitality.[20] This thoughtfulness toward the Leitgebel family, ensuring that his sister pay the family a visit, reflected the deep value Pier Giorgio attached to his friendships; they were neither utilitarian nor pleasure-seeking. Pier Giorgio cherished his friends and he did his best to remain in contact with them, taking time from his studies and activities to sit down and write to his friends.

In his correspondence of thirteen letters written to Leitgebel, Pier Giorgio discussed everything one could share with a close friend: numerous

---

18. See Col 1:24.

19. Father Sonnenschein certainly belonged to Pier Giorgio's circle of friends. The sociopolitical concerns that Pier Giorgio shared with Father Sonnenschein will be treated in chapter 7.

20. *Lettere*, Ital. ed., "To Willibald Leitgebel, Turin, April 13, 1923," 114. See also n1.

journeys, studies and exams, political concerns in Germany and Italy, people suffering, mountain excursions with his friends, and his sister's engagement to Jan Gawronski. In his last letter to Leitgebel, Pier Giorgio wished him a Holy Jubilee Year for 1925.[21] Pier Giorgio's religious beliefs reflected his love for the pope's teachings, making reference to Pope Pius XI's "warning" in his letter, but Pier Giorgio's views took on a distinctly eschatological dimension, not only for how God would reward the suffering, but also, as he stated in his letter to Leitgebel, "Our Faith helps us with the great hope that this life is short and that only afterwards comes the true Life, in which Justice will triumph."[22] The eschatological vision Pier Giorgio expressed, clearly biblical and wholly Catholic, was communicated to his friend: Pier Giorgio did not hide his beliefs; in keeping with his personality of courage, he verbalized his views unambiguously. This honesty made Pier Giorgio a true friend.

Pier Giorgio also wrote to Leitgebel's sister, Nisse, expressing his concerns for the unemployed who had been studying the sciences and did not find work after the war. His anti-Fascist views were a response to the violence caused by the Mussolini's *fasci*, "bundles," in different provinces of Italy.[23] Instead, Pier Giorgio aligned himself with the pope's repeated call for peace. He congratulated Nisse having had just married, sending his best wishes also to her husband.[24]

Pier Giorgio began his correspondence with Leitgebel from Hamburg, May 7, 1921. When he wrote the above letter from Turin in 1923, Pier Giorgio had already made several visits to Germany and through central Europe, and the two had been friends for almost two years. Pier Giorgio painfully observed how the economic situation was rapidly deteriorating in Germany due to the drastic devaluation of the German mark. The correspondence reflected the diversity of Pier Giorgio's friendships, they were not limited to Italian university classmates who balanced their life between studies and mountain climbing. Pier Giorgio's friends included Italians and non-Italians, men and women, his age group and outside his age group; they climbed mountains, but they were also priests, artists, professors, and politicians.

Catholicism united him with those who were committed to living according to Christ's teachings. These individuals sought peace in their troubled countries, believed in works of charity to alleviate the suffering

---

21. *Letters*, "To Willibald Leitgebel, Turin, December 30, 1924," 191–92. Correspondence with Leitgebel is based on letters in the Italian edition. Pier Giorgio's reaction to his sister's marriage will be taken up in chapter 9.

22. *Letters*, "To Willibald, Turin, February 3, 1923," 119.

23. *Fasci*, literally "bundle," treated below in chapter 7, section 6.

24. *Lettere*, Ital. ed., "To Nisse, Pollone, April 17, 1924," 208–9.

and misery of the poor, and worked toward a government that favored the interest and common good as taught by Christ and his church. Pier Giorgio valued his friends for their shared faith in Christ and their common social concerns. Social and moral issues were addressed through the different groups in which he actively participated, and through which he forged connections as shown with the FUCI and *Pax Romana*. While in Germany and central Europe, Pier Giorgio visited museums and went to operas, he never ignored the reality of poverty; he believed in the duty to help—however he could offer help, to respond to the needs of the poor.[25]

3. Letter to Antonio Villani—Forte dei Marmi, August 17, 1924[26]

In Pier Giorgio's letter to his friend Villani, many of the values that characterize the twenty-three-year-old Pier Giorgio surface in this Italian "lunch." Areas relevant to the life of Pier Giorgio contained in this long letter include: social life, studies, spiritual values, and finally, his political life. Missing in his letter were his numerous works of charity; but, Pier Giorgio seldom discussed works of charity, preferring modesty and discretion.

3.1. Pranzo "Lunch" with His Friends

The only lunch Pier Giorgio described in detail that he prepared for his friends was on Sunday afternoon July 27. A full appreciation of this lunch needs to be read with his letter written to Franz Massetti August 6.[27] Pier Giorgio had invited his good friends, Tipi Loschi—Marco Beltramo (Citizen Perrault) and Antonio Severi, and non-Tipi Loschi—Isadore Bonini (Commissioner Bonini) and Checchi Bonini.[28]

The date, July 27, was significant: Pier Giorgio had an exam the next day. He would not have invited his friends for lunch had he not prepared for his exam, and as he pointed out in his letter to Villani, "I was well-enough prepared." The relevance of this lunch invitation showed that he found time for his friends, to enjoy himself with them, and he was not obsessed with high grades to the detriment of his friendships. Pier Giorgio, as with any student, would be delighted with high grades. At what expense were these

---

25. The sociopolitical issues are addressed in chapter 7.
26. *Letters*, 168–70; Ital. ed., 238–39.
27. *Lettere*, Ital. ed., "To Franz Massetti, Forte dei Marmi, August 6, 1924," 227–28.
28. Details of the configuration of the *Tipi Loschi* is given below.

high grades obtained? Pier Giorgio admitted he was not inclined toward studying more than he had to; at the same time, he had a value for friendship that studies and grades could not match: academic knowledge could not replace human experience and this was at the core of Pier Giorgio's personality: people came first, not grades, careers, status or success.

Pier Giorgio mentioned that he was the cook and so he wore a white apron and for the chef's hat, he put on the "Becco Giallo," *Yellow Beak*, the name of the satirical newspaper. By making and wearing a chef's hat Pier Giorgio constructed from the newspaper he read, a political statement he shared with his close friends the same anti-Fascist sentiments as the satirical newspaper that often ridiculed Fascist politics. Details on the cooking were provided in the letter written to Massetti, "The dinner, without 'boasting,' went incredibly well and was eaten in perfect joy; truly the guests were received poorly by the cook because they arrived punctually late by half an hour and so I could not guarantee pasta *asciutta*.[29] Having finished the lunch we sang beautiful mountain songs and others." The details Pier Giorgio offered were revelatory of his personality, both in terms of humor, but also attentiveness to his guests. His friends arrived late and Pier Giorgio's concern was the pasta being overcooked. *Pasta asciutta* or "dry" pasta is distinguished from pasta *minestra* or noodle soup. The detail may seem irrelevant but for his Italian guests, they knew what *pasta asciutta* should taste like. Pier Giorgio wanted to avoid overcooked pasta and so *pasta asciutta* he "could not guarantee" because the timing needed to be fairly accurate: covering the pot with a lid meant the heat would continue to cook the pasta; and adding hot water the pasta would acquire a watery texture. In both cases the pasta would not be *asciutta*. Pier Giorgio could not be careless about the timing of the pasta being dropped into the boiling water.

3.1.1. Attitude toward Studies

In the same August 17 letter to Antonio Villani, Pier Giorgio stated that he was prepared for the exam; he "calmly went," only to find out the exam was postponed. Having called Pollone to speak to his father, Pier Giorgio anticipated his father's reaction, "you can imagine the lectures I received." Pier Giorgio's father was involved in the progress of his education, and so, Alfredo Frassati called Professor Grassi, his electrotechnology professor. The exam was postponed due to the regular students who withdrew from the exams. Professor Grassi stipulated the conditions upon which Pier Giorgio

---

29. *Pasta asciutta* in the original Italian; literally "dry pasta," compared to pasta *minestra* or pasta *in forno* "baked pasta."

might take the exam. Clearly, his father wanted him to take his exam rather than having to wait until the autumn, and Pier Giorgio himself was anxious to complete the exam.

Having obtained the permission by the students as one of the conditions to take the exam on the Friday, Pier Giorgio could say, "I was thus freed from a heavy burden." Pier Giorgio mentioned that he could have known the material better but his relationship with studies was doing the necessary work to obtain a reasonable grade, and not having the "burden" of endless studies for his exams, "I was fed up walking up and down for a few days," and he realized he had already forgotten some of the material—the anxiety experienced by a student preparing to take exams. Although he admitted that 70/100 was "not too bad," his real satisfaction was, "it's always one less exam," and that reflected Pier Giorgio's main concern, not so much the grade, but completing the exam. Pier Giorgio realized that concentration was difficult because of the many "distractions"; he admitted in this area his "will" was lacking. One could imagine the challenge studying toward the end of summer, while staying at the beautiful beach town, Forte dei Marmi on the Ligurian coast. A stoic effort would be needed not to succumb to the temptation of going sailing or swimming, or other outdoor activities, especially with Pier Giorgio's outdoor interests. He confided in his aunt Elena in a letter the previous day that he had been sailing "only" a few times.[30] He had a schedule during the vacation as well as "free time" from studies as he told his aunt.

3.1.2. Asking for Prayers

"I entrust myself to your prayers," Pier Giorgio wrote Villani. This formula Pier Giorgio used asking for someone's prayers came naturally to him as he often requested prayers. Pier Giorgio turned to a friend upon whom he could rely for prayers, also suggesting his dependency on the "other." Furthermore, these prayers were ultimately directed to a divine source, whether Villani turned to the saints who in turn brought the petition to God, whether they were directly addressed to God, prayer remained fundamental in Pier Giorgio's life. Showing that he was dependent on others to help him get through his studies, Pier Giorgio acknowledged he could not succeed on his own. Pier Giorgio relied on others, knowing "The prayer of a righteous man has great power in its effects."[31] This reflected Pier Giorgio's humility and ultimate dependence on God.

30. *Letters*, "To Aunt Elena Ametis, Forte dei Marmi, August 16, 1924," 168.
31. Jas 5:16.

His letter to his aunt Elena expressed with depth the value Pier Giorgio attached to prayer, the sacramental life, but also, his understanding of the communion of saints. He told his aunt, "For your feast day I will not be able to give you my best wishes in person so I will pray a lot for you and I will receive Holy Communion for you and Luciana."[32] Whether family or friend, Pier Giorgio was deeply united with them through prayer. In the case of his aunt, he remembered her namesday, offered to pray for her, and received communion for both his aunt and his sister.

What does this mean, receiving communion for someone? Pier Giorgio knew this was the best way he could obtain graces for an individual: receiving the body and blood of Christ for that person. The spiritual needs which Pier Giorgio might not know, even needs others might not be aware of, but God knew, and so Pier Giorgio received communion for those very spiritual needs to which God could respond through Pier Giorgio's communion. The communion of saints, living, suffering, triumphant, included the intercessory prayer of this communion.

Truly a person does not die even at "death" because the baptized individual who dies in a state of grace, only needs to be purified in purgatory before joining the saints in heaven. This communion is made possible by Jesus Christ, crucifixion, death and resurrection. Pier Giorgio increased in understanding of Catholic teaching, especially while attending the Social Institute and listening to the teachings of the different apostolates and confraternities of prayer. Pier Giorgio's faith was more than a series of coherent concepts that fit nicely together; his was a faith lived—a faith embracing the mystery of God's love.

3.2. Sociopolitical Issues[33]

Pier Giorgio's letter moved into a political tone, but the Catholic Associations to which Pier Giorgio belonged also took political positions. Pier Giorgio took a clear position against Fascism. Any kind of negotiation with Fascists for him was simply unacceptable even if such "alliances" served the interest of Catholics. For Pier Giorgio one did not negotiate with a party whose objectives and the means of attaining them conflicted with Christian values. He had originally hoped that the FUCI could establish a merger with Catholic Youth, a university movement associated with working-class Italians. When this alliance was not realized, even though both university clubs shared a Catholic identity, Pier Giorgio started a Catholic Action section at

---

32. *Letters*, "To Aunt Elena Ametis, Forte dei Marmi, August 16, 1924," 168.

33. The sociopolitical context will be developed in further detail in chapter 7.

his home parish, *La Crocetta*. By mid-August 1924, Pier Giorgio discovered that its Catholic Action members maintained "ambiguous" positions with regards to Mussolini and the Fascists. Mussolini had agrarian reform policies that undoubtedly attracted the Italian working-class, but Pier Giorgio gave reasons for keeping a distance from the Fascist government, "How can a party call itself Catholic, when it supports a government that has no morals, namely when it has made the morals of assassins and robbers its own?" His reference to the Catholic Center referred to the party that drew from different left- and right-wing parties.[34]

The significance of this last part of Pier Giorgio's letter reflected his personality: his religious principles governed his social life, his political views, and his actions. People might have agreed or disagreed with him, but they knew what Pier Giorgio thought and how he lived, and the coherency between the two—the truth he pursued and the truth he advanced. Pier Giorgio did not use calculating strategies or manipulative tactics to make himself accepted or his views attractive. He was not a man of many faces, but rather, one truth that he desired to live to its fullest, and that was in conformity to the teachings of Jesus Christ. Pier Giorgio the son of Alfredo and Adelaide, Pier Giorgio the student at Turin Polytechnic, Pier Giorgio climbing mountains, Pier Giorgio swimming in the Italian Riviera, Pier Giorgio praying at *La Crocetta*, Pier Giorgio combatting Communism, Pier Giorgio the anti-Fascist, were one and the same, and his friends knew this.

4. Proclamation to Marco Beltramo—Forte dei Marmi, August 1924[35]

In his "Proclamation" from the "Terror Section," Pier Giorgio unveiled the *Tipi Loschi*.[36] On May 18, 1924, at Pian della Mussa, Pier Giorgio and his friends founded the *Tipi Loschi*, the "Shady Ones." Pier Giorgio's letter of August 1924 to Beltramo expressed the fundamental bond of the Tipi Loschi: their faith uniting all its members. The tone of Pier Giorgio's letter also reflected the humoristic and joyful means employed by the society bringing together the members in their mountain activities.

---

34. Political climate of Italy during Mussolini's rise to power will be taken up in chapter 7.

35. *Letters*, 164–66; Ital. ed., 231–32.

36. *Tipi Loschi* literally means "Shady Ones." I will keep the original Italian.

4.1. Tipi Loschi Members

The photo of the original members constituting the Tipi Loschi Society shows ten individuals together on the founding day:[37]

Pier Giorgio Frassati—Robespierre, Terror section: name based on the figure Maximilien Robespierre, the French Revolutionary leader, associated with the "Reign of Terror." Pier Giorgio's ironic humor was suggested in the name of their club, the "Shady Ones," and their Tipi Loschi names conveyed elements of truth: Pier Giorgio as Robespierre played the role of an incorruptible leader.

Marco Beltramo—Perrault/Perôl, Terror section: Pier Giorgio along with Marco constituted the Terror section of the Tipi Loschi. Perrault got his name from the play *Il Conte di Bréchard* by the Italian playwright Giovacchino Forzano. Situated during the French Revolution, the play included the name Perrault; Beltramo was now the "new Perrault."[38]

Clementina (Tina) Luotto—president* [permanent position]:[39] Clementina was especially known for her poetic use of language, and so while admired, she was also teased for her Dantescan thirteenth-century Italian.

Ernestina (Tina) Bonelli—direct of excursions*/D.d.g. [permanent position], also *Englesina*, "young English lady": D.d.g as Pier Giorgio employed in his letters referred to the Italian *direttrice di gite*. Tina's visit to England accounts for her nickname.

Laura Hidalgo—secretary* [permanent position][40]

---

37. Names of Tipi Loschi (section 4.1) is based on the ten members in the picnic photo at Pian della Mussa, May 18, 1924, with some variation: Clementina Luotto refers to six members in Frassati, *I giorni*, 136, and biographies on Pier Giorgio have given other names creating some confusion. Based on Wanda Gawronska's conversations with her mother, Luciana Frassati, Gian Maria Bertini and Isidoro Bonini were definitely not members of the society. Reference to Franz Massetti, "Petronio," Isidoro Bonini, "Danton" and Gian Maria Bertini, "La Gaffe," are nicknames given outside of the Tipi Loschi Society. Siccardi lists twelve members but four members are missing from her list that appear at Pian della Mussa, and six that she included are not at the founding picnic. See Siccardi, *Pier Giorgio Frassati*, 227–28 and n.1. Antonio Severi's sister has been identified in a photo and the same woman appears in the founding picnic of the Tipi Loschi (Wanda Gawronska, personal communication November/December/April/August 2015–16 / August 2019). Left-right in the Pian della Mussa photo appear as follows: Maddalena Guglielmini; Marco Beltramo; Antonio Severi; Antonio Severi's sister; Ernestina Bonelli; Emilio Randone; Laura Hidalgo; Clementina Luotto; Giuseppe Grimaldi; Pier Giorgio Frassati.

38. Frassati, *I giorni*, 127; *Beatitudes*, 93.

39. Asterisk * refers to "permanent position."

40. Laura Hidalgo will be considered in further details in chapter 9.

Giuseppe Grimaldi—"figaro here figaro there* [permanent position]": Araldus
Maddalena Guglielmini[41]
Antonio Severi
Antonio Severi's sister
Emilio Randone

4.2. Tipi Loschi Motto

"Few but good, like maccheroni," *Pochi ma buoni come maccheroni*.[42] The motto is not simply humorous, but the motto also contains a deeper meaning. People like good food, and one knows well that quality is of greater value than quantity. The Tipi Loschi are not a large group, but they are good, and applying this to real situations, the maccheroni they eat during mountains excursions may be "few," but they are good. It is the "good" that matters at the end. The choice of the attribute "good," as much as it may apply to food, can also apply to people, "a good person." Even if the "good" in the two phrases are analogical, "good maccheroni" and "good people," share a common property: the "good" as something desirable.

One could add that the motto along with Pier Giorgio's creative thought for a social group operated at two levels: the natural level of jokes and mountain hikes, at a deeper supernatural level, as his letter expressed to Marco was this fundamental bond of faith: joking playfulness created a human bond, and together, climbing mountains is analogous to pilgrims journeying toward God—the supernatural. The creative efforts of Pier Giorgio and his close friend Beltramo, with the input from the Tipi Loschi board members produced the fun-filled, faith-motivated society.

4.3. Proclamations and Statutes

Greetings were commonly transmitted with "canon blasts." Connections were made with the French Revolution by employing their own calendar with reference to the "non-Fascist era." Farewells included *Terror omnia vincit*, "Terror conquers all things," in this case a play on the expression, *Omnia vincit amor*, "love conquers all." Proclamations were used with a first person plural pronoun, "we," giving the letter an authoritative tone, not unlike the

---

41. Guglielmini sisters, see *Lettere*, Ital. ed., 320.

42. Motto first appears in, *Letters*, "To Marco, Turin, end of November, 1924," 185–86.

classical royal or papal "we." These proclamations concerned matters of the Tipi Loschi Society. Sections besides the "Terror Section," typically determined where Pier Giorgio was writing his letter, appearing as a subsection, from the mountains, "Alpinistic," at Pollone, "Talpinistic," or by the beach, "Aquanistic," the center, being Turin. Proclamations also served to keep society members informed as to what the others were doing, ending the proclamations with terroristic greetings and canon blasts.

4.4. Santa Pece de' Pazzi

The Society's protection was placed under *Santa Pece de' Pazzi*.[43] The tongue-in-cheek patronage stemmed from an incident which undoubtedly caused great laughter. Pier Giorgio's sense of humor reflected the society's statutes with male and female "swindlers," pranks and jokes as a way of keeping three unifying elements of the society: purity, joy, and faith. Love, for Pier Giorgio, represented more than feelings: love manifested itself in acts of goodness toward the other.[44] The ultimate goal was communion with God. Love had its source in God, and a person's purified love was the result of prayer and sacrifice. For Pier Giorgio this purity of love was manifested precisely in the joy of the Tipi Loschi. Such love depended upon faith: with faith one was willing to make sacrifices, one could love with a pure heart. Faith would ultimately create this "bond" as Pier Giorgio had so much desired.

In a slip of the tongue, the expression *Santa Pace*, "Holy Peace," *pece* replaced *pace* and the laughter due to the slip led to *de' Pazzi* "of the crazy ones," referring to himself and the Tipi Loschi.[45] Given the joking nature of the members and respect for the sacred, no doubt, the name stuck, *Pece de' Pazzi*, placing the Society of "crazy ones" under the patronage of *Santa Pece* which appeared in the August statutes.[46]

---

43. See #5 of Tipi Loschi statutes.

44. For a discussion on the distinction between love of "friendship" and love of "concupiscence," see Aquinas, ST IIa–IIae, q. 23, a. 1.

45. *Santa Pece de' Pazzi* appears in, *Lettere*, Ital. ed., "To Clementina Luotto, Forte dei Marmi—Dal Grand Hotel, August 15, 1924," 235.

46. The noun, *Pace*, "peace," is feminine, while the adjective, *Santa*, means either "Holy" or female "Saint."

SOCIETY OF TIPI LOSCHI[47]
INDUSTRY OF ALPINE TOURISM, ETC.

SOCIETY WITH ALL CAPITAL COMPLETELY DEPOSITED
(so much deposit that there isn't any left)

STATUTES

1st) The Society of the Tipi Loschi is founded, composed of members, male and female, who are divided into two groups: male swindlers and female swindlers.

2nd) The Society is directed by a Board Council constituting:
    A President—
    A Director of Excursions, etc.—
    A Secretary—
    A "Figaro here—Figaro there"—

3rd) To be accepted as swindlers >male / >female a request must be made to the founding Swindlers and the approval of the Council.

4th) The motto of the society is: "Few but good, like maccheroni" and individual members of the Society must aspire to this motto.

5th) The Society is placed under the protection of the +/- celestial protection of "SANTA PECE DE' PAZZI."

6th) The Solemnities of the Society are celebrated the:
    29th of April—New Era
    18th of May—Foundation

7th) It is absolutely forbidden for all swindlers >male / >female to bring dogs of whatever breed, especially Mongrenica.

Also, it is prohibited to bring any kind of pepper or similar insects.

---

47. *Letters*, 165 (my translation).

5. Pier Giorgio and Friendship

In the Tipi Loschi Society one not only discovers the creative personality of Pier Giorgio, but his spiritual desires uniting himself with his friends in the Catholic faith journeying together toward eternal life. The Tipi Loschi were rooted in the Holy Spirit acting in each one of them, and each of the members, working together, collaborating with God's Spirit of Truth and Love. They had as a point of reference, not subjective feelings, or new claims to Christian morals, but the unchanging teachings of Christ and his church. The experience of joy being together was the fruit of the Catholic faith they shared. Each one of them sought to grow in sanctity through friendship, not pursuing their passions or corrupted pleasures, but conforming themselves to the truth of the gospel, their ongoing purification through their encounter first of all with Christ and then with each other. Conversion for the Christian is real, a change of heart, not seeking the disordered pleasures of the world, but the true joy that only Christ can give to those who follow him. This was the message Pier Giorgio strived to live and to share with his friends.

Pier Giorgio came from a wealthy bourgeois family with a prominent reputation, his father, owner of *La Stampa*, senator, and ambassador to Germany, his mother an artist, Pier Giorgio knew that his friends could be seeking ulterior motives in their friendship with him; in other words, utilitarian-based friendships. Yet, Pier Giorgio did not reject such friends nor did he dwell on such possibilities, whether the poor in the slums, or from his own social class. Pier Giorgio used his social status, even his apparent connections through his father, for this ultimate end—bringing friends to Christ.[48] Pier Giorgio led his friends to think about fundamental existential questions: "faith, family, affection, work, leisure, the future . . ."[49] Pier Giorgio's goal with his friends was dialogue with Christ, participating in the sacramental life of the church; Pier Giorgio desired for his friends to share in this communion of saints.

His personality came across as a "natural leader," not because Pier Giorgio sought a leading role in activities with his friends, but his personality showed moral integrity, courage, purity and coherency, which drew university friends and others to him. He knew what he believed and adhered to what was true. This contrasted sharply with the increasing positivism marking Italy at the turn of the twentieth century leaving truth for those who still believed in it. Intellectual relativism Pier Giorgio rejected; political

---

48. Soldi, *Verso l'assoluto*, 46.
49. Soldi, *Verso l'assoluto*, 46.

manipulation he regarded as evil; the sins of impurity he battled against. The individual was in need of purification—this came with sacrifice. These virtues understandably made Pier Giorgio a leader.

The fraternity among Pier Giorgio's intimate friend sharing a common faith, and common mountain adventures, were united by prayer; growing in their faith was the objective of the Tipi Loschi Society. Pier Giorgio made this clear in his letter to Beltramo above, "You have stated very well that there will always be an indissoluble bond which will unite us forever and this bond we hold is Faith, which made us companions on beautiful trips and made it possible for our Society to be founded on solid rock." The Tipi Loschi were founded on an "indissoluble bond" which was possible through their common "faith." Pier Giorgio made an indirect allusion to Saint Peter who is the rock of Christ's church. The language of friendship reflected one of community, "oneness," and "church," the church built on the confession of Saint Peter which had a rock foundation.[50] Clearly, he had an eschatological vision in mind because of the very nature of "indissoluble bond" which was only possible by the action of the Holy Spirit. Pier Giorgio's society of joyful friends were rooted in the love of Jesus Christ, living in the hope of eternal life: on this eschatological path Pier Giorgio directed his friends.

6. Letter to Tina Bonelli—Cogne, September 13, 1924[51]

The structure of the Tipi Loschi letter had clear elements identifying the society. Greetings began by connecting the addressee by the name/function in the society, in the case of Bonelli, the "D.d.g." or "director of excursions." The letter of September 1924, addressed to [Ernes]Tina Bonelli contained the nickname *Englesina*, "Young English lady," with reference to Clementina Luotto, the president of the society, immediately followed by some "blast."

6.1. Mt. Grivola—the "Forbidden Fruit"

Mount Grivola was known to the Tipi Loschi by its nickname, *Il frutto proibito*, "the forbidden fruit." In his letter, the twenty-three-year-old Pier Giorgio immediately proceeded to its objective: his ascent of the dangerous mountain, the "forbidden fruit." Pier Giorgio's tone was rather teasing, if not provocative, by pointing out Bonelli's "maternal prohibition" which prevented her from climbing the mountain due to the danger of loose and

---

50. Matt 16:13–19.
51. *Letters*, 173–74; Ital. ed., 252–53.

falling stones. The description "maternal prohibition" signifies the values of the family ties within the Tipi Loschi, and the openness of the members with each other. Rather than Bonelli concealing from Pier Giorgio the fact that "my mother doesn't want me to climb the mountain," Pier Giorgio was informed of the prohibition. Moreover, Bonelli respected her mother's concern and prohibition, and did not climb the mountain with Pier Giorgio even though both Pier Giorgio and Bonelli were skilled climbers. One may assume that Bonelli would be around Pier Giorgio's age since they were university friends, possibly one or two years difference. Teasing her of what might have been a shocking discovery turned out to be the recognition of her mountain skills. The alpine guide, Cavagnet, provided the details, confirming Pier Giorgio and Beltramo's choice to confer upon Bonelli the position of D.d.g.

Pier Giorgio's gift to her was a "small stone" precisely because of the mountain's falling stones, which he had brought back from Mt. Grivola serving as an incentive for Bonelli to make the ascent. But he also included in his letter a "gentian," quoting Abbot Henry, who stated, "Maidens are like flowers." The gift of the flower, with the words coming from the abbot, conveyed a spiritual dimension to Pier Giorgio's letter, a message that came from the abbot, rather than just his own thoughts, to value female friendship comparable to flowers. Pier Giorgio sent gentians not only to Bonelli, but he included the flower in his letters to Laura Hidalgo, the secretary, and Clementina Luotto, the president, in each instance making reference to Abbot Henry's quotation. He recognized in this personal gesture not only the value of friendship, but specifically, female friendship, prudently offering each of the three women in the Tipi Loschi Society a gift by which to remember him and his ascent to the summit of Mt. Grivola.[52]

Pier Giorgio wrote to all three Tipe Losche women, *lestofantesche*, "female swindlers," on the same day, September 13, sending them gentians which he had picked at the Vittorio Sella shelter. Not only did he write the three Tipe Losche on the 13th, but on the same day Pier Giorgio wrote a short postcard-size letter to his mother. The action of climbing the "Forbidden Fruit," metaphorically "conquering" the mountain, having reached the summit, demonstrated Pier Giorgio's act of courage and determination. The risks and challenges imposed by nature were conveyed in his correspondence with these three women and his mother. The virtue that characterized a man was "courage," the perseverance not to give up in spite of the difficulties, the challenges, the obstacles to be overcome. Pier Giorgio had learned

---

52. Pierazzi, *Così ho visto*, 159.

this since his childhood climbing mountains with his mother. It was fitting that he should send a note to his mother speaking of his "conquest."

The virtuous act, however, did not only reflect a human effort overcoming the challenges that nature could impose on a mountain climber. Another dimension of the ascent was the spiritual one, the encounter with God through his creation, conveyed in Pier Giorgio's letter to his mother, "I have returned safe and sound from a magnificent climb after having spent an hour of sheer bliss contemplating the magnificent glaciers."[53] The reward that virtue of perseverance promised, a virtue that was another way of speaking of courage, determination of the making ascent, overcoming continuous obstacles and even unexpected ones, fatigue, cold, danger, uncertainty, motivated by what awaited, the anticipation of something beautiful and extraordinary, even knowing that what lied ahead was something of a mystery, Pier Giorgio was convinced that the ascent was worth all the risks that went along with the "difficult climb." Finally, Pier Giorgio expressed in his letter the satisfaction, the fulfillment of the challenging ascent in a few simple words, "an hour of sheer bliss contemplating . . ."

6.2. Masses on the Mountains

After his descent from Mt. Grivola, Pier Giorgio did not say much more about his experience afterward. Unless somebody had been present to observe Pier Giorgio or someone who had been familiar enough with his pious practices, the intensity of Pier Giorgio's spiritual life could not have been known because as transparent as Pier Giorgio was, he preferred discretion rather than describing his personal religious habits and acts of piety. After Pier Giorgio descended from Mt. Grivola, he went to see the parish priest at Cogne, Father Cesare Gérard, informing him that he had ascended Mt. Grivola the day before, and because he was feeling lazy that morning, he was late for communion, which he desired to receive. As Don Gérard noted, "We entered the Church and at the foot of the altar had made a good one quarter of an hour of preparation and I gave him Communion which he received with an indescribable piety. We were the only two in the Church. He remained on one of the two pews which are close to the altar in the choir, in thanksgiving."[54] When the mountain excursions fell on a Sunday or Solemnity, Pier Giorgio made a point of planning the trip with Bonelli, the D.d.g, to include Mass with the priests at Cogne, Balme, Piccolo San Bernardo where there was a chapel for the hostel, or at Sauze d'Oulx. The

---

53. *Letters*, "To his mother, Saturday, September 13, 1924, 2:45 p.m.," 175.

54. Frassati, *La fede*, "Testimony of Don Cesare Gérard, rector of Cogne," 93–94.

weekends or religious holidays meant classes were cancelled so they could leave late Saturday evening or very early Sunday morning, depending on the Mass schedule, chapel or church, and the distance of the mountains.

One of the locations with chapels or parishes where they could arrive or arrange Mass was the Gestaldi Shelter of the Balme parish. The parish priest was Father Giuseppe Cargnino. Pier Giorgio served Mass for him at the summit of the Ciamarella, on July 20, 1924.[55] Father Cargnino described Pier Giorgio as having an "angel" serving the Mass; Pier Giorgio's piety and devotion were alive.[56] Pier Giorgio and his friends attended Mass early in the morning before leaving Turin, or at a mountain location where Mass was available, or they arranged an early Mass with a priest in Turin or an early morning Mass at one of the villages before their climb. In the case of Ciamarella, they attended Mass right on the summit, celebrating the twenty-fifth anniversary of the Image of *La Consolata* placed on the mountain. At Sauze d'Oulx where Don Felice Richetto resided as parish priest, when Pier Giorgio was in the area skiing with his friends, Pier Giorgio would arrive even before 7 a.m., help Father Richetto prepare for the Mass, marking the gospel with the ribbon, robe the priest, and during Mass respond to the priest's prayers, always in a clear, grave and deep voice.[57]

If Pier Giorgio could not be assured of a Mass on a day of obligation during an excursion, he would not join the trip.[58] Even obtaining ecclesial dispensation for the trip which his friends would remind him, Pier Giorgio replied, "I know it's possible to obtain it, but I prefer not to go on the trip."[59] Pier Giorgio would write to the parish priest of the closest village in such cases to be reassured that he and his friends would be able to participate at Mass, and not only Mass for himself; he would bring together all his friends to Mass during these trips, and this meant at times leaving as early as 4 a.m. to pick up his friends, especially the women at such an early time of day.

Bonelli, the Tipi Loschi D.d.g., gave her own testimony of her experience with Pier Giorgio during one of their excursions, "To understand him one would have to see him serve Mass. When we reached the chapel of the hostel after having left our room with a determined will, where the water was freezing in the thermoses and the snow hardened on the clothing, we

---

55. This climb involved *Giovane Montagna*, "Young Mountaineers."

56. Frassati, *La fede*, "Testimony of Theologian, Giuseppe Cargnino, parish priest of Balme," 95–96.

57. Frassati, *La fede*, "Testimony of Don Felice Richetto, parish priest of Sauze d'Oulx," 91.

58. Frassati, *La fede*, 77.

59. Frassati, *La fede*, 77.

found him—ready, serious, transformed—ready to serve Mass in that regimental correctness underlined by the alpine clothing."[60]

Bonelli's testimony, especially from one of the intimate members of the Tipi Loschi, is revelatory not only of Pier Giorgio's disciplined practices, but the seriousness with which he observed Sunday Mass. Under the icy conditions of the mountains, at Piccolo San Bernardo, Pier Giorgio not only got up early to prepare himself for Mass and serve it, but he also made sure the others were present to fulfill their Sunday obligation. One of the characteristics of the Tipi Loschi was to support each other in prayer and in their spiritual lives. Pier Giorgio was not concerned about disturbing or interrupting their sleep. He ensured they were all up for Mass even if the water was frozen in the thermoses and snow hardened on their clothes. Bonelli suggested a quality of "regimental" preparedness in his alpine attire, in the "correctness" of his presence and serving Mass. Bonelli took note of these details because Pier Giorgio was known for playing jokes, making pranks among the Tipi Loschi; after all, the spirit of the Tipi Loschi as the statutes suggested was one of teasing, provocative, tongue-in-cheek humor. However, the significant change in Pier Giorgio's composure occurred when he placed himself before God, in prayer, at Mass when he was serving, as Bonelli said, "To understand him one would have to see him serve Mass."

From the same hostel at Piccolo San Bernardo another testimony had been given by a member of the Tipi Loschi; in this case, the secretary, Laura Hidalgo. The precious testimony succeeded in capturing the intensity of Pier Giorgio's soul, "When we reached the chapel of the hostel of Piccolo San Bernardo he was already by the altar, quiet and serene, completely transformed in the sweet conversation with the Lord. There was in his way of kneeling, in his way of praying so composed, without show and indifferent to others, his way of serving Mass and to receive Communion something that was so special that it struck everyone even those looking after the hostel, admired him as they watched."[61] The two Tipi Loschi testimonies of the same excursion and Mass offer two distinct perspectives, but, one can also identify parallels in the testimony: "transformed," *trasformato*. In the presence of Christ, as with the childhood experience just before his first communion, Pier Giorgio knelt before the "King of kings," carried in the streets of Turin. In this secluded mountain hostel, the twenty-three-year-old Pier Giorgio was still transformed in the act of worship in the presence of his King.

---

60. Frassati, *La fede*, "Testimony of Dr. Ernestina Bonelli," 73.
61. Frassati, *La fede*, "Testimony of Professor Laura Hidalgo," 84–85.

7. Letter to Marco Beltramo—Turin, End of November 1924[62]

Pier Giorgio discovered the D.d.g. planned an excursion but he was concerned and expressed his views with humor to Beltramo. Two issues troubled Pier Giorgio: the dates which fell during Mass days of obligation, and the ambitious ascent of Mt. Cervino (Matterhorn, 3,412 ft.). Pier Giorgio clearly held reservations based on his previous experience with Ernestina Bonelli. His sarcastic humor indicated that at the rate Bonelli was going, she would soon be climbing Mt. Everest and the Himalayas.

Pier Giorgio wrote jokingly to Beltramo, having just been on a mountain excursion attempting the Bessanese. The Bessanese trip began on Sunday morning, November 23, at 6:15 a.m. From Balme they proceeded at 2 p.m. In his end-of-November letter to Beltramo, Pier Giorgio wrote with sarcasm as he intended to admire the D.d.g. from the Pian Pacias while she and others climbed Mt. Everest. He had just returned from the Bessanese where they endured the demands of the bivouac—a snow cave at high altitude.[63]

In the Bessanese excursion Pier Giorgio narrated events with superb details, and terrific humor, while at the same time, conveying the austere winter conditions and challenges of the mountain, "The good Cerutti put himself to work right away and, having found a rock with a kind of roof leaning toward a snowy slope, we began to dig out a small apartment composed of the following rooms: a bedroom for three, a dining-room, a kitchen, a reception room for entertaining, a long corridor with a balcony from which one enjoyed a magnificent view that our apartment shared with n. 100. Our magnificent apartment measured 4.9 ft. in length, 1.6 ft. in width and 1.3 ft. in height. Heating was inadequate, but to compensate, it was very well ventilated, the rules of hygiene were faithfully and rigorously observed."[64] The letters sent to Beltramo the third week of November immediately preceding the Bessanese excursion and the end of November after the climb were both connected and served to raise doubts about the D.d.g's proposed excursion. The conditions of the Bessanese climb and the time spent in the bivouac under freezing conditions conveyed Pier Giorgio's apprehension about the Mt. Cervino excursion suggested by Bonelli. At the Bessanese in fact, they were only two Tipi Loschi, Pier Giorgio and Giuseppe Grimaldi, "Figaro here, Figaro there," and Giuseppe Cerutti.

62. *Letters*, 185; Ital. ed., 274–75.
63. *Letters*, 185n2.
64. *Letters*, "To Marco, Turin, November 1924," 183; Ital. ed., 272. Italian edition is in metric units.

Pier Giorgio's end-of-November letter revealed his sentimental side as he reflected on past events during different moments of his climb of the Bessanese, and one senses a nostalgia of not having the other Tipi Loschi with him, "The time would have seemed shorter because Clementina could have enthralled us with fourteenth-century-style dissertations. Tina with her famous flair for organization could have raised our already high morale, Laura not only to prepare delicious meals but also to provide excellent company."[65] This reference to the female Tipe Losche and their absence echoed the side of Pier Giorgio's personality that sought the presence of his friends to enjoy himself, the sense of spiritual communion in nature; he longed for their presence, and yet, he accepted the reality of their absence. This absence was not unlike longing the presence of his aunt at the beach, or his mother when he visited an art gallery.

7.1. Marco Beltramo

His co-citizen in "Terror," Marco/Perrault, could not join Pier Giorgio on the excursion to the Bessanese as much as Pier Giorgio would have enjoyed his presence with other Tipi Loschi. In considering his Tipi Loschi friends, Beltramo deserves special attention because the two were Tipi Loschi "co-citizens" of the city of "Terror," Turin. Yet, already a physical distance was expressed in Pier Giorgio's letter to Beltramo because the latter was the first to leave Turin for the Airforce Academy in Livorno, suggesting a "change" from the original Tipi Loschi who formed the group. Pier Giorgio was sensitive to these kind of changes; he reminisced in his November letters of previous trips and felt the absence of certain members. Yet, Pier Giorgio was a person of determination and when he could be part of an excursion, he would, so long as it did not conflict with Mass, and if possible, not with his studies, either.

Out of the nine fellow male and female swindlers Pier Giorgio had the most frequent exchange in his letters with Beltramo. This did not mean that his personal issues were only shared with Beltramo; but, a friendship, an affinity, and a spiritual bond was clearly expressed with Beltramo. His nickname would soon be "Wing of Terror" reflecting Beltramo's new career: from the month of August Beltramo would leave for the Airforce Academy starting with medical exams, until it became clear that he was beginning a new life. He and Beltramo remained united in the faith but as the autumn and winter months of 1924 moved into 1925, personal matters became heavier for Pier Giorgio to carry and this included the absence of his good

---

65. *Letters*, "To Marco, Turin, November 1924," 183; Ital. ed., 273.

friend.[66] Pier Giorgio wrote a moving letter to Beltramo in October telling him, "This is my last letter before you abandon the civilian way of life.... On the 27th I will go up to Oropa and pray for you at the feet of the Brown Virgin, even if my prayers are of little worth.... I will send you a souvenir that, let's hope, should always bind the 'Terror' in a non-material way; it is a rosary made of Seeds from the garden and to which I shall attach a medallion of the Madonna of Loreto, so that the Virgin will protect you."[67]

Anticipating his departure, Pier Giorgio wished to remain united with Beltramo leaving him in the "trust of Providence" and confident that everything would follow "according to His plans." Pier Giorgio's faith allowed him to offer up his close friend, and yet, at the human level, the experience could not be one of simple detachment. Instead, he remained united with Beltramo, first by praying for him at the feet of the Madonna of Oropa, and then, the Rosary that would always bind them in a spiritual way, made from seeds that Pier Giorgio cultivated in his garden. The medallion of the Madonna of Loreto which he added to Beltramo's Rosary was the patroness of pilots, her feast day being December 10; and so, Pier Giorgio would also remember and pray for Beltramo specifically on the feast of Our Lady Loreto.

During the mountain excursions with the Tipi Loschi, Pier Giorgio's religious observances changed little. During one of the evening departures for Sauze d'Oulx anticipating an arrival at 10 p.m., but due to the heavy snowfall, the train was required to stop and proceeded slowly arriving 6 a.m. the following morning. For Beltramo who was traveling with Pier Giorgio, the night was unforgettable: for the first time Beltramo noticed that Pier Giorgio, apart from being a good person, an excellent friend, joyful and pleasant, he found in Pier Giorgio something "superior" almost "transcendent." While the Tipi Loschi friends were kept warm in the train, Pier Giorgio was outside helping with the luggage. After returning to the compartment, he sat in the corner and quietly prayed the Rosary. He did not eat anything after midnight to observe the communion fast, receiving communion the next morning on the Sunday in the little church of Oulx.[68]

---

66. Pier Giorgio's relationships at an affective-emotional level, but especially spiritual, will be taken up in chapter 9.

67. *Letters*, "To Marco Beltramo, Pollone, October 23, 1924," 176; Ital. ed., 260.

68. Frassati, *La fede*, "Testimony of Dr. Marco Beltramo," 92–93.

7.2. Mountain Activities[69]

The mountain excursions involved the Alps of northwestern Italy, in Piedmont and Valle d'Aosta, bordering France and Switzerland. Pier Giorgio had been climbing these mountains since his childhood. Faith experience was part of the alpine activities; and since 1918 Pier Giorgio belonged to both the Italian Alpine Club and the Young Mountaineers. Besides being custodians of the mountain, the objectives of the Young Mountaineers ensured the obligations for Sundays and Solemnities were fulfilled.[70] So, Pier Giorgio's mountain excursions were planned with a cohesive group sharing a common faith, but his mountain trips were by no means limited to the Tipi Loschi. The members, as shown with Beltramo, were not always available to go mountain climbing; and so, Pier Giorgio would go with Young Mountaineers, Italian Alpine Club, or with other friends.

The ascent to Pian della Mussa (5,741 ft.) of May 18, 1924, constituted the foundation of the Tipi Loschi and its statues that followed. On July 4, Pier Giorgio made the ascent to Picchi del Pagliaio (4,787 ft.) with his friend Cesare Randone. On July 20, on the Ciamarrella (12,060 ft.) of the Graie Alps, Pier Giorgio served two Masses. September 13–14, he climbed the grueling Mt. Grivola, "Forbidden Fruit," (13,022 ft.). November 23–24, he ascended the Bessanese (11,916 ft.). January 18, 1925, he climbed Monte Tre Denti di Cumiana (4,492 ft.), the expedition which comprised Cerutti, the guide, Randone, Pasquali.[71]

Members of the Tipi Loschi went to Bardoneccia for the February carnival. Participating in the ski competition on February 22, 1925, Pier Giorgio came in twenty-sixth place out of forty-nine, as he stated, "I didn't believe I was among the first 30 given the total lack of training and the course being rather difficult.[72] On March 1, at Sauze d'Oulx (4,951 ft.) during the overnight train, Pier Giorgio fasted from midnight for Sunday Mass the next morning. March 15 and 22, Sauze d'Oulx, Pier Giorgio closed off the ski season with his Tipi Loschi friends and others.[73]

On May 10, with the planned ascent to Monte Valendino (6,929 ft.), Pier Giorgio almost cancelled his trip because of arriving late for Mass

---

69. Frassati, *Calendario*, "Pian della Mussa, May 18, 1924," to "Turin, June 26, 1925."

70. Casalegno, *Pier Giorgio Frassati*, 180.

71. *Letters*, "To Marco Beltramo," 200–201. Emilio Randone was part of the Tipi Loschi; Cesare, Emilio's brother, was also a friend. Pier Giorgio did not say which Randone.

72. *Letters*, "To Marco Beltramo," and "To Isidoro Bonini," "Turin, February 27, 1925," 213–14.

73. *Lettere*, Ital. ed., "To Marco Beltramo, Turin, March 23, 1925," 319–20.

unable to receive communion; but the hike was resumed once his religious observances were fulfilled.[74] Then on May 18, the one-year founding of Tipi Loschi, an excursion was organized to Rocca Sella, Graie Alps (4,948 ft.). The celebration began on Sunday, May 17, with Mass at 5:30 a.m. at the Church of the Visitation.[75]

Climbing on June 7, Lunelle, Val di Lanzo (9,095 ft.), Pier Giorgio was accompanied by Carlo Pol and Guglielmo Unterrichter where on the summit they prayed the *De Profundis* for Cesarino Rovere, a first-year polytechnic student who died in an accident ascending the Lunelle.[76] During this excursion, which would be his last, Pier Giorgio wrote *verso l'alto*, "towards the summit," on the photo taken of him climbing the mountain rock. The last excursion was planned for June 29, Pier Giorgio's namesday, but Father Cargnino the parish priest at Balme could not celebrate Mass at the Gistaldi Shelter; so the planned excursion was canceled.[77]

One can understand Pier Giorgio's relationship with the mountains and the Tipi Loschi excursions from a spiritual perspective. The mountains brought Pier Giorgio physically to intense heights through the endurance needed in these activities, but also the exhilaration that nature brought, that spiritual awe, "contemplating bliss." His Tipi Loschi friends were those with whom he could share these experiences, if not by their presence, then by relating events to them as the society gradually began to disperse with their commitments. Their common bond as Pier Giorgio emphasized, reflected the commitment to their common faith: enjoying themselves together, but even greater, the prayers they offered for each other in their absence. Pier Giorgio showed the value of praying for the deceased with the *De Profundis* he prayed at the summit of the Lunelle, June 7, just a month before his own death. The mountains had their summit, penetrating the eternal; and friends had their faith adhering to the promises of Christ.

Pier Giorgio's correspondence showed the extensive network and diversity of friendships from the Tipi Loschi to outside of Italy. His active involvement in charitable associations, Catholic university movements, and *Pax Romana*, expressed his ardent desire to show Christ's love for the poor, and to offer Christ's peace to wounded communities. Following the call of Pope Pius XI Pier Giorgio knew that peace could only be brought to the world with the love of Christ.[78]

---

74. Frassati, *La fede*, "Testimony of Jean Margherita," 80.
75. *Letters*, "To Marco Beltramo, Turin, May 13, 1925," 233.
76. Casalegno, *Pier Giorgio Frassati*, 188.
77. Frassti, *La fede*, "Testimony of Father Giuseppe Cargnino," 96.
78. Pope Pius XI, *Ubi Arcano di Consilio*, par. 29–35, December 23, 1922.

Questions

(Note: *ST* refers to *Summa Theologiae* of Saint Thomas Aquinas—part [I/II/III], question, article, response)

1. What does his letter to Miss Fischer focus on (§1)? Where did Pier Giorgio meet Maria Fischer (1.2)? What is Pax Romana (1.3)?

2. How did Pier Giorgio and Willibald Leitgebel meet (2.1)? What characterizes their friendship based on Pier Giorgio's letter (§2, January 1923)?

3. Why is Pier Giorgio so attentive to cooking pasta (3.1)? How does Pier Giorgio describe his lunch with his friends in his letter to Antonio Villani (3.1)?

4. Who is Marco Beltramo and what is his connection to the *Tipi Loschi* (§4)? Who are the *Tipi Loschi* members (4.1)? How does the name of the group describe the friends (4.2; 4.3; 4.4)?

5. How does Pier Giorgio live his friendships (§5)? How does St. Thomas Aquinas distinguish friendship with people from friendship with God? (See note 44 above; *ST*, IIa–IIae, q. 23, a. 1.)

6. What was Pier Giorgio's concern about mountain excursions and Masses (6.2)? Which Mass on the mountain seems of historical significance (6.2)?

7

Christian Society

God has not created us for the perishable and transitory things of earth, but for things heavenly and everlasting; He has given us this world as a place of exile, and not as our abiding place.

RERUM NOVARUM, 33
POPE LEO XIII, 1891

The socioeconomic context of Italy in the early 1900s is reflected especially in the country's political turmoil. Pier Giorgio's family background, social status and political activities need to be understood within this unstable environment. Pier Giorgio's sensitive temperament and deep Christian values permeated his political choices and activism. Another controversial matter concerned both the Catholic Church and the Italian State: the "Roman question." Rome was the See of the Bishop of Rome, Vicar of Christ, and Pope of the Universal Church, but since 1861, Rome became officially the capital of the Kingdom of Italy. The capital of imperial Rome was chosen as capital of the newly united Italian peninsula. The Church of Rome was directly affected by Italy's political choices. Pier Giorgio staunchly defended the papacy, but he also believed in a united Italy.

1. Letter to Antonio Villani—Berlin, March 17, 1921[1]

Dearest Villani,

I just got to know Dr. Sonnenschein, a charming priest, who speaks Italian quite well and also takes care of Italians residing in Berlin. I asked about the Catholic student movement and I found out that about one tenth of the Berlin students profess our same religion.

However, the work of Dr. Sonnenschein, which for the last 15 years was directed towards preparing young students to live in society, today, due to the misery manifested in this class, has had to perform tasks to protect them, to help them find work, so that they could confront the cost of living.

The organization is more specific than ours, and independent of all other Catholic organizations; however, Clubs exist that are composed of university students and workers.

Dr. Sonnenschein will kindly invite me to the meetings that these mixed Clubs will have and so I would be able to know the two environments.

Write to me soon giving me your impressions of the Emilian student convention in Rome: also give me news about our Club. Have you organized something for that society of help between friends? Greetings to all the friends and to you an affectionate farewell.

Pier Giorgio

The opening of Pier Giorgio's letter suggests ongoing communication between him and his good friend, Antonio Villani. The two studied at the Turin Polytechnic and Pier Giorgio looked up to Villani as an older brother. Villani had been active in Catholic Action in the Emilia region and he was the president of Catholic Youth.[2] When Pier Giorgio wrote to Villani, March 17, it was the first letter describing Pier Giorgio's meeting with the Rev. Dr. Karl Sonnenschein. One of the first pieces of information that Pier Giorgio transmitted to his friend was the number of Catholic students in Berlin, 10 percent of the student population, reflecting Pier Giorgio's concern to remain connected with students, who, "profess our religion."

---

1. *Lettere*, Ital. ed., 35–36 (my translation).

2. *Gioventù emiliana*, "Emilian youth," comes from the Italian regional name of Emilia (Romagna-Emilia).

1.1. Rev. Dr. Karl Sonnenschein

The influence Sonnenschein had on Pier Giorgio's spirituality was not insignificant. The social views of the twenty-year-old Pier Giorgio would be considerably sharpened by his meetings and observations with the "Saint Francis of Berlin," especially Pier Giorgio's understanding of the political economist Giuseppe Toniolo.[3] Sonnenschein already had established close ties with Italy. The German priest was born on July 15, 1876, and died February 20, 1929. He was forty-five years old when Pier Giorgio had met him. Having studied at the German College in Rome, his knowledge of Italian placed him within Italian Catholic culture and society. Sonnenschein studied the Italian philosopher Toniolo, and collaborated in establishing in 1906 the Popular Union between Italian Catholics.[4] He also made known the encyclical of Leo XIII, *Rerum Novarum*, creating ties with trade unions in Italy. Sonnenschein enthusiastically contributed to the International Catholic Congress in Rome in 1900, a model which he hoped to bring to Catholic student movements in Germany. Having directed numerous social movements in German universities, Sonnenschein's pastoral activities also included a Catholic newspaper in Berlin that dealt with contemporary religious, social, and cultural problems.[5]

Pier Giorgio's presence in Berlin was motivated in his desire to spend time with his father. Withdrawn from the family ambassadorial social life, Pier Giorgio soon discovered and visited the factories to acquaint himself with the condition of the workers.[6] Sonnenschein helped Pier Giorgio with a network of Catholic contacts in Germany, both university students and professors. The close proximity between the German priest and his poor students helped Pier Giorgio appreciate the benefits of mixed associations of Catholic workers and students.

Sonnenschein's ministry had changed from working in a unified organization of poor students and workers focused on living in society, to one of assisting students who were living in poor conditions due to Germany's economic crisis after the First World War. This union of students and workers appealed to Pier Giorgio because it also meant unifying two classes which were typically separated, the wealthier student body and the poorer workers.[7] Pier Giorgio never ceased to "speak with, or of Sonnenschein, or

---

3. Frassati, *I giorni*, 167.
4. Trabucco, introduction to *L'impegno sociale*, 9.
5. Frassati, *L'impegno sociale*, 66 and n1.
6. Frassati, *L'impegno sociale*, 66.
7. Frassati, *L'impegno sociale*, 66n1. Luciana Frassati provides a vivid and rather humorous description of Sonnenschein. She was not impressed with the German priest

salaries of miners or para-social questions, or strictly social ones like the union of workers and students."⁸

These mixed clubs, as the letter suggests, interested Pier Giorgio, hoping to create a FUCI-CA club in Turin.⁹ Pier Giorgio wished to apply Catholic thought and values in a concrete social framework where both students and workers were brought together by charity. He trusted in Villani's judgment by asking him what he thought of the Emilian Youth Convention in Rome. In his final question, "Have you organized something of that society of help between friends?" Pier Giorgio wished to know—even if he was writing from Berlin—in concrete terms at what stage Villani and the others had reached in the project of mutual assistance for poor students.

1.2. Pier Giorgio's Reaction to WWI

The assassination of Archduke Franz Ferdinand of Austria on June 28, 1914, triggered an international conflict and the outbreak of WWI. Italy was divided between interventionists, who supported a "three-month war," and neutralists, who were not in favor of Italy's involvement in the war. The neutralists consisted of Giolittans, Socialists, and Catholics, while opposing the neutralists were nationalists, liberal conservatives, reformed socialists, trade unionist revolutionaries including Benito Mussolini. *Il Popolo d'Italia* was an interventionist newspaper that Mussolini founded, while Alfredo Frassati's paper, *La Stampa*, was against intervention.¹⁰ Alfredo Frassati's views against the war were made clear in the columns of his paper, pointing out the errors and incongruence "accomplished on the skin of the soldiers and the nation."¹¹ Alfredo criticized the "inefficient military plans, the bad faith of a thuggish journalism, the irresponsible men lacking a conscience." Pier Giorgio shared his father's non-interventionist position.¹²

Italy's decision to intervene was motivated by nationalist sentiment, and on May 24, 1915, Italy declared war on Austria. During the wartime period, Pier Giorgio pursued summer studies at the Bonafous Institute to

---

when Pier Giorgio first introduced him at their residence in Berlin (*L'impegno sociale*, 68–69).

8. Frassati, *L'impegno sociale*, 69.

9. Federation of Italian Catholic Universities and Catholic Action.

10. Casalegno, *Pier Giorgio Frassati*, 76. *Giolittan* refers to followers of Giovanni Giolitti who led the Italian government from 1903–1914. Mussolini's newspaper, *Il Popolo d'Italia*, "The People of Italy," was one of the most widely read interventionist newspapers. See Frassati, *Beatitudes*, 27.

11. *Positio*, 57.

12. *Positio*, 57.

help at home with the gardening.[13] Natalina Novo, the wife of the gardener, lost her brother in the war; Pier Giorgio discussed the war with Novo. Hearing the news of two thousand Alpine troops separated from Italian troops, shelled by the enemy, Pier Giorgio asked Novo, "Wouldn't you give your life to stop the war?" While Novo replied in the negative since she believed she was too young to die, and her life was more precious than that of the soldiers, the fourteen-year-old Pier Giorgio had replied, "I would, I would today."[14] Pier Giorgio was especially close to those who had been wounded and effected by the war. Whenever Pier Giorgio could, he joined Professor Augusto Monti to visit the hospital where he sought to bring some consolation and joy to the bandaged and traumatized soldiers at the Military Hospital.[15]

With Italy's powerful offensive in Austria and the conquest of Trento and Trieste, the armistice was signed on November 3, 1918. On November 4, 1918, when WWI ended Pier Giorgio was seventeen years old; he had rushed to the bell tower of the Pollone parish church to announce the war had ended.[16] Pier Giorgio also wrote to his friend Carlo Bellingeri to send him good wishes on his namesday, November 4, telling his friend how blessed he was that his namesday should coincide with the end of the war.[17] The American President Thomas Woodrow Wilson visited Turin on January 2, 1919, and Pier Giorgio with great enthusiasm welcomed him with other Piemontesi in the northern Italian city. Pier Giorgio appeared with his alpine hat, screaming the entire day, "Long live Wilson," *Viva Wilson*, only taking a break for lunch.[18]

With the Treaty of Versailles the German Weimar Republic was expected to pay war damages and reparation after having been defeated. Germany, unable to fulfill the excessive demands, suffered further humiliation with the occupation of the Ruhr Valley, an especially rich mining region occupied by French and Belgian troops. While visiting his father in Berlin and studying German in Freiburg im Breisgau, Pier Giorgio had visited the Ruhr region traveling on the Rhine on his way to Düsseldorf. Alfredo Frassati, serving as Italian ambassador to Germany, warned the Italian government

---

13. See chapter 4, section 5.2, above.
14. Frassati, *Beatitudes*, 32.
15. Casalegno, *Pier Giorgio Frassati*, 79.
16. Frassati, *Calendario*, "Pollone, November 4, 1918."
17. *Lettere*, Ital. ed., "To Carlo Bellingeri, November 4, 1918."
18. *Positio*, 57.

that the humiliating treatment of the Germans would serve to reinforce German nationalism.[19]

2. Letter to Gian Maria Bertini—Freiburg im Breisgau, October 23, 1921[20]

Pier Giorgio opened his letter to Bertini with an apology, "for not having written." Such apologetic tones characterized his personal writing. Pier Giorgio's excursion details through the Black Forest and his impressions climbing Schonberg Mountain with his friend Rev. Dr. Emil Eiffler were contained in his letter.[21] In his conversations with Eiffler, when they began to speak of Jesus Christ, "Then, Pier Giorgio's eyes could brighten and his words almost burst into enthusiasm to glorify whom he loved most profoundly from his heart."[22]

The October 1921 letter written from Freiburg contained valuable information as the twenty-year-old Pier Giorgio developed his sociopolitical concerns, writing to his dear friend Bertini. Each part of the letter assumed information that Bertini understood. To appreciate Pier Giorgio's letter at both the social and political levels, inseparable from his Catholic religious convictions, further background to the letter is needed.

The first subtle reference to the post-WWI political tension was expressed in his letter viewing the German plateau, "as far as the borders of our dear unfortunately French friends." Pier Giorgio made indirect reference to the Versailles Treaty and the harsh conditions imposed upon the Germans. Pier Giorgio naturally supported the vulnerable and suffering, and during this post-bellic period, it was undoubtedly the Germans who had won Pier Giorgio's sympathy and support.

Pier Giorgio regarded the Italian government as being run by "Freemasons," the ones responsible for "ripping" their flag during the Catholic Youth march in Rome.[23] Pier Giorgio's letter takes on an increasingly political tone with the PPI, Popular Party of Italy, claiming that the Party was

---

19. Malgeri, "Pier Giorgio's World," xxvi.
20. *Letters*, 58–60; Ital. ed., 74–75.
21. Fr. Sonnenschein was a mutual friend of Pier Giorgio and Rev. Eiffler.
22. Frassati, *La fede*, "Testimony of Monseigneur Emil Eiffler," 260–61.
23. Giovanni Giolitti was forced to resign after Italy's 1921 spring elections; he was replaced by Ivanoe Bonomi followed by Luigi Facta. Paradoxically, Giolitti's Liberal government, unable to form a coalition with moderate Socialists brought Mussolini into the chamber by forming a National bloc with the Fascists. See Seton-Watson, *Storia d'Italia*, ch. 13, for details.

"only out for votes" by making promises which were not fulfilled. While in Germany, Pier Giorgio remained connected with developments in Italy, including the Cesare Balbo activities in Turin. The letter's political tone presupposes a religiopolitical awareness of late-nineteenth-century Italy. Before his postscript Pier Giorgio made reference to a "fundraiser for our banner, ripped on the orders of the Freemason government." This passage frames the letter within the context of the Catholic Church's relation with the Italian government.

2.1. Rerum Novarum

Pope Leo XIII began his pontificate in 1878 and addressed the contentious issues of the period concerning labor and capital, rights and duties, in his 1891 encyclical *Rerum Novarum*. The encyclical expressed concern for the unjust working conditions, "wretchedness," afflicting the working class.[24] Communicating the rights of workers, which included the right to form unions, as well as the rights of individuals to own private property, the papal encyclical rejected, however, both, uncontrolled capitalism and state-controlled socialism. Drawing from the Scriptures, Leo XIII conveyed the "value" attached to the poor, "God Himself seems to incline rather to those who suffer misfortune; for Jesus Christ calls the poor 'blessed'; (Matt 5:3) He lovingly invites those in labor and grief to come to him for solace; (Matt 11:28) and He displays the tenderest charity toward the lowly and the oppressed."[25] To understand, therefore, Pier Giorgio's sociopolitical views, one must take *Rerum Novarum* into account, which Pier Giorgio knew well. His views on the suffering due to unjust governments was Pier Giorgio's primary concern. Whether in Italy or in Germany, Pier Giorgio kept the misery of the individual in mind, as the encyclical underscored, "God Himself seems to incline rather to those who suffer misfortune." Pier Giorgio undoubtedly found this misfortune among the poor of Turin and of Berlin and his closeness to the poor was precisely because Christ called the poor, "blessed." Pier Giorgio took the example from Christ himself, a reminder from the encyclical, "He displays the tenderest charity toward the lowly and the oppressed."

Pier Giorgio made reference to the papal encyclical *Rerum Novarum* in his letter to Villani on the anniversary of the encyclical, May 15, 1924. Including the anniversary date of the encyclical was not simply remembering the date of its promulgation, but acknowledging the date conveyed Pier

24. *Rerum Novarum*, 3.
25. *Rerum Novarum*, 24.

Giorgio's familiarity with the church's official social teaching. For Pier Giorgio the encyclical was his point of reference when it came to expressing his positions and concrete practices concerning the poor. Pier Giorgio never attacked wealthy individuals or families, but instead, he focused on finding a way to improve the conditions of the forgotten and destitute. Reading the encyclical and discussing it with his friends who were laborers as well as fellow students, Pier Giorgio supported and defended church initiatives in social and economic matters.

Pier Giorgio's sensitive and empathetic personality meant he suffered with suffering individuals, united with them in their misery; the gospel of Jesus Christ and Catholic social teaching motivated Pier Giorgio's response. Pier Giorgio's political expression was firmly rooted in Christian values reflecting his own empathetic personality.[26] To suffer with others also meant to suffer for them. Christ carried the misery of human sin himself on the cross out of love.[27]

2.2. Catholic Church–Italian State Relations

In the body of the October letter Pier Giorgio expressed to Bertini, "I am pleased that you have launched the fundraiser for our banner, ripped on the orders of the Freemason government." The comments referred to one of two incidents of political violence to which Pier Giorgio had been subjected. The event concerned the blessed FUCI flag, the flag Pier Giorgio carried during the Catholic Youth march in Rome. To think of Pier Giorgio's flag as simply a purchased flag that was ripped would fail to capture the spiritual value attached to the flag, and therefore, the significance of the violent event.

The flag, having been blessed, carried with it a sacramental value; moreover, the flag represented the Cesare Balbo Club, the Turin Polytechnic division of Catholic university students of Italy, FUCI. The significance of flag-blessing ceremonies was conveyed especially in Pier Giorgio's two letters addressing Cesare Balbo, the flag blessing where he was the godfather; then, the abusive display of the flag.[28]

---

26. See chapter 1, section 3.1, above. "Empathy" can be found early in Pier Giorgio's personality.

27. Col 1:19–20.

28. The value of the FUCI flag and its religious symbolism will be taken up in section 5, below.

2.2.1. Pier Giorgio and the Catholic Student Flag[29]

The incident that led to the desecration of the flag which Pier Giorgio was carrying occurred during a GCI convention in Rome celebrating the fiftieth anniversary of its foundation which had been postponed to September 1–8, 1921.[30] Catholic Youth wanted to reaffirm in Rome an unquestionable reality: the strong presence of the Catholic youth of Italy.[31] Their destination from the Vatican was the Tomb of the Unknown Soldier. Although the Mass was to be celebrated at the Colosseum, the Ministry of Internal Affairs prevented the ecclesiastical assistant, Monsignor Giandomenico Pini, from celebrating. A group led by Pier Giorgio ordered that any violent instrument should be thrown away and that no violence was to be committed, and to even be prepared to die, for the defense of the faith.[32]

After their meeting with the pope, the Catholic Youth had received permission by ministry officials to participate in the procession to the monument dedicated to Vittorio Emanuele.[33] Ex-combatants wanted to respond to the Masonic accusations launched against the Catholics; provocations began when men armed with clubs shouted, "Long live the Pope King."[34] Chaos unleashed, the students tried to defend themselves the best they could. The civil adversaries were reinforced by the Royal Guard holding rifles hitting the backs of Italian university students. Pier Giorgio took notice of a student being mistreated by the Royal Guard and battled to release his fellow Catholic and friend. The students proceeded to Santa Maria in Vallicella (Chiesa Nuova) once the first confrontation was over.[35] At the church the troops were placed under "Masonic" orders and barriers prevented the Catholic university students from making their way to the Vittoriano Monument. A second barrier, however, awaited at the Piazza San Pantaleo and Piazza Argentina. Overcoming the barriers, the fifty thousand youth continued to the Vittoriano Monument.

---

29. Superb details are given in Frassati, *L'impegno sociale*, 55–62.

30. GCI = Gioventù Cattolica Italiana, "Italian Catholic Youth." The fiftieth anniversary, in fact, was in 1919, but could not be celebrated due to the conditions after WWI. See, *Positio*, 98.

31. Frassati, *L'impegno sociale*, 55.

32. Frassati, *L'impegno sociale*, 55.

33. Also known as the "Vittoriano Monument" in Piazza Venezia and *Altare della Patria*, "Altar of the Fatherland."

34. Frassati, *I giorni*, 100.

35. Chiesa Nuova, Santa Maria in Vallicella Parish, Church of the Congregation of St. Philip Neri, "Oratorians."

Marching east, at the Piazza del Gesù the cavalry of the Royal Guard blocked the students requiring the students to change routes to via del Plebiscito. Another two hundred guards appeared arriving from Palazzo Altieri with orders to remove the Catholic university student banners.[36] Father Enrico Bobola led the students to the Jesuit Church of the Gesù, believing the doors to be open; but they were locked, and the students found themselves caught in the Piazza del Gesù.[37] The guards began by striking the students with the muskets, pulling and ripping the flags. Students attempted to defend the desecration of their flags. Pier Giorgio was confronted by the Royal Guard on horses, "with his flag between his teeth, a red face, his hair in the wind, he defended himself whirling a pole with agility and extraordinary precision."[38] Pier Giorgio with the other Catholic youth were taken to Palazzo Altieri by the Royal Guard, still harassed by the authorities, and released later in the afternoon.

Throughout the streets of Rome, the Italian university students could hear Pier Giorgio shouting, *Viva il Papa*, "Long live the Pope." Pier Giorgio believed that in relations between the Vatican and Italy, the temporal power would be harmful to the Church of Rome. Italy would need to eliminate differences, ceding to the pope, head of Catholicism, enough territory to construct around the Vatican the necessary buildings to satisfy an exchange between the Vatican and the world. Pier Giorgio knew for biblical reasons that the pope must remain above all governments, all nations, "We can only hope in Him."[39]

2.2.2. Pope Pius IX and Italian Nationalism

In the nineteenth century, Italian nationalists sought to unite the divided peninsula between rival city states and Pontifical States. It was in 1861 that in Turin the House of Savoy united northern Italy and the southern kingdom. Pope Pius IX, governing the church during the period, refused to cede the Pontifical States which created a political obstacle in uniting the Kingdom of Italy with Rome as its capital. The royal army of King Victor Emmanuel led by the nationalist Giuseppe Garibaldi invaded the Pontifical territory on September 20, 1870. The nationalists claimed and expropriated the rich territory of monasteries, palaces, gardens and art galleries which belonged to the church. The one thousand years of papal temporal

---

36. Palazzo Altieri is on via del Plebiscito just opposite the Piazza del Gesù.
37. Piazza del Gesù in front of the Church of the Jesuit Fathers.
38. Frassati, *L'impegno sociale*, "Testimony of Don Enrico Bobola," 57–58.
39. Frassati, *L'impegno sociale*, "Testimony of Orazio Coccolo," 62.

rule in central Italy ceased.[40] The Savoyard King confiscated Pope Pius IX's residence at Quirinale Palace.[41] As a result Pope Pius excommunicated the invading royal army, the new government, and the Savoyard monarch, indicating that the government and monarch were illegitimate.[42] A decree was promulgated in 1874 which prohibited Italian Catholics from voting in elections, participating in Italian political life, or occupying government posts in a decree known as *Non expedit*. This decree was upheld by Pope Leo XIII who followed Pope Pius IX.[43]

Italian Catholics such as Pier Giorgio were loyal to the pope as the Roman incident revealed; he defended the Catholic banner from the Royal Guards attempting to desecrate it during the Catholic Youth convention. Italians who staunchly expressed their Catholic faith, as did Pier Giorgio, found themselves ridiculed or even persecuted as the events in Rome demonstrated.

2.3. Italian Post WWI Politics

With migration to the northern Italian industrial triangle, Genoa, Milan, Turin, and Italian soldiers returning from WWI—Italy was hit by a socioeconomic crisis. Factory workers demanded rights throughout northern Italy. The Russian Revolution of 1917 produced a Bolshevik movement in Turin with violent conflicts between the "Red" Communists and "White" Catholics. Turin itself became the *città rossa*, "Red City," perceived as anticlerical where confrontation between workers and industrialists exploded in strikes and barricades.[44] Pier Giorgio's home city had been the center for neutralists—Catholics and liberals, while interventionists and nationalists—in opposition, defended their own interests.

Pope Benedict XV lifted the *Non expedit* in 1919 after WWI during a period of social and political tension in Italy. Father Luigi Sturzo, an Italian priest from Sicily founded the PPI, *Partito Popolare Italiano*, "Popular Party of Italy," in 1919 based on Pope Leo XIII's social teachings in *Rerum Novarum*. Pier Giorgio, who knew the encyclical, was also a supporter of Father Sturzo's socioeconomic politics; and therefore the PPI, the "Popularists" as they became known, were opposed to both socialists and communists since

40. Seton-Watson, *Storia d'Italia*, 12; Malgeri, "Pier Giorgio's World," xxiii–xxiv.

41. "Savoyard" refers to the House of Savoy. Since 1720 the Duke of Savoy was also King of Sardinia.

42. Seton-Watson, *Storia d'Italia*, 14, 63.

43. Seton-Watson, *Storia d'Italia*, 71–73.

44. Malgeri, "Pier Giorgio's World," xxv.

the PPI sought to "vindicate" a Catholic Italy in the culture of the Italian workers. The threat came from both directions: materialist Marxism and Liberal atheism.[45] In fact, the PPI entry into Italian politics represented a militant Catholicism which characterized the Popularists.[46] Pier Giorgio belonged to this militant political expression of Catholicism and propagated its Catholic newspaper, *Il Momento*. Reflecting the differences with his father and his newspaper, *La Stampa*, and his liberal economics, Alfredo Frassati asserted, "Good Pier Giorgio. I heard that you are publicizing *Il Momento*. That means that when you are hungry, you will go eat at *Il Momento*."[47]

3. Letter to Antonio Villani—Turin, July 18, 1922[48]

At twenty-one years old, Pier Giorgio's letter reflects his considerable social and political commitments: the letter to Villani opens and closes seeking assistance to find concrete solutions to help individuals. His sociopolitical vision is directed toward the ultimate hope of divine justice: the meaning of this life is contingent upon a higher and ultimate good God.

3.1. Conference of Saint Vincent

On November 28, 1918, when Pier Giorgio was seventeen years old, his name appeared among the members of the Conference of Saint Vincent.[49] The conference served as the charitable branch of the Jesuit Social Institute where Pier Giorgio had studied for two years.[50] Four years later, in 1922, as a student at the Turin Polytechnic, Pier Giorgio transferred to the Saint Vincent Conference associated with the Cesare Balbo branch of the FUCI. The two conference sections also held meetings at two different parishes, Our Lady of Mount Carmel (Social Institute) and Our Lady of Peace (Turin Polytechnic).[51]

The Social Institute's Saint Vincent Conference was founded in 1905 and soon placed under the patronage of Turin's own "saint" of charity,

---

45. Frassati, *I giorni*, 120.
46. *Positio*, 11.
47. Frassati, *L'impegno sociale*, 122.
48. *Letters*, 86; Ital ed., 116–17.
49. Casalegno, *Pier Giorgio Frassati*, 70.
50. See chapter 4, section 4, above for details on Pier Giorgio's education.
51. These parishes in Italian are *Madonna di Monte Carmelo* and *Madonna della Pace*. For Pier Giorgio's presence at Cottolengo, see Frassati, *I giorni*, 116; and for Pietro Occelli's testimony at *La Madonna della Pace*, see 171.

Giuseppe Cottolengo. The Cottolengo Conference was under the direction of the Jesuits, while the Cesare Balbo Conference made use of a large room offered by the Fathers of the Missions.[52] The objective of the conferences was to help young students by visiting the poor, familiarize themselves with the tragic conditions of the deprived in comparison to their own privileged status, and to offer them material help, thereby filling the gap between study and the Christian message, offering charitable services for the love of God and one's neighbor.[53]

At Our Lady of Mount Carmel, Francesco Bertagna had been president for thirty-seven years. Pier Giorgio was working closely with him as a "novice" visiting homes in the poor quarters of Turin. Pier Giorgio brought to the poor vouchers to purchase bread, linen, clothing, covers, medicine, wood and charcoal; Pier Giorgio went as far as looking for work for the unemployed, often making use of his father's Saturday Charity or other benefactors for this purpose.[54] His letter to Villani expressed Pier Giorgio's sense of justice and his deep desire to help others, prompting him to find solutions to help individuals overcome their misery often due to a lack of income.

3.1.1. Charity for Sinners

Four months after writing to Villani, Pier Giorgio wrote to Bellingeri to express his disappointment with developments in the conference concerning a family.[55] The controversy involved the Zanatta family; Pier Giorgio articulated his charitable principles. With the family in moral crisis, Pier Giorgio emphasized compassion and catechesis. How did a person support individuals whose lifestyles were morally dubious? Was charity withdrawn or withheld in such instances? Were these individuals excluded from charity? Pier Giorgio did not deny the moral irregularity of those receiving charity, but he also recognized their genuine need for help. The conference to which he belonged, Cottolengo Conference, was under the direction of individuals who believed that charity should be withheld from those living a morally questionable lifestyle. Pier Giorgio believed that charity was charity and should go to whomever needed help. The letter raised the moral problem to which

---

52. Fathers of the Missions, *"Padri della Missione,"* San Vincenzo Italia website, lists Blessed Pier Giorgio Frassati as one of the Vincentian Blesseds. See http://www.sanvincenzoitalia.it/chi-siamo/la-famiglia-vincenziana/congregazione-della-missione-padri-della-missione.

53. Casalengo, *Pier Giorgio Frassati*, 70–71.

54. Frassati, *La carità*, "Testimony of Francesco Bertagna," 247–48.

55. *Letters*, "To Carlo Bellingeri, Berlin, December 14, 1922," 105–6.

the director appeared to respond: charity offered to people living immoral lives would reinforce their immoral lifestyle. Pier Giorgio took a different position: if such individual needed assistance, Christian charity would help transform their lives. As they discovered God's love and compassion, they had a greater chance of abandoning their sinful ways. A person did not receive charity on the basis of how morally they lived but on the gravity of their situation. Pier Giorgio wrote to Bellingeri telling him, "Carlo, if you really want to know, one of my ideas is that I would abolish certain conferences of Saint Vincent; when there are men from another generation, so full of Christian zeal, who don't even know how to warn the parents about the alleged misconduct of their daughters and thus try to do good work, but instead they prefer to abandon that family, it's better that the conference didn't exist."[56] The solution to moral problems was not "abandonment," but rather, finding a way to correct the individual, to help lead the person toward conversion; and, in this case, Pier Giorgio suggested to talk to the parents, to help by teaching what was true, catechizing, but not abandonment. In other words, the "older generation" preferred not to support the Zanatta family because they were considered unworthy of charitable support; one of the four daughters lived in Rome as someone's "mistress."[57] So, when Pier Giorgio transferred to the Cesare Balbo Conference, he continued to support the Zanatta family in which he took particular interest. His intuition of "non-abandonment" proved correct: with his ongoing charity, the family had eventually morally and materially improved.[58]

3.2. Social Justice and Politics

Pier Giorgio believed that a socioeconomically just society in Italy could only come about by a political system that most closely aligned itself with gospel values. For Pier Giorgio the gospel and the teachings of Jesus Christ meant necessarily offering help and hope to the poor. In Turin and Berlin, he was a witness to how politics could create unjust societies where the poor were neglected and forgotten in their misery.

The July 1922 letter to Villani indicates the Italian Left had dominated Italy's 1919 general elections. The Socialists and Populists, first and second position with votes, respectively, were followed by Giolitti's Liberals in third position. Pier Giorgio made reference in his letter to the two "Filippos": Filippo Meda a politically active Roman Catholic elected to office in 1922

---

56. *Letters*, "To Carlo Bellingeri, Berlin, December 14, 1922," 105–6.
57. Frassati, *La carità*, 254.
58. Frassati, *La carità*, "Testimony of Francesco Bertagna," 249.

for the Popular Party of Italy (Populists), and the Socialist Party of Italy (Socialists) led by Filippo Turati.[59]

During the social and political upheaval in Italy after WWI, besides the concern of rising Communism, the Roman Catholic hierarchy and Catholic politicians such as Meda (Populist) had reason to fear a coalition between Populists and Socialists because such an alliance would bring Turati's Marxist sympathies into the Italian government. While Catholic politicians agreed on a socially just society in responding to the gospel values, the solution could not have been negotiating with atheists or an atheistically-driven ideology. Instead, Luigi Facta was appointed prime minister in February 1922, allowing Mussolini and his Fascists to continue with their nationalist campaign. Neither Pope Pius XI nor the Catholic hierarchy was prepared to negotiate with the Left. Catholicism had the bitter experience of witnessing its faithful persecuted, martyred, slaughtered, and even wiped out by despots, both political and religious.

For Pier Giorgio, his political "purity" was to be found in the gospel, and his youthful ideal—a vision of a just society on earth. But he also knew that divine justice would ultimately reward or punish accordingly, "If a Good and Just God didn't exist, our life would be useless." This led to Pier Giorgio's eschatological vision; although he believed one should do the best to live according to the gospel on earth, for those who suffered unjustly, just as those who sinned obstinately, divine justice would be applied.[60]

4. Letter to the Members of the Milites Mariae Club— Turin, October 30, 1922[61]

Pier Giorgio's extraordinary letter contains profound spiritual objectives addressed to *Milites Mariae*, and served to appeal to the members of the Italian Catholic Youth the need for improved organization. Referring to the Catholic Youth convention in Rome of September 1921, which he described as "deplorable," Pier Giorgio hoped to see the union between FUCI and GCI.[62]

---

59. The complex developments in the crisis conditions of July 1922, are found in Seton-Watson, *Storia d'Italia*, 692. See chapter 13 for details.

60. Pier Giorgio's eschatological vision is taken up below in chapter 10.

61. *Letters*, 97–99; Ital. ed., 135–37.

62. FUCI = *Federazione Universitaria Cattolica Italiana*, Federation of Italian Catholic Universities; GCI. =*Gioventù Cattolica Italiana*, "Italian Catholic Youth" ("Catholic Youth").

4.1. Milites Mariae

Pier Giorgio had hoped for a more socially-oriented FUCI, addressing concrete problems experienced by students and workers reflected in the majority of Italian youth. He had experienced at both, the Ravenna Convention in August 1921, and the following month at the Rome Convention—the latter convention in particular was representative of Italy's Catholic youth—the need to address social issues. Pier Giorgio's frustration with FUCI was its lack of social representation of Italian youth. A Catholic youth organization should have been active, transforming, and even militant. Pier Giorgio was not only a student at the Turin Polytechnic, but he also participated in the outskirts of Turin where he acquired a wealth of knowledge from the experience of workers in the Savonarola Club at the FIAT plant. Both the intellectual elite of a bourgeois lifestyle and the low-income workers could benefit from each other's experiences: this was Pier Giorgio's fundamental message—the transformation he wanted to see in the FUCI.[63] The majority of the FUCI members, however, rejected the formal proposal, including Monsignor Giandomenico Pini who preferred a FUCI formation of an intellectual and spiritual caliber of students to prepare for future responsibilities.[64] As a result, while Pier Giorgio remained a member of the FUCI, he also belonged to the GCI through the *Milites Mariae*.[65]

Milites Mariae was founded by Pier Giorgio and other youth belonging to *La Crocetta*, Pier Giorgio's home parish. He started religious classes at the parish for Catholic Youth. Unfortunately, apart from the lack of space at the church, and lack of moral support on the part of the part of the parish priest, Monsignor Roccati, even his assistant, the theologian, Giorgio Formica who was the ecclesiastical assistant of *Milites Mariae*, was unsupportive. While Pier Giorgio sought a federation between FUCI and Catholic Youth, Don Formica obstructed the federation of the two groups.[66]

---

63. *Positio*, 95.
64. *Positio*, 96.
65. *Positio*, 96.
66. *Positio*, 96–97.

4.1.1. Catholic Youth / Catholic Action[67]

Catholic Youth (*Gioventù Cattolica*) was founded in 1867 and later became part of Catholic Action *(Azione Cattolica)*.[68] Their motto was "prayer, action, sacrifice," and also contained in their mission by which they were inspired, "devotion to the Holy See, study of religion, testimony of Christian life, and charitable works." The project was formalized when the first congress met in Venice in 1874.[69] Catholic Action emerged out of the religiopolitical tension of Italian nationalism and the need to protect Italian Catholics "uncontaminated from liberalism."[70] In 1923, Catholic Action was divided into four sections: the Federation of Italian Catholic Men, the Society of Italian Catholic Youth, the Federation of Italian Catholic Universities, the Union of Italian Catholic women.[71]

As indicated in section 2.2 above, in September 1921, Pier Giorgio participated in the Catholic Youth convention in Rome celebrating fifty years since its foundation with fifty thousand students in procession.[72] Pier Giorgio did not become an official member of Catholic Action until May 1922. Due to the difficulty to create a merger between Catholic Action and FUCI, Pier Giorgio's only option was become a member of Catholic Action. He received the permission to found *Milites Mariae* by the parish priest of *La Crocetta* making him a member of Catholic Action.[73] In November 1922, Pier Giorgio participated at the Catholic Action convention in Novara.

4.1.2. FUCI—Federation of Italian Catholic Universities[74]

Catholic Italian university students found themselves in an environment hostile to their beliefs as Roman Catholics in the late eighteenth century, around the time of Italian political unification. Between the positivism and anticlericalism, Italian Catholics who had studied in a Catholic context were alienated in the universities when Catholic clubs did not exist. "May 26,

---

67. I wish to thank Luca Manzon, a member of Azione Cattolica in Turin who took the time to describe their activities and goals.

68. Originally, Society of Italian Catholic Youth, *Società della Gioventù Cattolica Italiana*. ACI = *Azione Cattolica Italiana*, "Italian Catholic Action."

69. Seton-Watson, *Storia d'Italia*, 71.

70. Seton-Watson, *Storia d'Italia*, 71.

71. Developments expressed in the letter of October 1923, to the FUCI Board of Directors. See section 6, below.

72. Frassati, *Calendario*, "Roma, 1–8 September, 1921."

73. Frassati, *Calendario*, "Torino, May 14, 1922."

74. http://www.fuci.net/index.php/chi-siamo/storia.

1889, in Rome the San Sebastian Club was formed with the objective to oppose itself to 'lay tendencies' that were anticlerical and positivistic present in the world and university schools, and to claim the presence of a young and active Catholic laity capable to assert itself through cultural commitments and even in the area of science; in this way, showing the irreconcilability between faith and science did not exist."[75] Cesare Balbo Club already was founded in 1894, in Turin, and at the XIII Italian Catholic Convention held in Turin in 1895, the proposal was made to create a federation of Italian Catholic university clubs.[76] At the XIV Italian Catholic Convention in Fiesole in 1896, FUCI was formally established. Monseigneur Giandomenico Pini was chosen as the ecclesiastical assistant who remained in this position until 1923. Pier Giorgio was a member of FUCI since he began his studies at the Turin Polytechnic in 1919, and in August 1921, he participated at the XXV FUCI convention in Ravenna.[77] Pier Giorgio as an active FUCI member, expressed his desire to have a club united with *Gioventù Cattolica*, Catholic Youth, and he also communicated his concerns over the direction FUCI was taking with regards to Mussolini.[78]

4.2. Objectives of Milites Mariae Address

Pier Giorgio's first concern was education: rejecting the "corrupt" instruction transmitted in public schools, he wanted the Catholic students to be trained in apologetics where they could learn and defend their faith. The corruption to which he referred was the positivist developments in Italian education distorting or rejecting Catholic beliefs. This made Catholics vulnerable to the "dangers in life." Pier Giorgio believed with public education morality was threatened due to political ideology. For this reason, a person needed to be properly educated to vote with a conscience enlightened by Catholic teaching, and this he wanted to assure the Catholic Youth through an apologetics program.

The letter expressed Pier Giorgio's personality to "act": discussing and planning must be transformed into a concrete program of action. The indifference of the FUCI he found unsettling, and offered the Catholic Youth the "lofty mission" entrusted to Italian Catholic university students by divine providence. He acknowledged the Catholic youth by reminding them,

---

75. FUCI, "Who are we, history," *Chi siamo, storia*.

76. Casalengo, *Pier Giorgio Frassati*, 128.

77. Frassati, *Calendario*, "Ravenna, 29 August, 1921."

78. Dealt with below, section 6, "To the Board of Directors of 'Cesare Balbo,' 26th of October, 1923."

who, "by the grace of God are Catholics." The letter was clearly built around "our own formation." For Pier Giorgio, "youth" was not about wasting life "preoccupied enjoying the good life" leading to "immorality." Instead, Pier Giorgio asserts, "to be ready to carry on the battles." If the youth were to be engaged in battle, it represented a good cause: the construction of a moral society that was built on Catholic principles. Without God's grace and personal sacrifice, reaching the goal of a moral society was not possible. The emphasis, therefore, in obtaining the goal Pier Giorgio sought for the *Milites Mariae*, was teaching its members on "religious and philosophical matters," reflecting the Catholic Action motto: "prayer, action, sacrifice."

5. Letter to the Board of Directors of "Cesare Balbo," October 26, 1923[79]

Pier Giorgio's letter to the Directors of the Cesare Balbo Club withdrawing his membership reflected his response to the unacceptable conduct of Club members during Mussolini's visit to Turin. The letter follows a complaint written the same day, October 26, by both Pier Giorgio and Bertini concerning the display of the flag—as if the displayed flag served to honor Mussolini's presence—a decision and act Pier Giorgio found absolutely unacceptable. In the October 26 letter following his complaint, Pier Giorgio made additional biblical allusions to convey his message. Following his conscience, the one responsible for "violence" being done to clubs, namely Mussolini, could not be honored, and so, Pier Giorgio responded by disassociating himself from the Cesare Balbo Club altogether. Pier Giorgio insisted he did not act out of anger or passion, but a rational decision that was based on the coherency between belief and action; in other words, truth was manifested in personal conduct. The Federation of Italian Catholic Universities diverged from Catholic Youth / Catholic Action. Although united in the Catholic faith, the two associations expressed a difference in their objectives, intellectually and socially, manifesting a significant difference in political orientation.[80]

5.1. Sacredness of the FUCI Flag

Pier Giorgio withdrew his membership after having written a letter to the directors of the Cesare Balbo Club expressing his disapproval of the president's actions. The letter sent to the board of directors, along with Bertini's

---

79. *Letters*, 142–43; Ital. ed., 197–98.
80. *Positio*, 26–27.

protest, expressed grievances on three points: (1) Msgr. Pinardi requested only the flag of the Catholic Associations' headquarters to be displayed while he disapproved of Catholic Associations participating in Mussolini's reception; and so, (2) the claim of the Cesare Balbo Club president to be taking orders from above did not have any real foundation; (3) the president of the Cesare Balbo Club acted on his own initiative.

The flag displayed during Mussolini's visit to Turin was the basis of Pier Giorgio's complaint and ultimately his resignation from Cesare Balbo. He discussed the matter with Monsignor Pinardi for clarification, and the explanations offered by the monsignor conflicted with those of the board of directors; besides, they already knew the disapproval of displaying the flag.[81] The distinction was made between the blessed flag of the Cesare Balbo Club that was also carried in Rome by Pier Giorgio "gloriously damaged," and a flag at the headquarters that was given permission to be displayed.

The blessing of the flag conveyed not only its symbolic value representing Catholic Italian students at the Turin Polytechnic, "Cesare Balbo," but the spiritual value associated with the flag, with blessed water and sign of the cross, sprinkled by the priest. Therefore, Pier Giorgio's reaction, along with Bertini's, was not sentimental or political, but fundamentally, religious: the Catholic flag could not be displayed before someone who had promoted violence and murder.

Only three months earlier Pier Giorgio had made a speech in Pollone, precisely expressing the value of the blessed flag.[82] In his address to the Catholic Youth of Pollone, Pier Giorgio asserted, "So that every one of you may be worthy of this Flag and may defend it against every attack." Pier Giorgio reminded the youth that "God's minister" had just blessed their prayers as well as calling upon "blessings from heaven"; with such blessings, they might be "worthy" of the flag with the duty to defend it against "attack." The flag was treated with great respect and great value. Pier Giorgio pointed out that the flag "represents in a symbolic way" the teachings of Jesus Christ, and Pier Giorgio drew from this flag the motto of Catholic Action, "Prayer, Action, Sacrifice." Pier Giorgio ended his delivery once again in reference to the flag, "Therefore keep this beautiful white flag immaculate, and if the occasion should present itself tomorrow, defend it, because from now on it is sacred: it not only represents your club, it also represents the most beautiful patrimony of our Italy and the civilized world." Pier Giorgio expressed

81. Msgr. Giovanni Battista Pinardi (Servant of God) was the Auxiliary Bishop of Turin and the Diocesan Assistant for Catholic Action. See Casalegno, *Pier Giorgio Frassati*, 209.

82. *Letters*, "To the Members of the 'Catholic Youth,' of Pollone, July 29, 1923," 128–31; Ital. ed., 178–80.

his complete allegiance to the Holy Father by crying out, "Long live Jesus Christ! Long live the Pope!"

5.2. Interpretation of Scriptures and Politics

To explain his decision on religious principles, Pier Giorgio drew from two biblical passages which reflected how he approached society and interpreted politics. Scriptures served to warn those who were followers of Christ and strived to build a Christian society, that cunning political strategies were used to lead believers away from the light, away from the truth, away from goodness.

The passage Pier Giorgio employed showed that "sons of darkness are more cunning than the sons of light" (Luke 16:8). In the context of the biblical narrative, the steward being released from his employment expected to rely on friends to welcome him into their homes: he manipulated the debtors by reducing their payments. The "astuteness" of the steward secured him the "benefits" he needed but the cunning tactics only proved that he was a son of darkness. The allusion was to politicians who sought power and would find ways of "paying" off even rivals; after all, the debtors owed money, but would become the steward's friends by a self-interested reduced debit. Pier Giorgio had the astuteness of politicians in mind, especially Mussolini's cunning tactics in his rise to power.

Pier Giorgio added a biblical text to reinforce his position, "'Beware of false prophets, who come to you in sheep's clothing but inwardly are ravenous wolves'" (Matt 7:15). The verse repeated the sense of deception. One might be led astray by the cunning words and acts or outright "false" language disguised as "sheep." Pier Giorgio focused on the problematic of individuals portraying themselves to be helpful friends, as in the self-interested steward, who was nothing more than dishonest, though he appeared kind and considerate. Pier Giorgio believed Mussolini's increasing popularity was achieved through the deception of political language that disguised Mussolini's self-serving ambitions, ultimately, taking vulnerable followers with him. This reflected the success of cunning language; the enemies, dangerous "wolves" portraying to be innocent "sheep."

Pier Giorgio was aware of deceptive political maneuvers, and therefore, such political figures failed to win his support. These maneuvers surfaced most clearly in the flag controversy. Mussolini was winning more sympathizers and even political alliances bringing him to power. Pier Giorgio remained unconvinced of Mussolini's moral credibility. Undoubtedly, for Pier Giorgio the greatest pain for him was to have witnessed Roman Catholics giving their support to Mussolini.

6. Letter to Antonio Villani—Turin, June 23, 1924[83]

Pier Giorgio's letter addressed to *Tonini* (Severi) related the dramatic events of Fascist breaking into his family home which he referred to as a "little catastrophe," *piccola devastazione*. The language Pier Giorgio used to describe the event also showed once again Pier Giorgio's tremendous control and use of the Italian language; in this case, a descriptive narrative with a choice of nouns and adjectives which allowed Villani to imagine the events that took place. "It was a cowardly enterprise, but nothing more," reflected Pier Giorgio's modesty. The moment Pier Giorgio realized it was the Fascists cutting the telephone wires, "my blood raced to my veins even faster." He colorfully described his reaction; "I threw myself at . . ." and the series of adjectives to describe the intruders, "crooks" and "cowards" followed by a "punch." Being ironic, Pier Giorgio stated, "courageously," when the "swindlers" heard the voice of "one" man, they "ran for the door," while he and Italo Pavoni, the family chauffeur, chased after them.

6.1. Christian Democracy

The value of the letter is not only that it revealed the violent maneuvers of the Fascists which Pier Giorgio was already aware of, but the event confirmed his and his family's views about the coercive tactics used by the Fascists. Pier Giorgio turned to the concrete events in his home to prove that the government was "corrupt" and intervention was needed to "surgically remove" the Fascist party that was becoming a "cancer." The metaphor anticipating death if surgical intervention was not immediate, conveyed a tragic end: "there will be no more hope for us not even a little bit." To have hope in government, therefore, required immediate action when dealing with politicians, just like a disease, otherwise, the deadly disease would spread. Pier Giorgio closed his letter with a chant opening with, "Long live Matteotti. Long live Liberty."[84] Pier Giorgio closed the chant in a sense of victory because Pier Giorgio was a man of hope; he "poured out" his soul to Villani because of

---

83. *Letters*, 156–57; Ital. ed., 219–20.

84. Giacomo Matteotti (1885–1924) leader of the PSU (Democratic Socialist Union) which advanced a moderate socialism. Matteotti was staunchly anti-Fascist. In June 1924, a few weeks before Pier Giorgio wrote his letter, Matteotti had been kidnapped and killed. Fascists were held responsible. See Seton-Watson, *Historia d'Italia*, 739.

their common Christians ideals, "I leave you yelling . . . Long live Christian Democracy." The political message Pier Giorgio delivered was a democratic state based on Christian principles, but Christian democracy was not in any way compromise for Pier Giorgio: Christian democracy meant the gospel of Christ—what the Roman Catholic Church believed, upheld and taught as in *Rerum Novarum*.

After Pier Giorgio and Italo chased the men out the door, Pier Giorgio asked his mother if she had been frightened, and Mariscia whether she had been hurt; he was relieved to know that nobody had been injured. He went to wash his hands, placed himself in front of the table, and had his second dish of risotto.[85] Pier Giorgio's modest testimony of the intruders which he dismissed as a "little invasion" and a "cowardly undertaking but nothing much" in his opening lines to Villani reflected actions of "justice that must coincide with the affirmation of supreme human, moral and religious values."[86]

Pier Giorgio shared with his father fundamental democratic principles, which were in opposition to the two extremes, Fascism and Communism. Alfredo's paper, *La Stampa*, also had to deal with Fascist repression of the newspaper because *La Stampa* was critical of Fascist politics. The Fascist intervention in *La Stampa* and the Frassati residence were gazetted in the June 24, 1924, *London Times*, "After the meeting a strong column of Fascists tried to storm the offices of the *Stampa*, but were driven back by the Carabinieri. At the same time, some Fascisti in a motor-car raided the private residence of Senator Frassati, proprietor and editor of the *Stampa*."[87] The father and son differed, however, on political economics: Alfredo Frassati supported a liberal economy whereas Pier Giorgio defended a gospel-inspired society.

The social democracy advanced by the PPI and the Sicilian priest Don Luigi Sturzo cannot be confused with a later development of "social democracy"—the radical reinterpretation of Christian ethics. Moreover, social democracy in Italy emerged in a Catholic society where moral codes were shaped by the teachings of the Roman Catholic Church reflected in the fabric of Italian society. Divorce, artificial contraceptives, abortion, were all illegal; homosexual unions and polygamy were socially inconceivable in Catholic Italy. In a letter Pier Giorgio wrote to his sister, Luciana, he reminds her that the father needs to fill out a form to be sent to Verona, "Civil Committee against Blasphemy."[88] Pier Giorgio's politics emphasized Catho-

---

85. Frassati, *L'impegno sociale*, 106.
86. Frassati, *L'impegno sociale*, 108.
87. "The Matteoti Crime," *London Times*, June 24, 1924.
88. *Letters*, "Luciana, Pollone, October 9, 1922," 94–95. Italy introduced the

lic social values and Catholic morality. As Pierazzi asserts, Communism simply worsened since Pier Giorgio's time.[89]

6.2. Fascism Governs Italy

In 1919 Turin, as with other industrial centers of Italy, namely, Milan and Genoa, entered a period of socioeconomic crisis exacerbating political instability. Agitation of workers, and the arrival of migrants from other regions of Italy, created a disproportion between wages and cost of living.[90] Between strikes and worker unrest by September of 1920 factories were occupied not just in the northern centers but at the national level. During the same period as workers made their demands a block was gradually constructed made up of ex-interventionists and combatants; thus, nationalists who defended Italy's intervention in WWI solidified themselves with the conservative Right, beginning the advance of Fascism.[91] The "comrades" maintained a powerful "warrior" spirit even after the war and in 1919 they founded the "Combat bundle" *Fasci di combattimento*," from *fascio* "bundle," developing national interests, recognized by their black shirts, "and their members soon became called: fascists."[92]

The rise of Mussolini was attributed to the Popular Party of Italy which did not support Giolitti's government, resulting in the Giolitti's resignation. The departure of Giolitti created a political vacuum giving Mussolini the opportunity to consolidate political power. Mussolini's March on Rome on October 28, 1922, was not only accomplished with the approval of King Victor Emmanuel III, but the latter also entrusted Mussolini with the task of forming a new government. In 1924 Mussolini had won the elections removing all opposition to install a dictatorship.

6.2.1. Mussolini and Pope Pius XI

The election of Pope Pius XI to the See of Saint Peter in 1922 coincided with Mussolini's rise to power. Mussolini and his Fascist government were at the pope's door steps. The leader of the Fascists employed political rhetoric

---

Anti-Blasphemy Law in 1930 during Mussolini's government making it illegal to blaspheme, "against the Deity or Symbols or Persons venerated in the religion of the State"—Roman Catholicism (art. 724, Italian Penal Code).

89. Pierazzi, *Così ho visto*, 113.
90. Casalegno, *Pier Giorgio Frassati*, 117.
91. Casalegno, *Pier Giorgio Frassati*, 118.
92. Seton-Watson, *Storia d'Italia*, 688–89.

that linked the Popular Party to atheistic socialism, and the liberal thinkers with irreligiosity. Instead, the Fascist government returned crucifixes to the hospitals and schools, removed the objectionable masonic lodges, defended priests from the invasions of communists, and finally, Mussolini was prepared to treat the "Roman question."[93] Associating directly or indirectly the Popular Party with Bolshevism and the Liberals with anticlericalism, Mussolini reassured the Vatican he was the man with whom Pope Pius XI could negotiate. Undoubtedly, Mussolini succeeded in winning the sympathy and support of not only Catholics, but even the Supreme Pontiff stated, "We needed even the man whom Providence made us meet." The church hierarchy was horrified by events followed by the 1917 Bolshevik Revolution in Russia, the same Bolsheviks killing priests and sisters in the churches of Poland.[94] In the 1920s the Mexican church had suffered the slaughter of thousands of lay faithful, priests and bishops due to the anticlerical government. The pontiff could not permit the socioeconomic conditions in Italy to create a Communist government or an anticlerical regime. Mussolini bluntly stated the church's option: "either Rome or Moscow."[95] These two extremes were precisely the only options though many moderates would have sought a middle-road solution with the Socialists.

6.2.2. Pier Giorgio's Political Purity

The founding of the Popular Party meant reconstructing society that raised the economic, moral, and juridical life of workers built on the politico-economic principles of the Catholic thinker Giuseppe Toniolo. Pier Giorgio identified the Catholic values reconstructing society inspired by the thought of Toniolo.[96] When Pier Giorgio sought membership in the Popular Party

---

93. Seton-Watson, *Storia d'Italia*, 684. A few weeks after Mussolini's March on Rome, crucifixes reappeared in schools and in tribunals at the Vatican's request. The Vatican was also successful in obtaining from Mussolini obligatory Catholic religious education in elementary schools which had been abolished with the unification of Italy and its anticlerical government since 1877 (Seton-Watson, *Storia d'Italia*, 720). The radical secularizing laws in Italy began in 1871 which included: suppression of the faculties of theology with seminaries placed under government control; laws expropriating church corporations and the confiscation of their property was further extended to Rome. With pressure coming from the Left this included confiscating the buildings of forty international Catholic Orders. See Seton-Watson, *Storia d'Italia*, 66–67.

94. Seton-Watson, *Storia d'Italia*, 66–67.

95. Seton-Watson, *Storia d'Italia*, 66–67.

96. Trabucco, introduction to *L'impegno sociale*, 13. Trabucco quotes from Toniolo who influenced both Fr. Karl Sonnenschein and through Sonnenschein, Pier Giorgio. It is beyond the scope of this book to examine Toniolo's thought and influence on Pier

he was refused membership: the son of a liberal, Alfredo Frassati, hardly the influence of socialist economic principles. Pier Giorgio belonged to the "upper-middle class"—*alta borghesia*—and the father owned *La Stampa* which did not support the PPI and its leader, Don Luigi Sturzo.[97] Pier Giorgio's compelling desire to obtain membership was reflected in his coherency: honesty, frankness, religious expression, charitable works, and these qualities led to his admission into the PPI registering in his home parish of La Crocetta.[98] Pier Giorgio's letters attacked Fascism while he defended and promoted the Popular Party of Italy until finally the PPI—paradoxically—aligned itself with the Fascists in 1922. Devastated, Pier Giorgio discontinued to support the PPI.[99]

Pier Giorgio's political position could not be found so much in his ideas because Pier Giorgio was not ideologically driven. Rather, Pier Giorgio's political views were shaped by his Christian values. For Pier Giorgio things were black and white, no nuances, no grey area, no perhaps: one either follows Christ and lives the gospel or one does not. His personality did not allow for compromise and negotiation of truth. Pier Giorgio believed in Word of God as the truth, not as an optional way of life, or a diluted form of teaching. Christ's teachings were transmitted by the Catholic Church and that was precisely what Pier Giorgio strived to live. Politically this transformed into values that Pier Giorgio perceived as being closest to gospel. The word used to describe Pier Giorgio, "pure"—*un puro*—reflected his personality and his political position founded on truth.[100]

Questions

1. What was Pier Giorgio's experience in Berlin when he writes to Antonio Villani (§1; March 1921)?

2. How did Pier Giorgio and Rev. Dr. Karl Sonnenschein become friends (1.1)?

Giorgio. Toniolo himself was beatified in 2012 by Pope Benedict XVI.

97. Trabucco, introduction to *L'impegno sociale*, 14.

98. Trabucco, introduction to *L'impegno sociale*, 14.

99. The implications of the Fascist-PPI alliance have been treated in, David C. Bellusci, "Pier Giorgio Frassati: Italian Nationalism, Mussolini and the Vatican," paper given at the Canadian Jacques Maritain Association, Ryerson University, Toronto, May 20–21, 2017. See also, Frassati, *I giorni*, 111.

100. Frassati, *I giorni*, 69.

3. Pier Giorgio's letter to Gian Maria Bertini (§2; October 1923) made reference to the papal document, *Rerum Novarum*. What was the subject of *Rerum Novarum* (2.1)? How did *Rerum Novarum* influence Pier Giorgio's concern for the poor (§2; 2.1)?

4. What motivated Pier Giorgio's membership in the St. Vincent Conferences (3.1)?

5. What does *Milites Mariae* mean? Why did Pier Giorgio write a letter to the members of *Milites Mariae* (§4; 4.1)?

6. What conflict occurred in Rome between the Catholic Youth rally and the Italian State in the summer of 1921 (2.2.1; 2.2.2)? What happened to Pier Giorgio holding the FUCI flag (2.2.1)? Why was the FUCI flag considered "sacred" (5.1)?

8

Pier Giorgio's Spirituality

> You must follow him along the way of the cross, choosing to be crucified in his way, not yours.
>
> SAINT CATHERINE OF SIENA, *LETTERS* [T354]

Pier Giorgio's letters reflect a maturing of values, religious, social, and political, influenced by several Dominican figures. Dominican spirituality and the associated saints featured prominently in the life of Pier Giorgio, some more than others, but they each contributed to his spiritual growth. Unquestionably, Fra Girolamo Savonarola represented the Dominican figure whom Pier Giorgio desired to follow; both shared a willingness to die for truth in the name of the gospel. His meetings with the Dominican Father Filippo Robotti at Cesare Balbo Club in Turin led him to discover more fully Dominican spirituality and Dominican saints: Saint Dominic, Saint Catherine of Siena, Saint Thomas Aquinas and also Saint Augustine of Hippo.

1. Letter to Antonio Villani—Pollone, August 31, 1923[1]

August 1923, Pier Giorgio, twenty-two years old, replied to two of Villani's previous letters. The theme of the letter with the exception of his closing paragraph focused on Dominican spirituality. Pier Giorgio became a Third

---

1. *Letters*, 138–39; Ital. ed., 191–92.

Order Dominican taking the name "Fra Girolamo." He expressed his gratitude for Villani's "kind words," an allusion to Pier Giorgio's uncle, zio Pietro, who had recently died.[2] The thoughts expressed by Villani were received by Pier Giorgio as a further expression of friendship, the bond present Pier Giorgio's words, "feelings from the heart since your heart is so close to mine."

1.1. Saint Dominic

Following the Rule of Saint Augustine, the Dominicans were formally approved by Pope Honorius III on December 22, 1216.[3] The Fundamental Constitutions of the Dominican Order gives its founding purpose as follows: "Since it is known that our Order was founded, from the beginning, especially for preaching and the salvation of souls. . . ." Emerging in the context of widespread heresy, Saint Dominic realized the significance of studying and teaching. The suggestion of battle to fight heresy, no doubt, attracted Pier Giorgio, as he wrote to Villani, "he instituted it as an army to do battle against heretics." While preaching reflected the mission of the order, it also meant the members of the Dominican family together supported and contributed to the "preaching" objectives bringing the light of truth to those who dwell in darkness of sin, symbolized in the Dominican shield of light penetrating the dark. The Dominican mission, Pier Giorgio certainly believed he belonged to with his own individual charism. Catechizing, whether the faithful, the fallen away, or the nonbelievers, required studies in order to instruct and enlighten, and to form authorized preachers. Pier Giorgio recognized the increasing social and political disorder around him in Turin, Italy, and Europe, which was why he followed not only the path of *veritas* of Saint Dominic, but more specifically, the radical Dominican who was executed, Fra Girolamo, who did not compromise the gospel of Christ. Like Saint Dominic, Pier Giorgio had a preference for the Gospel of St. Matthew because it contained the Beatitudes.[4]

Pier Giorgio conveyed his joy with Villani expressing interest to belong to the great family of Saint Dominic, citing Dante's *Paradiso*, X, 96, "You grow fat if you don't rant and rave," where figures from the Dominican family appear in Dante's *Paradiso*, namely, Saint Dominic, Saint Albert of Cologne, and Saint Thomas Aquinas. In his enthusiastic response to Villani's

---

2. Pier Giorgio's reaction to his uncle's death will be taken up in chapter 10.

3. For Constitutions see, *Liber Constitutionum et Ordinationum*, "Constitutio Fundamentalis," Curia Generalitia, Romae, 2010, I–III. In English, *The Book of the Constitutions and Ordinations of the Brothers of the Order of Preachers* (Dublin, 2001).

4. Frassati, *I giorni*, 166.

own wish to belong to the Dominican family, Pier Giorgio informed him that there were few obligations, and added, "I wouldn't be able to belong to an Order that required a lot." While Pier Giorgio made reference to his choice of Dominican name, "Girolamo Savonarola," he did not provide details of his spiritual journey as a Tertiary Dominican.[5]

1.2. Third Order Dominicans[6]

As Pier Giorgio related in his letter to Villani, "We need to recite the Dominican Office of Our Lady or the Rosary every day, but if you deliberately omit this for one day or for a few days you don't commit a mortal sin." Pier Giorgio belonged to the Confraternity of the Holy Rosary since he was seventeen years old while studying at the Jesuit Institute.[7] His Marian devotion as a child, praying the Rosary, later offering Rosaries as gifts which he made, appeared to find its fulfillment in an order that had a Marian spirituality specifically attached to the Rosary. Since Saint Dominic founded the order in the thirteenth century, the Rosary represented an integral part of Dominican devotion. Pope Leo XII, who died a few years after Pier Giorgio's birth, was also known as the "Pope of the Rosary"; Pope Leo had written eleven encyclicals on the Rosary.[8]

Pier Giorgio being an "observant" person by nature, taking duties and responsibilities seriously, remained committed to the daily Dominican Office. His reference to "heretics" and the earlier practices reflected the objective of the Tertiary Rule; to protect the faithful from falling into the errors of heretics, whether moral or doctrinal. The vocation of the Third Order Dominicans: to live in their own home, married or unmarried, or diocesan priests who followed the rule praying the Office or Rosary like all the religious. They gather in their communities, male, female, or mixed communities, where together they pray, contemplate, study, and act in the world where the Lord has put them.[9] The source by which the Tertiary Dominicans attained their force was listening, studying and praying the Word

---

5. Girolamo Savonarola is in section 2, following.

6. I have retained the use of "Third Order" and "Tertiary" corresponding to texts I am citing. It should be noted that the terms "Third Order" and "Tertiary" have been replaced with the usage "Lay" as in "Lay Dominican."

7. See chapter 4, section 4.3 above; also, chapter 3, section 5.1, above.

8. Calloway, *Champions of the Rosary*, 126.

9. Spiazzi, *Beato Pier Giorgio*, 20.

of God, participating if possible to daily communion which presupposed frequent confession as well as the Daily Office or Rosary.[10]

1.2.1. Pier Giorgio's Entry into the Dominicans

Pier Giorgio's Dominican itinerary began in 1918 when he began his studies at the Turin Polytechnic and where he met Fr. Filippo Robotti. Attending the Cesare Balbo meetings of the Cesare Balbo Club, he got to know Fr. Filippo who was the chaplain to the club. The Dominican chaplain himself of the Turin Polytechnic belonged to the Province of Saint Peter Martyr. The patron of Dominican Province to which Piedmont belonged was named after the thirteenth-century saint, also known as Peter of Verona, who actively preached against the Cathar heresy spreading in northern Italy. Saint Peter Martyr was eventually killed by a heretic with an axe striking his head. The martyr was known to have written in his own blood, *Credo in unum Deum*, "I believe in one God."[11] Pier Giorgio's first encounter with the Dominican Province, therefore, was one named after a saint fighting heresy and who died a martyr.[12]

Fr. Filippo was also involved in the Savonarola Club named after another Dominican who was executed.[13] The club supported the FIAT workers, but Fr. Filippo was also actively involved in promoting the PPI and Pier Giorgio even joined Fr. Filippo with the political campaigning.[14] Fr. Filippo had been military chaplain for the Italians during WWI, and was later elected prior of Saint Dominic in Turin.[15] Fr. Filippo's opposition to Fascism led to his departure for the United States, where he remained until 1936.[16] Occasionally, Pier Giorgio visited Fr. Filippo at the Dominican priory of Turin, and during one of the meetings, Fr. Filippo had spoken to Pier Giorgio of the Third Order Dominicans without making any reference that

---

10. Spiazzi, *Beato Pier Giorgio*, 22.

11. See "St Peter Martyr," *Dominican Saints*, 2009. *Provincia Lombardiae Superioris*, "Upper Lombardy," was confirmed and created at the Dominican General Chapter of Besançon in 1303. The renaming of the "Province of St. Peter Martyr" took place in 1410. See Hinnebusch, "Peter Martyr, St," 192.

12. In Dominican iconography with which Pier Giorgio would have been familiar, St. Peter Martyr is identified with an axe on his bloody head.

13. I am using Fr. Filippo Robotti's first name to avoid confusion with his brother, Fr. Francesco Robotti, also a Dominican with the Turin community.

14. This will be taken up in the next section on Girolamo Savonarola.

15. Casalengo, *Pier Giorgio Frassati*, 129.

16. *Lettere* (Ital. ed.), "Filippo Robotti," 365.

he should enter.[17] Fr. Filippo gave the Dominican Rule of the Third Order to Pier Giorgio in 1921 and Pier Giorgio spent the following year pondering about Dominican spirituality, the Third Order, reading the rule and its obligations.[18] *L'Ordine Domenicano*, "The Dominican Order," was given to Pier Giorgio with the dedication, "To my dear friend Frassati. Fr. Robotti, 2-IV-1920."[19] Pier Giorgio's initial contact with the Dominicans reflected a social justice and sociopolitical context, participating at the Savonarola Club meetings, and helping Fr. Filippo with PPI electoral campaigning, besides the interaction between the two during Cesare Balbo meetings, and Pier Giorgio's personal visits to the Dominican priory in Turin.

To join the Third Order a request was made to the father director of the fraternity; and if accepted, the investiture took place in which the habit of the order was received, along with the Dominican name. After a period of "trial and formation" the Council of the Fraternity decided whether to admit the novice to the Rite of Profession in which the lay person committed himself to follow Saint Dominic and Saint Catherine of Siena according to the norms of the Rule until death.

Fra Girolamo was the name of a zealous preacher, a messenger of truth and justice, certainly not a diplomat, and resolutely nonnegotiable in his position, coherent to his death. Pier Giorgio desired to take "Girolamo" as his name as part of the Order of Preachers.[20] He was discouraged from taking the name because a religious name was chosen among the Blessed and Saints; but, as his letters to Bertini and Villani indicated, he even encouraged his friends to take the same name.

Father Francesco Robotti was the prior of Saint Dominic in Turin when he made the request for admission, "He entered my cell somewhat red with timidity desiring to be a tertiary Dominican. Then, to my last request regarding the name to take without hesitation he answered, 'Fra Girolamo' as if it had been an irrevocable resolution. . . . I knew that others had already informed him of the religious rule that he was about to embrace, I also knew that the choice of the name was the result of discussions, therefore, I was happy to register him with the good number."[21]

---

17. Robotti, essay, in *Beato Pier Giorgio*, 97. The Dominicans had been in Turin since the middle of the thirteenth century. The Mediaeval Church is located at 1 Via San Domenico, Turin. The Dominicans closed their priory in 2015; the church, however, is opened for religious services.

18. Robotti, essay, in *Beato Pier Giorgio*, 97.

19. Frassati, *La fede*, 203n10.

20. Spiazzi, *Beato Pier Giorgio*, 27.

21. Frassati, *La fede*, "Testimony of Father Francesco Robotti," 200.

1.2.2. Profession as Third Order Dominican

Personal meetings with Fr. Filippo Robotti, discussion on Saint Dominic and Dominican figures and spirituality, obligations of the Third Order, shared social and political concerns, one year after reading *The Dominican Order*, in 1922, Pier Giorgio applied to the Third Order novitiate.[22] In 1922 the Dominicans were also commemorating the VII centenary of the death of the order's founder, Saint Dominic. It was on April 23, 1922, that Pier Giorgio was admitted into the Dominican Third Order Novitiate of the Province of Saint Peter Martyr.[23]

With the investiture falling on the solemn liturgical Dominican seventh centenary celebrations of 1922, Pier Giorgio's admission into the Dominican Tertiary community and with his own extensive preparation produced a ceremony of spiritual and emotional intensity. Father Angelo Arrighini, the Dominican spiritual assistant for youth associations, vested Pier Giorgio with the scapular of the order.[24] Father Filippo witnessed the ceremony, "He wore the white scapular with twenty-two other youth on April 23, 1922, taking the name, as noted, Fra Girolamo. My brother Father Francesco Robotti, who succeeded me in charge of the priory was the prior of the convent. One can imagine the joy I experienced when a soul so beautiful asked me to enter the Third Order Dominicans.... It was a decision that came spontaneously from his heart, when he knew the ideal of religious apostolate which fermented in his heart, it was in harmony with the objectives of our Third Order."[25] The father provincial was invited to preside the liturgy, Fr. Benedetto Berro. The Dominican friars, Fr. Filippo, along with Fr. Reginaldo Giuliani and Fr. Enrico Ibertis were also present. Father Stanislaus Gillet, who was to become the general master of the order a few years later (1929), was in Turin giving conferences in French and participated in the centenary celebrations, and at Pier Giorgio's reception into the novitiate.

Pier Giorgio presented himself to pronounce his novitiate commitments, "his head straight, his expression lucid, quality suggesting he could lead and dominate. From his person emitted the power of attraction full of sweetness."[26] Fr. Giuliani knew Pier Giorgio's commitment to Dominican

---

22. Concerning the "Angelic Militia" to which Luciana Frassati makes reference starting in 1921, see section 4, below, St. Thomas Aquinas.

23. More precisely, it was the first Vespers of the Solemnity, making it Saturday evening, April 22, 1922, according to Fr. Giuliani who was present. See Giuliani, essay, in *Beato Pier Giorgio*, 92–93.

24. Arrighini, essay, in *Beato Pier Giorgio*, 117–18.

25. Frassati, *La fede*, "Testimony of Father Filippo Robotti," 202.

26. Frassati, *La fede*, "Testimony of Father Martin Gillet, OP," 202. Father Gillet was

prayer life, "He was scrupulous in observing the Rule of the Third Order. Even though he could practise like other Tertiaries, reciting daily one third of the Rosary, he chose the oldest custom to pray the entire Office of the Blessed Virgin Mary according to the Dominican Rite."[27]

Instead of following the usual formation period due to his departure for Germany and his plans to possibly remain in Germany for his studies in mining engineering, Pier Giorgio asked to have his profession before his departure, as Fr. Francesco Robotti stated; "A month later, May 28, 1922, in a late afternoon there was the Profession of the new Fra Girolamo, profession date changed because Pier Giorgio had to go to Germany."[28] Fr. Francesco Robotti, the same prior who had received Pier Giorgio for his investiture the previous month, had also received Pier Giorgio for his Profession. On May 28, Pier Giorgio made his profession in the chapel of Our Lady of Grace in the Church of Saint Dominic. Although the profession was liturgically less solemn than the VII centenary celebrations of April 23, several Dominican Tertiaries were present besides Dominican Friars from the priory. Fr. Francesco Robotti, the prior, received Pier Giorgio into the order, "I asked him to stand according to the Rite and I embraced him after the formula of the Rite of Profession, his cheeks were wet with tears."[29]

2. Letter to Gian Maria Bertini—Pollone, October 31, 1923[30]

Pier Giorgio addressed his letter to "Fra Girolamo," his friend Maria Bertini who shared the same religious name as Pier Giorgio, and who had also become a member of the Third Order Dominicans; signing off his letter, Pier Giorgio used his religious name, "Fra Girolamo." As with the fiery Dominican preacher, Pier Giorgio boldly defended truth—even in sensitive

---

master general of the Dominican Order from 1929–1946.

27. Giuliani, essay, in *Beato Pier Giorgio*, 94.

28. Frassati, *La fede*, "Testimony of Francesco Robotti," 201.

29. Frassati, *La fede*, "Testimony of Francesco Robotti," 201. References to Pier Giorgio's investiture and profession in the Third Order Dominicans are inconsistent with the following dates: Casalegno, *Pier Giorgio Frassti*, 236; Comíns, *Il Beato*, 73; Siccardi, *Pier Giorgio Frassati*, 150; Spiazzi, *Beato Pier Giorgio*, 23, suggest 1923, by stating, "following year," as the date for Pier Giorgio's profession; *Positio*, 79, gives May 28, 1923, as Pier Giorgio's investiture; Frassati, *Calendario*, "Turin, May 28, 1923," refers to Pier Giorgio as becoming a "Tertiary in the Church of St. Dominic." My dates for Pier Giorgio's investiture and profession rely on the testimonies of the Dominican Fathers who were present.

30. *Letters*, 143–44; Ital. ed., 198–99.

political matters. The letter focused on the tension within the Club caused by the display of the Cesare Balbo flag during Mussolini's visit to Turin.[31] Although Pier Giorgio resigned, he was still waiting for an explanation from the president, Constantino Guardia-Riva. Pier Giorgio disapproved of the female members meddling in the men's club because the FUCI women had their own club, "Gaetana Agnesi."

The display of the blessed Cesare Balbo flag with Mussolini triumphantly parading through the streets of Turin was clearly unacceptable. To complicate matters, Guardia-Riva received the permission of Canon Bues, the new ecclesiastical assistant for Cesare Balbo to display the flag. The anti-fascist Father Filippo Robotti would have refused such a request, but now Pier Giorgio had to accept the decision of Canon Giovanni Bues, and with Mussolini's March on Rome in October of 1922, the Roman Catholic Church was moving cautiously with the Fascist government. Pier Giorgio found himself in the painful situation of an ecclesiastic authorizing the display of the club flag just after having had previously the supportive exchange with a priest who shared in Pier Giorgio's concern for a society that reflected the gospel values. Pier Giorgio, nevertheless, maintained in his letter that, "after having heard the contrary opinion of the few members present some evenings beforehand," gave reason why the flag should not have been displayed. In other words, Guardia-Riva acted on his own. Pier Giorgio asserted, "I can't approve of Guardia-Riva's methods of leadership, he hasn't known how to be popular with his advisers, and he has always acted politically or diplomatically . . . out of place in a Catholic Club where actions ought to be as clean and clear as spring water."

Pier Giorgio recognized in Guardia-Riva political maneuvers, and such "diplomatic or political motivation" did not belong in a Catholic club. The sense of Pier Giorgio's transparency, his coherency in belief and act, his "purity" reflected the moral integrity of a leader: a person who led did not seek political motives, or self-interest. Writing to Bertini, he listed his four complaints directed toward the club leadership: nonexistent internal life, miserable external life, bureaucracy in relations with FUCI, and diplomatic "secrecy." Pier Giorgio referred to his "conscience" twice; first neither he nor Bertini voted for Guardia-Riva, and second, he could not approve of Guardia-Riva's "methods," considering him to ignore his advisors and act singlehandedly. Pier Giorgio made it clear to Guardia-Riva to approach Canon Bues on the matter on the authorization of displaying the Catholic flag with Mussolini in procession. The letter showed that Pier Giorgio battled and defended the principles he believed in even if it meant clarifying the matter

---

31. See chapter 7, section 5.

with the canon as he would not "hide" anything. He also expressed humility in his willingness to be corrected if he had been "wrong" in any way.

2.1. Fra Girolamo

In Pier Giorgio's earlier letter to Villani, Pier Giorgio explained to his friend the requirements for the Third Order Dominicans.[32] Pier Giorgio had taken the name of Fra Girolamo and with this name, Pier Giorgio made Dominican spirituality his own as a professed Tertiary. Pier Giorgio had turned to Father Giuliani seeking all the books on Fra Girolamo in order to study him well and to learn from him and even to defend him.[33]

One can say with reasonable certainty that the Dominican Friar, Girolamo Savonarola, was the most influential Dominican figure in Pier Giorgio's sociopolitical thought, and even the reason for which Pier Giorgio became a Dominican. A person who seeks the truth, and lives by the truth, and preaches the truth as Christ had taught, should be prepared even to die a martyr. The documents on the relationship between Pier Giorgio and Savonarola are substantial. Pier Giorgio would have come across Paolo Luotto's writings, Clementina Luotto's father, on Savonarola published in 1897.[34]

Girolamo Savonarola was born in Ferrara, in northern Italy, on September 21, 1452, and was burned at the stake on May 23, 1498, as a heretic and schismatic after his excommunication by Pope Alexander VI. Savonarola's fiery, prophetic, and political preaching won him many Florentine followers but also political and religious enemies. Florence was at the summit of its Renaissance splendor, but also seduced by worldliness. Savonarola preached to the Florentines in apocalyptic language that they were degenerating into paganism and needed conversion as expressed in "bonfire of the vanities."[35] With the invading forces of Charles VIII of France, the Medici who had governed the city were expelled by the followers of Savonarola; for their part, the disciples of the Ferrarese preacher wanted to establish a Florentine republic modeled on Christian principles. Savonarola drew the Florentine youth in campaigns to rid the city of Florence of immorality and vice.[36] According to Savonarola, "A good, 'more from God than from men,'

---

32. Section 1, above, Letter to Antonio Villani, Pollone, August 31, 1923.
33. Giuliani, essay, in *Beato Pier Giorgio*, 93–94.
34. Ginoli, *Fra Girolamo Savonarola*, 160.
35. Tocco, *Savonarola: Profeta e Ribelle*, 102–3.
36. For details on Girolamo Savonarola, see Ridolfi, *Life of Girolamo Savonarola*, 1959.

adhered to three principles: first, they will free themselves from the servitude of a tyrant and they will live in freedom . . . ; second, spiritual happiness will follow because each person can live as a true Christian, and nothing will prevent him . . . ; third, not only will they deserve eternal happiness, but even greater, they will increase their merits and their heavenly crown will grow."[37]

Pier Giorgio knew enough about Savonarola to choose the Dominican figure as his model in Dominican life, thereby, taking the name "Fra Girolamo." Although the custom of taking a name was that of a saint or beatified, Pier Giorgio, zealous about the truth, chose the name of a person who reflected his own principles. What were the principles Pier Giorgio found in Savonarola? Given his sociopolitical concerns, the role of a person inspired by the gospel, to seek holiness and promote justice, Pier Giorgio found in Savonarola the model who defended and died for the truth. The truth conformed to the gospel of Christ, a just society based not on greed, but sharing one's wealth, not on oppressing the weak, but helping them out of their misery, not a society that tolerates immorality, sin and vice, but a government that teaches, promotes, and rewards Christian virtue. These values Pier Giorgio found in Savonarola, especially two heroic qualities: Savonarola's willingness to die for the truth, and by his fiery preaching the call to conversion.[38]

2.2. Pier Giorgio and Girolamo Savonarola

Turin's workers' club attached to the new FIAT car manufacturer was founded in 1914 by the Dominican Father Filippo Robotti, along with Professor Serafino Dezani, a Savonarola scholar. The club had soon received ecclesial approbation by the archbishop cardinal of Turin, Agostino Richelmy, and was attended by Catholic workers who were against both revolutionary social-communism as well as against the nationalist reactionaries.[39] These workers preferred, instead, to follow the direction of Savonarola building a society on gospel teachings headed by Christ the King. Pier Giorgio began attending the meetings when he became a member in the autumn of 1919;

37. Savonarola, *Circa il reggimento*, ch. 3. Pier Giorgio was most probably familiar with this work as well as other writings of Savonarola, namely *De ruina mundi*, *Commento al Gloria*, *Esposzione sopra l'orazione della Vergine*, *Commento al Miserere*. Ginoli, *Fra Girolamo Savonarola*, 160.

38. The Dominican Innocenzo Venchi has presented the "Initiative of the Order of Preachers to promote the cause of Beatification for Fra Girolamo Savonarola."

39. Casalegno, *Pier Giorgio Frassati*, 129.

soon after, he became a member of Cesare Balbo, where Father Filippo Robotti was chaplain. With his desire to become closer to the workers, Pier Giorgio turned to the Savonarola Club to respond to this desire.[40] Pier Giorgio often gave talks to the workers in a way that was simple and sincere offering them his genuine warmth and friendship.[41]

Pier Giorgio's religious, theological, and metaphysical sources serve as the basis for his political acts and social commitment.[42] His Christian vocation in the world became clear: "a mission directly contemporaneous in virtue of an indissoluble solidarity in three directions: the expansion of the church, therefore, of grace and of truth; a 'reweaving' of Christian civilization; and a modification of Christian society."[43]

The name of the Dominican Friar, *Fra Girolamo*, reflected Pier Giorgio's fundamental "radicality." Based on his Christian experience taking on a new form of existence with his new name, the choice of *Girolamo* further "invests" Pier Giorgio with an inevitable responsibility whereby customs might not be further corrupted; that is, "that the ideal of Justice be realised."[44] In taking Girolamo's name Pier Giorgio wished to "imitate him in battle and in virtue."[45]

3. Saint Catherine of Siena

In a gift Pier Giorgio offered to his sister, Luciana, Pier Giorgio revealed his love and devotion to Catherine of Siena. In his letters, Pier Giorgio had already expressed his admiration for the Sienese Saint. Catherine, the twenty-third child of twenty-five children, was born in Siena in 1347, and since her childhood she was attentive to the voice and will of God. She refused marriage, but lived with her family while separated from them in her room. With the Dominican convent nearby, she embraced Dominican spirituality and eventually received the habit and cape of the *Mantellate* "invested with a cape" reference to the Tertiary Dominican women. Her charitable work extended from helping the poor with food and clothing, and visiting the sick in hospitals.[46]

40. Casalegno, *Pier Giorgio Frassati*, 129.
41. Casalegno, *Pier Giorgio Frassati*, 130.
42. La Pira, preface to *L'impegno sociale*, 29.
43. La Pira, preface to *L'impegno sociale*, 34.
44. *Positio*, 80.
45. Frassati, *I giorni*, 115.
46. For her complete biography written by her confessor, see Capua, *Catherine of Siena*, 2003.

In 1373, when Catherine was twenty-seven years old, the Dominican Raymond of Capua became her confessor and spiritual director. Catherine's apostolic zeal transformed into political mediation. With political tensions escalating between Siena and Florence, Catherine made her first political journey to Florence.[47] Catherine and her followers traveled throughout central and northern Italy calling the faithful to the "love of God" as a way to reform the clergy and lead believers to repentance and renewal.[48] The Sienese mystic defended the papacy of Pope Gregory XI while anti-papal conflicts continued to spread. Catherine succeeded in preventing Florence and Pisa in allying themselves in an anti-papal front.

In 1375, Catherine began dictating to scribes her thoughts intended for her followers. Her letters spread while she defended peace between republics and principalities as her audience began to include political figures including Pope Gregory XI.[49] Catherine maintained a correspondence with Pope Gregory, "Dear Christ on earth."[50] In her correspondence, Catherine implored the pope to reform both the clergy and administration of Papal States. By 1376, Catherine was sent as ambassador of Florence to Avignon with the intent of securing a peace treaty between Florence and the Papal States. Her unsuccessful mission resulted in criticism on the part of the Florentine leaders, but Catherine replied from Avignon reprimanding the Florentines with severe language. Catherine made the opportunity of her stay in Avignon to persuade Pope Gregory to return to Rome, which he did at the beginning of 1377, six months after Catherine had arrived in Avignon.

Her short life both contemplative and active ended when Catherine was thirty-three years old. The bold Dominican woman, faithful to the Church of Rome and committed to a life of sanctity, politically engaged, offered sufficient motives for Pier Giorgio to be drawn to the spirituality of this *Mantellata*. Catherine's life contained numerous elements already present in the life of Pier Giorgio: concern for the poor, the ill, the vulnerable, and love for the church, which included political expression. Parallels are not difficult to find between Catherine of Siena and Pier Giorgio Frassati.

When Luciana completed her university degree in law in 1923, Pier Giorgio found the gift that he knew was most suitable for his sister: "To my good and dear sister, on the day of her degree, may this book be the guide

---

47. Capua, *Catherine of Siena*, 105–7.

48. Noffke, *Letters of Saint Catherine*, 1–3, and *Chronology*, 32–34.

49. Noffke, *Letters of Saint Catherine*, 1–3, and *Chronology*, 32–34. See also, Capua, *Catherine of Siena*, chapters on "Prophetess" and "Marvellous Ambassadress."

50. Noffke, *Letters of Saint Catherine*, 65, to Pope Gregory XI.

on her ascetic path to spiritual perfection."⁵¹ The book was *La Vita di Santa Caterina*, "The Life of Saint Catherine." Pier Giorgio chose for his sister the figure of a female Dominican Saint whom he found as a source of inspiration on the path to asceticism, a path he sought to share with the one whom he dearly loved. This path, as the dedication expressed, led toward not only an ascetic exercise, but one of "perfection." The commitment to the spiritual life represented not only responsibilities which were fulfilled by a devout Catholic, but beyond these duties, as Pier Giorgio desired to live himself, moving toward perfection. The twenty-three-year-old Luciana, already having achieved her law degree, suggesting "perfection" in her academic and professional life, Pier Giorgio wished to see his sister apply the same diligence, discipline and "perfection," in her spiritual life.

The description of "perfection" in the ascetic life showed that for Pier Giorgio himself, and for his sister, spiritual perfection was also possible outside the structures of religious life or the priesthood. A lay person—Third Order Dominican—he could reach "perfection." However, the fact that Pier Giorgio referred to "ascetic" life also meant the disciple of Christ, the committed Catholic, was not expected and had no reason to live a life of mediocrity. Luke-warmness comparable to the biblical metaphor of the believers who had lost their salt served as reminder, "'You are the salt of the earth; but if salt has lost its taste, how shall its saltness be restored? It is no longer good for anything except to be thrown out and trodden under foot by men.'"⁵² The "perfection," therefore, to which Pier Giorgio referred represented the "life" of the disciple of Christ, just as "salt" represented the "life" of food. Pier Giorgio desired this "life" for himself; he similarly desired this "life" for those whom he loved, and he found in Saint Catherine of Siena in her own *vita*, "life," the example by which he and his sister could both live the summit of the spiritual life.

Pier Giorgio was drawn to the life of Saint Catherine of Siena as revealed in the *Dialogue of Divine Providence;* letters and visions highlighted her communion with God.⁵³ In Saint Catherine, Pier Giorgio found spiritual support for his active side, like Fra Girolamo, social and political. Saint Catherine's life, a contemplative mystic politically active, seeking peace between states defending the Roman Papacy, Pier Giorgio identified with his own aspirations as expressed in Saint Catherine's motto, "doing is always

---

51. Frassati, *Calendario*, "Turin, July 15, 1923." The use of the third person singular in Italian indicates the formal register Pier Giorgio used in writing the dedication to his sister.

52. Matt 5:13.

53. Frassati, *La fede*, "Testimony of Don Pietro Occelli," 205.

good."⁵⁴ Pier Giorgio conveyed his love and devotion for the Sienese Saint in his desire to be united with Christ, "The Saint he 'envied' while living she had spoken to Jesus."⁵⁵ At the end of June, shortly before Pier Giorgio died, he was reading Johannes Jørgensen's *Life of Saint Catherine of Siena* that had been translated from the Danish, the same biography Pier Giorgio had given to his sister for her graduation.⁵⁶ He shared his thoughts on Saint Catherine with his good friend Franz Massetti, "Here, look Saint Catherine had in her own lifetime the gift to see Jesus . . . we instead, must wait until Paradise."⁵⁷

4. Letter to Franz Massetti, January 4, "Holy Year"[58]

Pier Giorgio's detailed letter to his friend Massetti presented his plan for the Holy Year of 1925. The twenty-three-year-old conveyed in his letter spiritual depth and maturity as Pier Giorgio continued to grow from a tiny seed to a rich fruit-bearing tree, nourished by water and sunlight, prayer and sacraments. His letter focused on the papal proclamation of a holy year; Pier Giorgio reflected on the theme of "peace." His project for the year meant in particular spiritual readings. Pier Giorgio's letter further unveiled his Dominican influences; namely, the purity of the Angelic Doctor, Saint Thomas Aquinas.

4.1. Saint Thomas Aquinas

Pier Giorgio made reference to the writings of Saint Thomas Aquinas when he was on his annual spiritual retreat at Santa Croce, March 26, 1923.[59] Pier Giorgio deepened his knowledge of Saint Thomas from the time he began interacting with Father Filippo Robotti and visiting him at the Dominican priory in Turin, in 1921 when he became a member of both Cesare Balbo and the Savonarola Club. Parallels have been drawn between Pier Giorgio

---

54. Massetti, *Pier Giorgio Frassati*, 35–36.

55. Frassati, *I giorni*,189.

56. Jørgensen's work on Saint Catherine was written in 1915. The Italian publication with a letter from the Secretary of the Vatican State, Cardinal Gaspari, November 26, 1919, gave ecclesial approval to the biography, included in the Italian translation. Pier Giorgio read Jørgensen's work on Saint Catherine soon after its publication. In English Jørgensen's, *Saint Catherine of Siena*, 1938.

57. Massetti, *Pier Giorgio Frassati*, 78–79.

58. *Letters*, 193–94; Ital. ed., 285–86.

59. *Letters*, "To Antonio Villani," 122–23.

and Saint Thomas in terms of the social status of the two families, and the radical break with wealth, in seeking to live among the poor, and unite themselves with the poor—Pier Giorgio as a Third Order Dominican, Saint Thomas as a Dominican Friar.[60]

A brief consideration of Saint Thomas's childhood and early adulthood serve to show possible parallels between Pier Giorgio and Aquinas. Thomas was born in 1225 in Aquino, the present-day Lazio region of Italy. Since both parents of Aquinas belonged to southern Italian nobility, they expected and planned for Thomas to follow their uncle as abbot of the Benedictine monastery at Monte Cassino, the abbey where Thomas began his studies at the age of five.[61] But Thomas's parents removed their son from the abbey during the territorial conflict between the emperor Frederick II and Pope Gregory IX when the emperor's soldiers brutally attacked the Benedictine monastery. Thomas's parents decided to send their fourteen-year-old son to Naples to continue his studies. Under the influence of Dominican preachers, a newly established order whose members lived a life of mendicant poverty, the Aquinate decided to join the Dominican Order. Aware that Thomas's mother might interfere with his vocation, the Dominicans decided to remove him from family intrusion, and sent Thomas to Rome and then to Paris. On his journey to Rome, he was captured by his brothers, as instructed by their mother, confined to their family castles for a year. Thomas's unrelenting commitment to his Dominican vocation resulted in his brothers scheming to tempt him with a prostitute, to have him seduced, in the hope he would abandon his Dominican vocation.[62] Instead, Thomas drove the prostitute away with his iron poker, branding a sign of the cross on his cell door. According to tradition, Thomas then dreamed of angels girding him with a cincture preserving him in chastity.

4.1.1. Unlikely Parallels

While parallels have been drawn between Pier Giorgio and Saint Thomas based on social status, and family projects, with both Dominican figures a rupture with the family and the world is suggested; such a reading remains questionable.[63] One needs to examine Pier Giorgio closely to establish the proper parallels between him and his attraction to Saint Thomas Aquinas.

60. Siccardi, *Pier Giorgio Frassati*, 153.
61. Weisheipl, *Friar Thomas D'Aquino*, 10.
62. Weisheipl, *Friar Thomas D'Aquino*, 31.
63. Siccardi makes such parallels between the family of Thomas Aquinas and Pier Giorgio, in *Pier Giorgio Frassati*, 153.

Certainly, the Aquino and Frassati families belonged to the nobility and upper-middle class, respectively; but in the case Saint Thomas a clear break had been made with his family's vocational direction when he was nineteen. The prestige and affluence associated with the nobility, aspiring to build for their son the future of a Benedictine abbot, Thomas flatly rejected and at nineteen years old, allowed himself to be taken by the Dominicans from Naples to Rome to Paris. Such a rupture never occurred with Pier Giorgio; at nineteen years old, Pier Giorgio revealed his own convictions in his numerous activities, spiritual, social and political, but they did not create an opposition between him and his family. In the case of Pier Giorgio and his parents, one sensed mutual respect, and Pier Giorgio did not perform actions that he knew would hurt his parents: where his intentions may have diverged with his mother and father, Pier Giorgio either sought their approval or might find ways to change their mind, if possible, by the intermediary of a priest.

This rupture is clear in the life of Saint Thomas once he decided to join the Dominicans, whereby he would become a mendicant friar, separating himself from his family and the world, and under the complete authority of his religious superiors, living a conventual life of poverty, living a chaste life. Pier Giorgio never broke with the world as such. Pier Giorgio's moral and spiritual life, since his childhood, enabled him to make the proper choices: he did not let enjoyment lead him to a hedonistic ethos or grave sin; he enjoyed the company of his friends who shared the same faith and values, and his involvement in the world was based on his Christian responsibilities both social and political. The rupture simply was not present in the case of Pier Giorgio; rather, the proper daily moral choices of a disciplined life, while in the world, meant Pier Giorgio desired and lived holiness as a lay person. Pleasure, for Pier Giorgio, was manifested in the gratuity of spiritual experience, just as St. Thomas taught: the person's true good is not the sensory pleasure of the body, but rather, the spiritual delight brought to the soul.[64]

4.2. Purity and Spiritual Battle

Pier Giorgio's primary attraction to Saint Thomas was based on Aquinas's purity. Even before Pier Giorgio was reading Saint Thomas's "sublime" works on his Santa Croce retreat in 1923, works offered to Pier Giorgio by his

---

64. *ST*, Ia–IIae, q. 2, a. 6, *resp*.

friend Villani, Pier Giorgio was already drawn by the life of Saint Thomas in terms of how the Angelic Doctor lived the beauty of purity.[65]

He first attached himself to Dominican spirituality in 1921, receiving the medal associated with the Angelic Warfare Confraternity.[66] The *Militia Angelica Divi Thomae Aquinatis*, "Angelic Militia of Saint Thomas Aquinas," was formally established by Pope Benedict XII in 1727; the Militia already began to spread after the death of Aquinas. Pier Giorgio was introduced to the Militia as any twenty-year-old who desired to live a chaste life following Jesus Christ and the teachings of the Catholic Church. The Militia also attracted Pier Giorgio because he was someone who believed in battles for a just and holy society, and Pier Giorgio knew, battles required relentless courage and openness to grace.

The life of Saint Thomas revealed a strategic temptation of the flesh— an attempt by his brothers to have him seduced in his parent's castle by a prostitute. Saint Thomas dreamed that he had been girded with a cord by angels. The cord served as a relic in the Dominican Church of Turin and to which Pier Giorgio was especially devoted— a veneration he desired to share with his friend Franz Massetti.[67] This battle to be pure and to be holy—to be girded—was part of the angelic warfare as described by Saint Paul's letter to the Ephesians, "Finally, be strong in the Lord and in the strength of his might. Put on the whole armor of God, that you may be able to stand against the wiles of the devil. For we are not contending against flesh and blood, but against the principalities, against the powers, against the world rulers of this present darkness, against the spiritual hosts of wickedness in the heavenly places. Therefore take the whole armor of God, that you may be able to withstand in the evil day, and having done all, to stand."[68] The sense of battle, being a member of the *Militia Angelicae*, "Angelic Militia," was so strong, even as an expression of his militant Catholicism, that Pier Giorgio encouraged his friends to join the *Militia* of Christ.[69] Living a chaste life, engaged in battle, represented foremost Pier Giorgio's connection with Saint Thomas.

---

65. "Purity" and relationships will be further considered in chapter 9.

66. Frassati, *La Fede*, 197; Massetti, *Pier Giorgio Frassati*, 49. Luciana Frassati gives the date as April 22, 1921, but Pier Giorgio was in Germany at this time. In fact, the medallion is not part of the Dominican rule, but rather a devotion associated with St. Thomas Aquinas. The Angelic Warfare Confraternity still exists and serves the purpose to defend and protect one's chastity.

67. Massetti, *Pier Giorgio Frassati*, 49.

68. Eph 6:10–13.

69. Frassati, *La fede*, "Testimony of Antionio Villani," 203.

5. Saint Augustine

Pier Giorgio tells Massetti in his Holy Year letter that his readings of Saint Augustine brought him "immense happiness." A few weeks later Pier Giorgio, writing to Isidoro Bonini, quoted Saint Augustine from his *Confessions*, "*Our heart is restless until it rests in you.*"[70] The writings of Augustine deeply moved Pier Giorgio because in Saint Augustine, Pier Giorgio found the same restless heart as his own. The search for true love, a central theme of Saint Augustine, had an impact on Pier Giorgio's own reflection on the experience of love.[71]

The Dominican Order took as their fundamental constitution the Rule of Saint Augustine, and it followed the Augustinian model of prayer, community, study, and apostolate that shaped Dominican life.[72] Pier Giorgio's Augustinian influence was felt in the Rule of Saint Augustine that the Dominicans had adopted. Each of these spiritual characteristics Pier Giorgio sought to realize: prayer which started early in Pier Giorgio's life and intensified in his adolescence with the sacraments; community through his close ties with his family and network of friends; study which Pier Giorgio approached as discipline, duty, and responsibility which he diligently observed; and apostolate which Pier Giorgio expressed concretely in his social and political work. His Third Order Dominican commitment served to deepen each of these four pillars of Dominican life with its Augustinian source.

Saint Augustine's struggles in his search for truth and love as the Doctor of Grace unfolds in his *Confessions*. In Saint Augustine's "restlessness" Pier Giorgio read his own journey seeking truth, and experiencing love, both human and divine. Saint Augustine also echoed the radical message of Saint Paul: the outpouring of love, the sacrifice of Christ.[73]

Questions

(Note: *ST* refers to *Summa Theologiae* of Saint Thomas Aquinas—part [I/II/III], question, article, response)

---

70. St. Augustine, *Confessions*, book 1, chapter 1. See *Letters*, "To Isidoro Bonini, January 25, 1925," 196–97.

71. See chapter 9, following, on "Love."

72. *Liber Constitutionum*, "Incipit Regula Beati Augustini Episcopi," 1–8; see Acts 4:32–35.

73. Rom 3:25.

1. Describe Pier Giorgio's entry and profession as a Lay (Third Order) Dominican (1.2.1).

2. Who was Girolamo Savonarola (2.1)? Why does Pier Giorgio take the name Fra Girolamo (2.2)? What is so radical about Pier Giorgio's choice (2.2)?

3. What are the human qualities, spiritual values, and historical significance in the life of St. Catherine of Siena that resonate with Pier Giorgio (§3)?

4. What especially attracted Pier Giorgio to St. Thomas Aquinas (4.2)? What is the Angelic Warfare Confraternity (4.2)? How does St. Thomas describe true pleasure? (See note 64; *ST*, Ia–IIae, q. 2, a. 6, *resp*).

5. What are the words of St. Augustine that Pier Giorgio connects with (§5)? In which works of St. Augustine are these thoughts expressed (§5)?

6. What is the significance of St. Paul's Epistle to the Romans 3:25 in relation to the quest for truth and love?

9

Love: Purity—Obedience—Sacrifice

> Blessed are the pure in heart, for they shall see God.
>
> MATTHEW 5:8

Pier Giorgio's profound relationships include family and friends experienced in the light of faith. His adult family relations are both emotional and intimate. In terms of Pier Giorgio's friends, one recognizes the sense of purity and sacrifice. The virtue with which Pier Giorgio embraced these relations was motivated by truth and love, obedience to his parents, and ultimately, the will of God. These relations, therefore, convey more than an affective bond or emotional ties. The value of these personal ties carries over to something supernatural because of Pier Giorgio's willingness to make sacrifices, to remain pure, to be obedient. With Pier Giorgio's receptivity to God's grace, he kissed the cross of Christ in his response to make sacrifices. With a pure heart and mind, certainly, Pier Giorgio discerned and collaborated with God's will.

1. Letter to His Mother—Freiburg im Breisgau, October 7, 1921[1]

Pier Giorgio wrote to his mother from Germany where the twenty-year-old was studying German. The letter reveals Pier Giorgio's emotional attachment to his mother; his openness with her had not changed. This relationship between mother and son meant Pier Giorgio could also rely on her to take care of personal matters such as university registration, and trust his mother's judgment in the appropriateness of a gift. Finally, the letter reflected the extent to which Pier Giorgio could share his daily activities with his mother, including German lessons, the cost of room and board, and travels along the Rhine. All this information, Pier Giorgio provided in his characteristic style of detail.

1.1. Maternal Attachment

The role Pier Giorgio's mother had in his education, his moral and sacramental life, and his mountain activities did not begin during his adolescence or adulthood, but Adelaide's involvement in Pier Giorgio's life was felt from the time he was a child.

As a young adult Pier Giorgio took a sip of his mother's Marsala after breakfast and he also smoked the same Tuscan cigars admitting with a smile, "Even my mother smokes Tuscan cigars."[2] The significance of the affective bond inevitably had an influence on how Pier Giorgio interacted with the opposite sex, and his sense of love, emotions and affection from the maternal bond to relational ties. His relationship with his mother enabled Pier Giorgio to experience the purity and gratuity of love that he sought, the selfless love of a mother who genuinely cared about her son's well-being, and he, who had so much love to give in return, to his family, and to his friends. But Pier Giorgio reserved, as the letter expressed, a special love for his mother, "You can't imagine with how much joy I read your letter today, and more so because I found in it a photograph of my dear mama." Pier Giorgio recognized his mother's handwriting on the envelope, and so, while away from home studying in Germany, he looked forward to the mail hoping to receive a letter especially from his mother, waiting for that recognizable calligraphy. His joy in this letter was even greater having the picture of his mother. The absence of his mother diminished somewhat having her picture in front of him: her handwriting—her words—her picture, the

---

1. *Letters*, 51; Ital. ed., 59–60.
2. Frassati, *I giorni*, 90.

visible signs of his mother. The joy Pier Giorgio felt was transmitted to his mother in the spontaneity of his expressed feelings. "So, I'll have you closer and every night I will be able to see you through it." One senses that Pier Giorgio placed the picture of his mother on a shelf where he could see her, think about her, feel her love and in a way, sense her presence. He desired to be with his mother; with the photo he could see her "through it." Pier Giorgio's heart was united with his mother's as he truly loved her, "I'll have you closer every night." Thoughtful words written by a son who longed to be reunited with his mother.

Certainly, Adelaide Frassati loved her son, but the expression was asymmetrical: the enthusiasm and excitement with which Pier Giorgio anticipated his mother's letters and more physically her presence, did not appear to be reciprocated on the part of his mother. This reflected Adelaide's personality; she wanted the best for her children, and she was involved in their lives, but at an emotional level, she remained distant. Pier Giorgio by comparison was thrilled to just have a picture of his mother with him.

Whether this emotional distance on the part of Adelaide was deliberate or not, it in fact, proved emotionally healthy for Pier Giorgio because his mother's distance provided Pier Giorgio the freedom he needed to develop other relationships, friendships; meaningful, genuine, honest friendships with men and women. In this regard, Adelaide's emotional ties with Pier Giorgio proved to be selfless and not self-focused. Pier Giorgio was pure, self-giving, and spontaneous in how he expressed his love because of his innocence in mind and heart. In return, Pier Giorgio's mother contributed to her son's emotional freedom manifested in his numerous friendships, healthy relations, and spiritual bonds.

1.2. Pier Giorgio's Mother Writes

The following year in July 1922, while Pier Giorgio's mother hiked in Antagnod d'Ayas, Valle d'Aosta, the Italian Alps, she wrote to Pier Giorgio who was in Turin at the time. The letter expressed the maternal sentiments from mother to son,

> Antangod d'Ayas 22-7-22,
> My dear Giorgetto, my beautiful and good boy, your letter did me so much good! I feel that even if everyone left me, that if I even felt everything fall apart around me, I will always have my strong and good big boy to support me. And when I lecture you for so many little things (the little things, at times in daily relations become big) is precisely why I think of your solid and good

qualities and I should perfect you (for your good) in the small things. I.e., that of shaving in the morning (5 minutes) would be a little thing and you would please everybody. And you can sleep—you must—for your health to sleep a lot of hours—either in the evening or in the morning (better in the evening) so, organize your schedule to have these hours—at your age they should be 8 and with the body and spirit rested you could with better and more success attend to your duties.

Papa writes a long enthusiastic letter that he is happy with your exam.

I embrace you very tightly and I send you every blessing,
Your Mamma[3]

The letter Pier Giorgio's mother wrote unveils something of their relationship. Adelaide wrote to her son addressing him in the diminutive, "Giorgetto," expressing her love for him, recognizing his goodness, *buono*, and his beautiful, *bello*, soul. She clearly described Pier Giorgio as a pillar of strength for her. Adelaide knew her son's heart, how much Pier Giorgio loved his mother. One can recognize the extent to which Adelaide fulfilled her role as mother who "lectures" her son "daily" for what may have appeared to be small things; she in fact, wished to see her twenty-one-year-old son continue to grow with a sense of moral responsibility and discipline. A key word that Adelaide employed in her vocabulary was the verb, "perfect." She recognized her son's goodness and wished to see Pier Giorgio perfected in that goodness. This perfection certainly fell within the Catholic tradition of how a person should continue to grow spiritually, morally and intellectually. Such growth formed the basis of Catholic education. Adelaide's concern for her son, and this Pier Giorgio knew, was not that of an intrusive mother, but rather, a mother who loved her son and truly cared for his good.

The letter also included a degree of humor, or sarcasm, which may also be a sign of where Pier Giorgio received his own sense of humor uniting love with joy. His mother brought up the main point of the letter; it was not written just to tell him how good and beautiful he was. The issue was "shaving in the morning (5 minutes)." She even indicated to Pier Giorgio how much time it would save him to shave conveying the message that something so small would please so many. The letter, therefore, served a twofold objective: to have Pier Giorgio shave, and to have him get a proper night's rest.

Adelaide also informed her son that she had heard from Papa who had written with pleasure regarding Pier Giorgio's exam results. This mutual love between mother and son did not diminish the sense of duty, nor was

---

3. My translation of Adelaide Frassati's letter to her son. I am grateful to Wanda Gawronska for the use of this letter.

this love at the expense of his responsibilities. Hygiene, proper rest, studies, were all included and expressed Adelaide's love for her son.

2. Letter to Laura Hidalgo—Forte dei Marmi, August 11, 1924[4]

Pier Giorgio's letter to Hidalgo contained three levels of thoughts, personal, relating daily activities, social, in reference to Tipi Loschi, and spiritual, when he considered their union in faith. Although Pier Giorgio had personal feelings for Hidalgo, one would never know how he felt by the way he wrote his letters to her.

2.1. Laura Hidalgo

Pier Giorgio got to know Laura Hidalgo February 11, 1923, at a Carnevale event which he experienced with his friends from the student section of the Italian Alpine Club.[5] The Carnevale activities in preparation for Lent, "farewell," *vale*, to "meat," *carne*, took place at the Piccolo San Bernardo. During these pre-Lenten activities on the Piccolo San Bernardo, Pier Giorgio discovered a personal affection develop for a friend, Laura Hidalgo.[6] His first letter to Laura was not written until he sent a postcard letter from Bergamo, June 8, 1924, well over a year after he felt an affection toward her.[7] Yet, Pier Giorgio had the chance to spend more time with her as members of the Tipi Loschi, having written to Laura after the Tipi Loschi foundation May 18. Pier Giorgio was very discrete keeping his affection a secret; even with his close friends; his letters do not make any specific reference to her, but rather, allusion to his suffering. In all Pier Giorgio wrote seven letters to Laura, the last one being April 30, 1925.[8]

Laura Hidalgo was actually three years older than Pier Giorgio and as her surname indicated, her father was of Spanish origin. At twenty years old, with her mother and father already deceased, Laura was left an orphan with her younger brother for whom she was responsible. Pier Giorgio knew Laura from Massimo D'Azeglio where they both studied; then, Pier Giorgio

---

4. *Letters*, 166–67; Ital. ed., 232–33.

5. CAI student section was abbreviated SUCAI, University Students Italian Alpine Club.

6. *Positio*, 147. Reference to the Carnevale is in *Letters*, "To Antonio Villani, Turin, February, 1923," 119–20.

7. *Lettere*, Ital. ed., 213–14.

8. *Letters*, 231.

also knew Laura from Gaetana Agnesi, since the Catholic female students shared certain activities with the male students of Cesare Balbo. During the Carnevale excursion to Piccolo San Bernardo, Pier Giorgio discovered his attraction to Laura.

Pier Giorgio had a spontaneous and energetic personality, but when it came to his personal life of affection and sentiments he was reserved and discrete. He asked Luciana if she could invite both Laura and another girl whom he met at the Carnevale events for tea. Inviting the two girls for tea with Luciana as intermediary, Pier Giorgio intended to observe his mother's reaction to Laura—a carefully thought-out means of maintaining discretion of his feelings toward Laura. Adelaide Frassati, however, knew Laura as a child as well as her family. The Hidalgo family lived in the same house as Pier Giorgio's paternal grandmother, Giuseppina Coda Canati Frassati, and Pier Giorgio's uncle, zio Pietro.[9] Neither Luciana nor their mother suspected that Pier Giorgio might have any feelings toward Laura, especially since Laura was identified by their mother as a typical "Azione Cattolica girl."[10]

Based on his August 2, 1924, letter, Pier Giorgio met with Laura at Quericianella three months following the foundation of the Tipi Loschi Society.[11] Pier Giorgio wrote eight letters to his friends in August 1924 making references to the planned visit to Quericianella and (or) Laura, then followed with reference to the actual visit.[12] In all these letters, except two, Pier Giorgio remained discrete, suggesting a casual visit without revealing his true feelings for Laura. The Tipi Loschi Society enabled him to refer to the D.d.g., Laura, within the context of the friendly society in which they both actively participated. Only in his letters to Bertini did Pier Giorgio convey his sentiments for Laura, and in his letter to Severi Pier Giorgio opened himself in terms of how he might approach this matter, "When I find the right moment to speak to my sister I will also tell the particulars of this visit,

---

9. Siccardi, *Pier Giorgio Frassati*, 256. Their residence was located at Via Avogadro, 26, Turin.

10. Frassati, *Beatitudes*, 97. Personal communication, Wanda Gawronska, May 2016.

11. *Letters*, "To Gian Maria Bertini, Viareggio, August 2, 1924," 162.

12. References to Pier Giorgio's planned visit (August 1924) to Quercianella/Laura Hidalgo, *Lettere*, Ital. ed., "To Gian Maria Bertini, Viareggio, August 2," 225; "To Marco Beltramo, Forte dei Marmi, August 5," 226–27; "To Marco Beltramo, Forte dei Marmi, August," 229–30; "To Laura Hidalgo, August 11," 232–33. After his visit with Laura Hidalgo, the crucial letter, "To Antoni Severi, Forte dei Marmi, August 13," 234. References to the actual visit, "To Clementina Luotto, Forte dei Marmi, August 13," 235; "To Marco Beltramo, Forte de Marmi, August," 237; "To Marco Beltramo, Pollone, August 24," 243–44. *Letters*, English edition, include, August 2, (Bertini), August 5 (Beltramo), August 11 (Hidalgo).

but for now diplomacy and my mother's poor state of health require me to be cautious."[13]

About four months later, Pier Giorgio finally revealed his sentiments for Laura to his sister, on December 18, telling Luciana that he was "in love."[14] Luciana transmitted to Pier Giorgio the "negative verdict" for a future with Laura.[15] Pier Giorgio did not wish to say anything to his mother, as he related to Luciana, as it "would be the final blow." With his mother's poor health and difficult marriage, Pier Giorgio was advised by Luciana not to see Laura, but Pier Giorgio expressed uncertainty in the matter since he and Laura shared the Tipi Loschi and other mountain activities. His apprehension built up under the difficult circumstances, even if he might have "plans for the future," but finally, "I cannot for I do not want to leave mamma."[16]

Pier Giorgio had not spoken to Laura of his love for her, not even any allusion to his sentiments. For this love, for both Laura and his mother, he was "the one to be sacrificed."[17] Pier Giorgio preferred to sacrifice his relationship with Laura in silence and in prayer. His own sister's marriage set for January 24, 1925, Luciana would leave home to join her husband moving to the Netherlands. With only Pier Giorgio remaining at home, Laura would serve only to exacerbate the already difficult marriage between his parents. If he also left his parents, the departure might have triggered the collapse in the marriage and separation. Sacrifice was the solution—sacrificing himself.

3. Letter to Isidoro Bonini—Modane Turin, December 28, 1924[18]

Pier Giorgio's letter to his friend Bonini, at the end of December 1924, made reference to a novel he had read by Italo Angeloni, *I Loved That Way*. Angeloni's romantic narrative, especially the first part, resembled Pier Giorgio's personal struggles, how much Laura meant to him, and the inevitable sacrifice being made of Pier Giorgio which he willingly accepted. A number of key terms and phrases were used to express Pier Giorgio's feelings, and the way he experienced love spiritually at the level of his faith: "I loved that way," "sacrificed," "Holy Will," "pure Love," "renouncing," "Christian strength," "Goal," and "true joy."

13. *Letters*, "To Antoni Severi, Forte dei Marmi, August 13, 1924," 234.
14. Frassati, *I giorni*, 137–38.
15. Frassati, *Beatitudes*, 97.
16. Frassati, *Beatitudes*, 98.
17. Frassati, *Beatitudes*, 98.
18. *Letters*, 190; Ital. ed., 281–82.

3.1. "I Loved That Way"

Referring to the Italian (Piemontese) novelist Italo Mario Angeloni and his romance, *Ho amato così*, the title reflects the depth of Pier Giorgio's "letting go," or *renuncio*, "I loved that way."[19] Angeloni's romance opens with the "The Escape." The tragic love story begins between the protagonist, "Giorgio," and a sixteen-year-old Andalusian; they share a passionate but chaste love.[20] The narrative is written from Giorgio's perspective of memory/reality, past/present, dream/delusion, but rather blurred, unsurprisingly, with a soldier reminiscing of his past after a war. Giorgio's mother and father, family and friends have all died. In the novel, the ex-combatant is afraid to die before shouting his poem of love, and closes his eyes as the sun sets as if the bell tolls for someone dying. He remembers in his youth falling in love with the sixteen-year-old, "Bianca," the daughter of the Contessa of Vamorello.[21] He sees his beloved's castle, and *La Madonna del Piola*, then, his own portrait, a "yellowed" twenty-year-old. The reminiscing soldier thinking of Bianca, asks, "How did you know how to suffer without dying?" and continues in his thoughts, "Solitude of war breaks the melancholy of the mountains in a scream." In the novel, Contessa Vamorello brings Bianca to the Convent of Santa Fosca to visit the Contessa's sister who is also the mother superior, Sister Claudia. Giorgio suspected this would be the "prologue of his drama," *il prologo del nostro drama*.[22]

As Giorgio describes his journey in the Ligurian countryside of northwestern Italy, across the snow-covered hills, accompanied by the sound of church bells, the white layered pines, changing trains, his thoughts remain focused on his beloved Andalusian. From one vignette to the next, Giorgio appears to physically journey to whatever his destination might be. As he exits the train, he approaches, she who sleeps, telling her not to wake up, "If you wake up, love will kill you. Love is anxiety. Love is agony in every hour for the entire life."[23] Giorgio is obsessed with his beloved Andalusian and their love story, "This heart, this white road, this perfume of spring, in the midst of winter, is the reality created from the dream to love you, and to love means to die."[24] Giorgio is traveling to Genoa by train, but the only reality

---

19. Angeloni, *Ho amato così*, 1925. The original publication date is given as 1922 which indicates that Pier Giorgio read the work soon after its publication.

20. The "Giorgio" in Angeloni's romance is not to be confused with Pier Giorgio who writes about the romance.

21. Angeloni, *Ho amato così*, 3–4.

22. *Ho amato così*, 34.

23. *Ho amato così*, 12.

24. *Ho amato così*, 13.

seems to be the Andalusian, the reality of his failed dream.[25] By the end of novel, *il renuncio*, "The Renouncing"—Giorgio renounces everything, and dramatically submits himself to the will of God.[26]

Pier Giorgio identified specifically with the first part, "The Escape," in which he identified with the Andalusian, who is willing to sacrifice her love knowing, "you will not return anymore."[27] Why does Pier Giorgio identify with the Andalusian, but himself as the one being sacrificed? Pier Giorgio's affection was chaste, deeply guided by religious sentiment, not unlike the Andalusian, but in Pier Giorgio's case, *io sarò il sacrificato*, "I will be the one sacrificed."

3.1.1. "That Way" in Pier Giorgio's Sacrifice

Pier Giorgio reflected on Angeloni's romance, "I am moved because it seems like my own love story." He then added in this letter, "only that in the novel it is the woman who made the sacrifice while in my case I will be sacrificed." Pier Giorgio considered the nature of "sacrifice," his entire reason for relating the story to Bonini. Pier Giorgio felt he was the object of the sacrifice. Whether a subject makes a sacrifice of one's own being, or whether a person is object of a sacrifice, the will is engaged. The individual accepts or refuses to make, or be made, sacrifice. In the case of Pier Giorgio, he willingly entered into the sacrifice: he chose to accept being made a sacrifice, he is subject and object.

The sacrifice was inseparable from the will of God.[28] In mid-December 1924, Pier Giorgio discussed the subject of Laura with his sister, and the letter which followed to Bonini two weeks after writing to Luciana expressed the "sacrifice." Pier Giorgio "renounces" what he described as "pure love" on the day he wrote Bonini, December 28. Not going to Piccolo San Bernardo where Pier Giorgio would have met Laura, he desired her happiness; Pier Giorgio renounced his love. He had been reflecting and praying for over two weeks since his conversation with Luciana; by not going to Piccolo San Bernardo, with a firmness of will, his painful decision was made concrete.

Pier Giorgio's absence from San Bernardo meant the beginning of carrying out this *rinunzio*, "renouncing," the start of months of inner turmoil and suffering. Pier Giorgio already understood he had to "bear the pain,"

25. *Ho amato così*, 14.
26. *Ho amato così*, 199.
27. *Ho amato così*, 36.
28. Angeloni's novel ends with Giorgio praying on his knees in a Dominican priory entrusting himself to the will of God. *Ho amato così*, 99.

but his will was not one of Stoic effort as he had admitted, but based on "Christian strength," and for this, Pier Giorgio "urged" Bonini to pray to God. Pier Giorgio did not just want to bear this "broken dream," but to bear it peacefully. The "Goal"—put in the first person plural, "for which we were created," and he cited Saint Augustine's *Confessions*, the "Goal" signified God.

Pier Giorgio made allusion to his condition from late-December 1924 onward, but his cryptic language avoided references to Laura and the nature of the "sacrifice." What mattered was doing the will of God. Instead, he repeatedly asked for prayers. He wrote to Laura January 22, 1924, congratulating her ironically on a "successful" mountain excursion.[29] The letter concluded with the possibility of the meeting of the two hiking groups on the summit of the Denti Di Cumiana. Even though a cordial mountain hike letter, the writing suggested that Pier Giorgio must have fought with tremendous difficulty not to be in the presence of Laura, though he allowed himself the hope of spending some time with her. Pier Giorgio had avoided going to Piccolo San Bernardo the previous month; so, did Pier Giorgio have second thoughts about Laura and this "renounced" love? They were members of Tipi Loschi and mountain activities were being planned. The hikes did not change; he played Robespierre, and Laura acted as secretary.

In his long letter to Bonini March 6, 1925, Pier Giorgio brought closure to the possibility of a future with Laura, "... only because the matter is now over and it's better not to talk about it anymore but to close this episode in my life forever."[30] While the "matter" might be closed it did not mean that Pier Giorgio did not continue to suffer. Writing to Beltramo April 29, 1925, Pier Giorgio explained he finally paid his debit to Laura and offered her as a gift Saint Paul's Letters in Latin with an Italian translation.[31] The last excursion together was connected to the Tipi Loschi foundation day, May 18, 1925. Pier Giorgio wrote to the president, Clementina Luotto, sending her two gentians that he and Laura picked.[32]

3.2. Will of God

The thoughts carried on in Pier Giorgio's letter to show his willingness to cooperate with God's will, "if that is how God wants it, His Holy Will be

---

29. *Letters*, "To Laura Hidalgo, Turin, January 22, 1925," 203. Further discussed in section 5, below.

30. *Letters*, "To Isidoro Bonini, Turin, March 6, 1925," 215–16.

31. *Lettere*, Ital. ed., "To Marco Beltramo, Turin, April 28, 1925," 337–38. See also, *Letters*, "To Marco Beltramo, Turin, March 30, 1925," 220–22.

32. *Lettere*, Ital. ed., "To Clementina Luotto, Turin, May 18, 1925," 346.

done." In other words, the resignation to the sacrifice was being reconciled with the will of God—how God wants it. Pier Giorgio interpreted the events around him in order to discern the will of God, not putting his own desires and dreams first, but what God asked of him which meant sacrificing his love for Laura. Luciana's "negative verdict" with regards to Laura remained decisive in Pier Giorgio's discernment. For Pier Giorgio, God's will was not simply a matter of what he wanted while ignoring events and others around him; he understood God's will included a sacrifice to be made of him.

Pier Giorgio sought to resolve the interior tension of sacrifice: the human desire of his heart and the supernatural desire to be united with the will of God. Franz Massetti, one of Pier Giorgio's close friends, wrote on this subject of God's will in his biography of Pier Giorgio.[33] Reflecting on the life of Pier Giorgio in his relationship with Laura, Massetti found in Pier Giorgio, "the fear not to correspond to the invitation of grace."[34] To create the dichotomy, between marrying Laura, according to Massetti, in what had become a fragile family context with the marriage and departure of Luciana, were not the reasons motivating Pier Giorgio's decision. The question for Pier Giorgio sought to answer: what God wanted of him. What would please God? Pier Giorgio needed to resolve this inner tension of love for Laura and love for his family, both loves being natural.[35] Perhaps his vocation was to work among the miners where he could continue his apostolate to bring Christ and his church to the workers. Testifying to the gospel and the teachings of Christ, regardless with whom or where, was what mattered. For Pier Giorgio, each vocation had the call to testify the love of Christ. As Massetti showed, at the end, what mattered was to give oneself to God for others without any limit.[36] In the same month of December, Pier Giorgio wrote to his friend Villani, telling him, "I hope with the Grace of God to continue along the path of Catholic ideals, and to be able one day, in whatever state God wills, to defend and propagate these rare and true things."[37]

One cannot overlook the depth of Massetti's observation when it comes to the life of Pier Giorgio, but a significant point is lacking in Massetti's writings: while love for neighbor whether a future spouse or family is something natural, as Massetti maintains, the sacrifice, which was unquestionably what Pier Giorgio was being asked to make was not at all natural. Sacrifice was not possible without God's grace, without the gratuitous love

33. Massetti, *Pier Giorgio Frassati*, 54.
34. Massetti, *Pier Giorgio Frassati*, 54.
35. Massetti, *Pier Giorgio Frassati*, 56.
36. Massetti, *Pier Giorgio Frassati*, 56.
37. *Letters*, "To Antonio Villani, Turin, December 16, 1924," 187.

associated with sacrifice of Christ offering himself. The Christian sacrifice Pier Giorgio understood: the oblation of oneself. The supernatural sacrifice for Pier Giorgio was possible because of his openness to the will of God, allowing himself to be "sacrificed" because he knew something greater awaited him, namely, eternal life.

4. Letter to Marco Beltramo—Turin, January 25, 1925[38]

In the midst of Pier Giorgio's suffering expressed in both letters to Bonini on December 28, and to Beltramo almost one month later, January 25, the day after his sister's wedding, Pier Giorgio manifested his capacity to recognize the work of God, the will of God, in the midst of his pain. Pier Giorgio's desire to be one with God enabled him to live his suffering in joy. Within one month he had experienced two emotionally dramatic events, the closed future with Laura and the inevitable departure of his sister. Yet, Pier Giorgio was capable of seeing God continuously at work, in spite of his emotional brokenness because he focused on the good of the other, rather than his own happiness. He desired Laura's happiness, and similarly he expressed happiness for his sister. Pier Giorgio did not deny his feelings, admitting, "yesterday the separation was terrible."

However, Pier Giorgio was not absorbed in self-pity, either, someone preoccupied with his own misery, and trying to find others to blame. He even communicated in his letter, and with good humor, Laura directing an outing to the Sagra of Saint Michael "without succeeding in arriving and finding the Sagra; "it doesn't get any better than that," *più di così muore*, literally, "more than that you die," a way of conveying the irony of the expedition, and no doubt, Pier Giorgio had a good friendly laugh.[39]

4.1. Luciana's Marriage

Pier Giorgio began his letter to Beltramo reflecting on the value of the "Rites of the Catholic Church." What the church taught, Pier Giorgio believed and adhered to, as he knew the church continued the salvific mission of Jesus Christ. The sacraments, therefore, he embraced wholeheartedly since he had chosen frequent confession and communion already as a young adolescent. He participated at the wedding of his own sister, emotionally intense, reflecting Pier Giorgio's sensitive disposition, a witness to the marriage

---

38. *Letters*, 203–4; Ital. ed., 295.

39. The sense of "joy" for Pier Giorgio will be taken up in chapter 10, section 4.1.

of his friend from childhood and daily companionship that Luciana had brought him. He acknowledged being ripped of his sister's presence, and the "separation."[40]

The letter Pier Giorgio wrote focused instead on the richness of the sacrament of marriage that he described as "magnificent," and recognized the spiritual emptiness of the civil marriage in comparison, calling it "comical." His appreciation of the sacrament reflected its richness not only liturgically, but its content, the lifetime commitment expressed in the sacramental union, the parallels between Christ's body and his church, the union between man and wife.[41] Pier Giorgio considered civil marriage comical because it lacked commitment, and civil marriage was emptied of its religious value. The sacramentality of marriage, its religious significance, reflected divine order, the union of man and woman leading to the generation of new life. Society, community, family, all have their source in this natural union between man and woman, as God created the world according to an order that he willed, "This is why a man leaves his father and mother and becomes attached to his wife, and they become one flesh."[42] Pier Giorgio accepted the validity of a civil marriage as a temporary solution, hoping that civil marriage would ultimately be abolished. He recognized the meaning of the sacramental marriage in which Christ himself was present. Pier Giorgio did not negotiate the truth: marriage was either true or false.

As a marriage gift Pier Giorgio purchased for his sister an ivory crucifix. While the crucifix to Luciana appeared "more suitable to the sadness of a funeral than the joy of the wedding,"[43] Pier Giorgio quite satisfied with the gift, had Archbishop Giuseppe Gamba bless it, the same archbishop who blessed Luciana's marriage to Jan Gawronski.[44]

Pier Giorgio described the separation from his sister as a "shot in the heart," *colpo nel cuore*, to convey to his friend Beltramo the intensity felt of Luciana's departure.[45] Pier Giorgio conveyed this pain in a few words, but

40. With Luciana's marriage to the Polish diplomat Jan Gawronski, she would be leaving with her husband for The Hague on a diplomatic assignment in the Netherlands.

41. Eph 5:22–33.

42. Gen 2:24.

43. The beautiful ivory crucifix is fixed over Adelaide's bed in her Pollone bedroom now used as an oratory.

44. Frassati, *Beatitudes*, 113.

45. Photograph in the *Letters*, 202, shows the glances exchanged between Pier Giorgio, very elegantly dressed, and his sister in her bridal dress and white veil. Luciana describes Pier Giorgio dressing himself for the occasion, "Pier Giorgio put on society clothes with moans and groans. He was helped by a maid to straighten the notoriously crooked tie, and insert the pearls in the tiny button holes, which drove him mad." Frassati, *Beatitudes*, 114.

Luciana's testimony provides for a far more vivid description of the event: "At the station, when it was time to leave me, he broke down crying desperately, unstoppable, such that he had even upset, besides me, all those present."[46] Luciana's comments related Pier Giorgio's reaction she had not expected, but also, the surprise of everyone present with Pier Giorgio's emotions, "desperate" and "unstoppable." Luciana Frassati realized she could not leave her brother in the painful farewell at the Turin train station, "He trembled all over, falling almost dry from his eyes burning with pain. He could not form whole words; they came out with a stammer that almost turned into a scream. I reassured him telling him we would see each other in a few days because it was impossible for me to leave Italy with that vision of him."[47] Pier Giorgio wrote to Luciana shortly after her departure from Italy, seeking some form of her presence to fill the physical distance and vacuum caused by his sister's absence: "Write to me often because at least receiving your letters can fill the great emptiness which you have left among us." With Luciana's departure, Pier Giorgio came to realize the separation meant more than a few days, "but for a life and only to see one another from time to time." His emotional and sensitive state did not only reflect Luciana's absence, but also his concern for their mother, "Write especially to mamma so that she can live happily, you were the one who lifted all of Mamma's burdens."[48]

The absence of his sister was felt, and Pier Giorgio did not hide his longing for his sister's presence, "write to me often." But he also explained why, "your letters can fill the enormous void." Luciana's departure came at a difficult time for Pier Giorgio because he was already attempting to resolve his relationship with Laura. As the director of excursions, Laura would be present at the Tipi Loschi activities. Whether Pier Giorgio should participate as he had done with the Piccolo San Bernardo on December 29, added to the anxiety, exacerbated by Luciana's departure one month later. The overall emotional context for the very sensitive Pier Giorgio proved extremely painful.

In the midst of this emotional upheaval, however, Pier Giorgio, having expressed the "void" he experienced, proceeded to thoughts of his mother in his letter. He asked Luciana to "especially write mama so she can live happily." He acknowledged the emptiness he felt but he did not end focused on his separation from his sister. Instead, he directed his thoughts to Luciana, "who lifted Mamma's burdens"; his mother's health especially worried Pier

---

46. *Letters*, 208n1; Ital. ed., 302n1.
47. Frassati, *Beatitudes*, 115.
48. *Letters*, "To Luciana, Turin, February 4, 1925," 208.

Giorgio. In the midst of his emotional turbulence, Pier Giorgio focused on the well-being of others, his mother in this instance, rather than himself.

Luciana's paternal grandmother, Giuseppina Coda Canati Frassati, gave to Luciana three thousand Lire as a wedding gift of which she sent one thousand Lire to Pier Giorgio. Luciana, however, told her brother that the one thousand Lire were meant for Pier Giorgio, "This is for you not for your poor." Pier Giorgio had never possessed such a significant sum of money, "the first thousand Lire note he possessed."[49] Instead, Pier Giorgio divided the amount between the Cesare Balbo Club and the Conference of Saint Vincent de Paul with the donations sent in Luciana's name.[50]

5. Letter to Isadoro Bonini—Turin, March 6, 1925[51]

In early March 1925, Pier Giorgio's letter to Bonini expressed a pivotal moment in his life, "a change within me." By the month of March, Pier Giorgio reflected especially on God's will, desiring obedience to his holy will, but also how sacrifices are made. He stated, "It was not his doing" because of the "firm measure" that this change in him entailed. Sacrifice seemed to suggest being "sad," having to "suffer," and all this "unwillingly." Pier Giorgio asked himself in his reflection whether he had felt this way because he lost his faith, and acknowledged he did not lose his faith. He realized that the one "joy" that the believer possessed was "faith." As a result, rather than focusing on his sacrifice, or that he was being sacrificed in his union with the will of God, Pier Giorgio recognized the "joy" of having "faith." Sacrifice, therefore, becomes "worthwhile" because it manifested the person's faith and, indeed, this brought joy.

Pier Giorgio considered the love that Catholics possess, "which surpasses every other love." The love of Catholics Pier Giorgio qualified as "immensely beautiful," just as the Catholic "religion" he described as "beautiful." In the midst of his suffering, Pier Giorgio's faith enabled him to experience not only joy, but also the beauty of love in the Catholic faith. A shift from what could have been sadness and suffering, to love, joy and beauty, all as a result of his sacrifice. But as he emphasized, this "change" in him was rooted in his faith.

Saint Paul's discourse on love, nourished Pier Giorgio's heart and soul, drawing from Saint Paul's Epistle, "If I speak in the tongues of men and of angels, but have not love, I am a noisy gong or a clanging cymbal. And if

---

49. Frassati, *Beatitudes*, 113.
50. *Letters*, "To Luciana, Turin, February, 14, 1925," 210–11.
51. *Letters*, 215–16; Ital. ed., 313–14.

I have prophetic powers, and understand all mysteries and all knowledge, and if I have all faith, so as to remove mountains, but have not love, I am nothing. If I give away all I have, and if I deliver my body to be burned, but have not love, I gain nothing."[52] Pier Giorgio's reflection on Saint Paul underscored the centrality of love for the Christian, and Pier Giorgio understood Saint Paul's message as Christ had taught, as the Catholic Church continued to teach "just as our religion is beautiful" that does not separate love from sacrifice. Pier Giorgio understood Saint Paul's Letter from his personal journey, and thereby, encountered Christ at the cross of sacrifice. The possession of talents, gifts and skills, even spiritual ones, without love, were all quite meaningless. Saint Paul's words Pier Giorgio lived by, fundamentally, placing his love for God above all and the sacrifices this entailed. Pier Giorgio understood with the grace of God, "love" motivated his life program, his "goal," which reflected the goal he had discerned, that goal for which his soul would "strive." Pier Giorgio also admitted that this plan, "God's Will," contained more "thorns" than "roses," and yet, with God's help, this he discerned as God's program for him to follow. He put his "trust" in God's "Providence" and God's "mercy."

Considering his own spiritual development, Pier Giorgio realized the value of Pope Pius X encouraging frequent communion, which Pier Giorgio enthusiastically responded to as a young adolescent. By acknowledging the role played by his family, teachers and friends, Pier Giorgio conveyed his humility, his incapacity to grow spiritually on his own: he depended on others, just as a plant depended on sunlight and water for nourishment to grow. While he recognized he needed others, Pier Giorgio drew from the sacraments of the church. This dependency on God, sacraments and community in the journey toward eternal life expressed what it meant to be a Catholic, walking together in prayer as part of the communion of saints, "parents, teachers, friends," guiding him, together, testimonies of Christian living.

Pier Giorgio's faith was equivalent to being alive, "If I had the misfortune of not believing, life would not be worth living." Faith, Pier Giorgio came to realize, gave life meaning. Without faith, sacrifice did not serve any purpose; without faith, sacrifice was not even possible. The letter to Bonini was the product of the mature experience and reflection on "sacrifice," the necessity of the offering ultimately of himself "because" the person whom he desired was "not willed." Pier Giorgio was willing to go as far as stating even if the sacrifice cost him his "earthly life," it mattered little. Life on earth, Pier Giorgio understood, prepared for something far greater, eternity, where all the believers would experience the perfection of love.

---

52. 1 Cor 13:2–3.

Questions

1. How does Pier Giorgio express his attachment toward his mother (§1; October 1921; 1.1)? In what way does Adelaide show concern for her son's well-being (1.2)?

2. Why does Pier Giorgio remain silent about Laura Hidalgo (2.1)? To whom does he confide his interest in Laura (2.1)?

3. What is the significance of Pier Giorgio's letter to Isidoro (§3; December 1924)?

4. Why is Pier Giorgio deeply moved by Italo Angeloni's novel, *I Loved That Way* (3.1)?

5. How does Pier Giorgio understand the role of sacrifice in his life (3.1.1)? How does Pier Giorgio understand the will of God (3.2)?

6. What is Pier Giorgio's emotional reaction when his sister marries (§4; January 1925; 4.1)? How does Pier Giorgio express himself in his letter to Isadoro Bonini (§5; March 1925)?

10

Pier Giorgio's Eschatological Vision

*Love or charity, endures forever or rather
I believe it will be even more alive in the next life.*

PIER GIORGIO, "LETTER TO CLEMENTINA LUOTTO, APRIL 23, 1925"

This final chapter brings together Pier Giorgio's Christian life firmly rooted in the reality of the world he lived in; yet, Pier Giorgio's sense of direction—or goal—motivated all his choices: Pier Giorgio's Catholic eschatological vision permeated his very being. Following Catholic teaching, Pier Giorgio experienced life as a pilgrim journey attentive to the needs of others. His sacrifices were directed ultimately toward the life Christ promised: the resurrection of the living and the dead. Final judgment, Pier Giorgio believed in, sustaining his receptivity to help others to the point of contracting a deadly disease as he visited and cared for the poor. Such commitment to the destitute within the framework of the Christian eschaton reflected the rapid maturation of Pier Giorgio's Catholic faith. The world's moral and social misery found ultimate expression in Pier Giorgio's eschatological vision.

1. Letter to Willibald Leitgebel—Turin, February 3, 1923[1]

In his February letter of 1923 to Leitgebel, Pier Giorgio reaffirmed the teachings of the Catholic faith, "this life is short," and reassured his distraught friend that, "only afterwards comes true Life in which Justice will triumph." The words of comfort Pier Giorgio offered had their source in Scriptures, "'Truly, I say to you, as you did it not to one of the least of these, you did it not to me. And they will go away into eternal punishment, but the righteous into eternal life.'"[2]

1.1. Divine Justice

The sense of justice where goodness will be rewarded remained clear in Pier Giorgio's eschatological vision: on earth evil may appear victorious, but God's justice does not allow this, and in the afterlife, where "justice will triumph," God will reward the good, the poor and suffering, accordingly.

Pier Giorgio's religious convictions prompted him to pray and he reassured his friends his prayers, but his desire to supplement prayer with material support remained fixed in his mind: what could he do to help those who suffered? Away from Germany and his German friends, he offered the little he saved from his frugal funds to put aside his surplus for the needy who relied on him, or who referred to him for help, "Take this money, please, for the poor children of Berlin: it's only a little but it's better than nothing." These acts of charity were indicative of Pier Giorgio's sense of moral responsibility not only to others, but what God expected of him as a believer, as a disciple of Christ, as the Scriptures clearly taught.

Pier Giorgio realized that the Versailles Treaty represented human justice, which was not true justice, that is, the justice of God. The sense of justice for Pier Giorgio effected his perception of society and government, and whether in the streets of Turin or Berlin, he admitted that human laws were deficient. Only the gospel could truly change society, but since governments failed to implement gospel values, and innocent people continued to suffer the consequences of political coercion and nationalist ambitions, Pier Giorgio believed the only hope was the justice of God, and as a result, true life would not be experienced until divine justice was executed.

---

1. *Letters*, 119; Ital. ed., 164.
2. Matt 25:44–46.

2. Letter to Antonio Villani—Turin, Thursday, July 19, 1923[3]

One of Pier Giorgio's longer letters was written to Villani in mid-summer, 1923. Four parts are present in the letter: (1) the preface: asking Villani a favor and reference to Luciana's law degree; (2) spiritual reflection: the theme of death based on his experience of seeing the decayed corpse of Spalassa; (3) studies: his slow progress due to the difficulty of the exams and the heat, and finally, (4) plans: mountain activities.

2.1. Prepared for Death

Pier Giorgio witnessed the decayed body of Bertini's friend at the hospital, Spalassa, just before being placed in the casket, describing him in a "pitiful state." Spalassa was cared for only by the nurses and some acquaintances. The odor in the room of the decomposed body forced Pier Giorgio to leave after two minutes. Yet, in spite of an unsettling experience, Pier Giorgio said, "But it was good for me to see this." Rather than remaining fixed on his displeasure of both sight and smell, the occasion became one of reflection: "Within a few years I will also be in that same state . . ." Yet, Pier Giorgio moved from the meditation on death, to an existential reflection on life, ". . . and yet I have sometimes been ambitious. And for what? Just for death?" It appeared to him that the brutal finality of "death" put into question the purpose of one's "ambitions": "Just for death?" It created the existential problem—"What is the meaning of life?" which Pier Giorgio inferred—the reality of death "which spares no one." These thoughts raised the question about the purpose of one's ambitions; after all, to what purpose, we all die? Pier Giorgio knew he would die like everybody else, and so death "will dissolve this body of mine and in a short time will turn it into dust." The existential problem: what meaning does life hold, let alone pursuing ambitions? Questions, no doubt, as the result of deep reflection, and it was in Pier Giorgio's nature to encounter reality through his senses and experience, and then, reflected on existential and metaphysical questions.

The decomposed body before him Pier Giorgio knew one day would be his own, "dissolve this body of mine" into dust. The lifeless body was separated from the soul: the brutal rupture of matter and spirit, body and soul, the sign of death, further indicated that, "beyond the material body there is the soul."[4] The living soul mattered, and this, Pier Giorgio understood;

---

3. *Letters*, 125–26; Ital. ed., 174–75.

4. For clarification on the separation of the soul at death and resurrection of the body, see, Aquinas, *ST*, III (Supplement), q. 69, a. 1, *resp.*, and q. 75, a. 1, *resp.*

that one's attention needed to focus on the soul so that it could present itself before the Supreme Tribunal; and on earth, the soul united to the human body was equally engaged in this preparation. Pier Giorgio's sense of divine judgment remained present in his language, his view of the afterlife, and judgment. The necessity, therefore of being prepared, adequately nourishing and cleansing the soul, so, the soul should be without fault, or as few faults as possible when it presented itself before God's judgment. For this purpose, after death, Pier Giorgio recognized the value of purgatory, for the last cleansing of the soul, "so that after having served some years in purgatory," the soul attains "Eternal peace."

Pier Giorgio asked Villani, as he questioned himself, "But how does one prepare oneself . . . ?" Not only did Pier Giorgio ask "how," but also, "when" in reference to what he called the "great Transition," when a body is separated from its soul leading to death, and preparing for judgment. Pier Giorgio provided a common sense conclusion as he thought to himself while he wrote to Villani: one did not know when "Death will come," and so, the most prudent thing would be to be prepared each day. Pier Giorgio qualified his conclusion by stating, "as if one is going to die that same day." Profound thoughts which Pier Giorgio concretized by applying them to his personal life, "and so from now on, I will try to make every day a little preparation for death." Such thoughts, desires and resolution, of this twenty-two-year old could only be the result of deep reflection and an intense prayer life. Writing to Villani, Pier Giorgio expressed his openness to the Holy Spirit so that his intuitions, his common sense discourse, reflected the work of God in him. Of further significance was Pier Giorgio's reflection on his youthful years: he did not think of them as a time to maximize fun, entertainment and pleasure, leading to a hedonistic ethics which he could have fallen into; but instead, he recognized the "beautiful years of youth" which he spiritually did not wish to waste, so as not to regret being unprepared at death.

2.2. Hope

The summer of 1923, however, put Pier Giorgio before the reality of death in its visible and odorous form, the death of a forgotten young man. But one month later, another death. In August, his father's brother, zio Pietro, was also on his deathbed.[5] Pier Giorgio experienced tremendous emotion as his uncle received the Blessed Sacrament, "when he received the Sacred Host tears of joy mixed with those of sorrow streamed down my face." In his letter to Severi, Pier Giorgio reveals his gratitude before God, "In his Infinite

5. *Letters*, "To Antonio Severi, Pollone, August 20, 1923," 137–38.

Mercy, God most certainly has not kept my innumerable sins in mind, but He has heard my prayers and the prayers of my family, and has given my uncle the great grace of receiving the last Sacraments while fully conscious." The experience of death permitted Pier Giorgio to reflect on life—and eternal life, "I believe that life should be an ongoing preparation for the next life, because one doesn't know neither the day nor the hour of our passing."

Pier Giorgio recognized himself as an "instrument of Divine Providence," although, in his humility, he considered himself "unworthy" of any such role. With his mother and a nun caring for his zio Pietro, Pier Giorgio considered his role to be an "instrument" because he succeeded in having his uncle "perform all his religious practises." His uncle, an agnostic who worked at *La Stampa* as administrator with Pier Giorgio's father was not a religious man, but with Pier Giorgio's intervention, he received Holy Communion. Pier Giorgio's Catholic faith manifested itself as his uncle received communion and "tears of joy mixed with those of sorrow streamed down my face." This passage where Pier Giorgio revealed his stirred emotions, conveyed to Severi the intensity of Pier Giorgio's experience to have witnessed his uncle finally receive Holy Communion.

Pier Giorgio desired to have his uncle receive communion and he prayed for him, and Pier Giorgio knew that God heard his prayers in infinite mercy, "God has surely not kept my innumerable sins in mind, but He has heard my prayers and the prayers of the family." His uncle, in a further blessing in what Pier Giorgio had witnessed, received the last rites, while still conscious, and thus, his zio Pietro recognized the two sacraments and prayers he received on his deathbed. Pier Giorgio also understood, "life should be a continual preparation for the next life, because one doesn't know the day nor the hours of passing." He recalled the tragic accident and death of the vice president of Young Mountaineers, Loretz, who fell to his death at the Chateau des Dames on an "easy" glacier.[6] Even though only twenty-two years old, Pier Giorgio's approach to death was "being prepared": death was inevitable, but one could not know when. A young man, healthy, energetic and strong, enjoying the goodness of life God offered, Pier Giorgio had no reason to think about death. But, his sense of reality, communion with God, connected Pier Giorgio with life and death.

---

6. *Letters*, "To Antonio Severi, Pollone, August 13, 1923," 134. Giovane Montagne, "Young Mountaineers" (Catholic youth mountaineering association).

3. Letter to Isidoro Bonini—Turin, January 15, 1925

Pier Giorgio's letter to Bonini opened with the introduction of the Holy Year, and then, focused on his personal state.[7] Although references to his interior life are interspersed with some brief reference to studies and photographs, one senses that the letter continues in the same tone as his previous letter to Bonini written only two weeks earlier, December 28.[8]

3.1. Quas Primas

The Encyclical *Quas Primas* issued by Pope Pius XI introduced the Feast of Christ the King in 1925. Undoubtedly, the kingship of Christ resonated well with Pier Giorgio; the Florentine Republic advanced by Fra Girolamo had also recognized Christ as the Sovereign King of the Republic. Pope Pius XI issued an encyclical focused entirely on the kingship of Christ as Savior of the Universe, words to which Pier Giorgio rejoiced; the spirit of his letters acknowledged, precisely, Christ as King. Already as a child, the Blessed Sacrament carried in the streets of Turin, Pier Giorgio knelt before his King.[9] Words from *Quas Primas* brought joy to Pier Giorgio's heart, even if the world around him appeared to collapse as one finds in the opening paragraph of the encyclical,

> We referred to the chief causes of the difficulties under which mankind was laboring. And We remember saying that these manifold evils in the world were due to the fact that the majority of men had thrust Jesus Christ and his holy law out of their lives; that these had no place either in private affairs or in politics: and we said further, that as long as individuals and states refused to submit to the rule of our Savior, there would be no really hopeful prospect of a lasting peace among nations. Men must look for the *peace of Christ in the Kingdom of Christ*; and that We promised to do as far as lay in Our power. *In the Kingdom of Christ*, that is, it seemed to Us that peace could not be more effectually restored nor fixed upon a firmer basis than through the restoration of the Empire of Our Lord.[10]

The "manifold evils in the world," as Pier Giorgio witnessed, "the majority of men had thrust Jesus Christ and his holy law out of their lives."

---

7. *Letters*, 196–97; Ital. ed., 288–89.
8. *Letters*, 190. See chapter 9, section 3, above.
9. See chapter 3, section 2.
10. Pope Pius XI, *Quas Primas*, 1, December 11, 1925.

Pier Giorgio's vision of a morally just world had not been achieved because the teachings of Christ had "no place either in private affairs or in politics." Pier Giorgio sought peace, he offered Bonini peace along with an olive branch as a symbol; but, neither individuals nor governments sought peace of Christ—true peace. The world, instead, sought a human peace based on ambitious alliances, false gods, and materialist ideologies. Pier Giorgio recognized in the words of Pope Pius XI his own hopes, "peace could not be more effectually restored nor fixed upon a firmer basis than through the restoration of the Empire of Our Lord."

3.2. Peace

Pier Giorgio had written his first letter of the Holy Year to his friend Franz Massetti offering him the "olive branch" of peace along with the sign of peace, and shared his ambitious plans for the Holy year. Pier Giorgio added in his letter to Massetti, "And this Peace, which is the burning Desire of us all, we hope will come in this year in which the Graces of the Lord are multiplied."[11] Peace in the light of *Quas Primas* served to bring the gospel of Christ to the world, a broken and suffering world, people trapped by the evil of sin. Only Christ could be true Peace and this Pier Giorgio shared with his friends, knowing that his own work to bring peace began in his own community.

Pier Giorgio also wrote to Beltramo on the same day as he wrote to Bonini, his opening words to Beltramo, "May peace be in your soul."[12] Compared to this gift of peace, as Pier Giorgio reminded his friend, "every other gift which one possess in this life is vanity just as all other things of the world are."[13] In his letter to Beltramo, Pier Giorgio pointed out that the world lacked both, "In the world which has distanced itself from God, there is a lack of Peace, but there is also a lack of Charity that is true and perfect Love." Peace and love go together, but Pier Giorgio qualified this meaning of "love": pure and perfect love—charity—brings peace to the world.

Pier Giorgio explained to Bonini that the Vicar of Christ "opened the doors of Justice," and the Holy Door with Grace became the means by which the faithful ought to fortify themselves. Through the grace of the Holy Door, the believer was strengthened in order that one might obtain the "Eternal Prize." Pier Giorgio examined the Holy Year from both the horizontal axis, the peace that the Holy Year intended to bring to the world through Christ,

---

11. *Letters*, "To Franz Massetti, January 4, Holy Year," 193–94.
12. *Letters*, "To Marco Beltramo, Turin, January 15, 1925," 198–99.
13. This echoes the *Imitation of Christ*. See chapter 4, section 4.4.

but also the vertical axis, whereby the strengthened individuals could prepare themselves for their prize; that is, eternal life.

In his Holy Year reflection, Pier Giorgio struggled with the paradox of the human condition, and a paradox that caused him to feel the world as "ugly" and this ugliness Pier Giorgio explained was due to "how much misery there is." The paradox that baffled and disturbed him was knowing that "unfortunately, good people are suffering while we who have been given many graces by God have alas! paid Him back so poorly." The pensive Pier Giorgio only needed to look around him to observe how often the wealthy and affluent individuals who lived well, rather than thanking God for all the blessings they have received, "paid Him back so poorly," while the suffering living in the misery of their poverty revealed themselves as "good people." The paradox where suffering led to prayer and hope, with empty hands and heavy hearts, while those with plenty, have their hands full with indifferent hearts.

In his reflections, Pier Giorgio wondered about his future, whether he would stay on, or stray from, the "right path"—whether he would "persevere to the end." While such questions were legitimate, Pier Giorgio found reassurance in his baptism where his journey of faith began, and in his deep reflection leading to Saint John's Gospel, "for apart from me you can do nothing," as Pier Giorgio rephrased the passage, "by yourself you can do nothing."[14] But with God at the center, as Pier Giorgio was reassured of his conclusion based on Saint John, "you will reach your goal." Moved by his baptismal faith, Pier Giorgio's goal was to do the will of God, ultimately to reach eternal life. He closed his first paragraph quoting Saint Augustine's *Confessions*, "Lord, our heart is restless until it rests in you," reflecting the interior tension of Pier Giorgio's soul to stay on the right path and finally, to find rest in God.[15]

The desire to convey the "peace" of the Jubilee Year was foremost on Pier Giorgio's mind, and he expressed this peace sharing his thoughts. Yet, the letter to Bonini also reflected the interior struggle Pier Giorgio experienced: he was only six months away from completing his studies; the suffering caused in his friendship with Laura; his sister's marriage less than ten days away; Beltramo, his close friend already left to study in Livorno. Pier Giorgio found peace, "Unfortunately, earthly friendships produce sorrow in our hearts because of the departure of those we love, but I would like for us to pledge a pact which knows no earthly boundaries nor temporal limits: union in prayer." He realized the only way friendship could be preserved

14. John 15:5.
15. See chapter 8, section 5.

was through prayer, just as the Tipi Loschi friends were bound together in their common faith. He continued in reference to the "happy-go-lucky" days he had spent with Bonini, "similar times won't ever return for me." Pier Giorgio revealed how he felt reflecting this conflict of "presence," that to be Catholic meant absence, past/future, and the paradox, suffering/joy: "I'll always be cheerful on the outside to demonstrate to our companions who don't share our idea that to be Catholic means to be joyful young people; but on the inside when I'm alone I give vent to my sadness." Pier Giorgio battled endless interior conflicts that he conveyed in his letters, but faith carried him through, and with this faith, in spite of what he suffered, he expressed his joy.

4. Letter to Luciana—Turin, February 14, 1925[16]

Pier Giorgio began his letter to Luciana with the question she had asked him, "You ask me whether I am in good spirits?" His letter to Luciana served to inform her that he was doing well, listing his usual mountain climbing activities, along with some details on her gift, and their father's visit to Rome. But Pier Giorgio's letter reflected overall what it meant to be "Catholic" and the "joy" of the Catholic faith.

4.1. Joy of Being Catholic

Pier Giorgio's tone in his letter changed considerably since Luciana's departure from Turin. The train station drama had troubled those who were present with Pier Giorgio's uncontrolled emotions. Luciana, worried about Pier Giorgio, not having expected her brother to be overcome with such grief, compounded with the "negative verdict" concerning Laura, Luciana understood her brother was alone without her. How could he be happy? And wondered whether Pier Giorgio was "in good spirits." Pier Giorgio's fortitude meant reaffirming himself in his faith, the correct path, not to succumb to emotions, or even worse, despair. His reply to Luciana clearly showed his sister the normalcy and joyfulness of his life, the joy of his faith, the joy of his companions—especially with Beltramo's return—the joy of the mountains.

Pier Giorgio's joy ultimately came from his faith, "As long as Faith gives me strength I will be always joyful." He intensified the sense of joy for Catholics by stating "every Catholic cannot but be joyful," and he further

---

16. *Letters*, 210–11; Ital. ed., 305–6.

added, "sadness ought to be banished from Catholic souls." Pier Giorgio maintained a clear logic in his argument: Catholics have this wonderful faith as members of the church, so, they should truly be joyful; therefore, the faith of Catholics should "banish" sadness. In his deep reflection during a period of struggle, Pier Giorgio experienced the anguish of separation, his sister's and Laura's, but he also realized rather than dwelling on what caused him suffering which deprived him of joy, that thanking God for his Catholic faith, any sadness he might have, would be banished by his faith.

Pier Giorgio distinguished between "sadness" and "sorrow" maintaining that, "Sorrow is not sadness. This illness [sadness] is nearly always caused by atheism." Sorrow enveloped both the Blessed Virgin Mary and the humanity of Jesus Christ where they both shared in the experience of "sorrow": the Virgin Mary witnessing her son's passion and crucifixion; Jesus Christ, the sorrow caused by the sins of humanity. Pier Giorgio recognized the Christian journey does not exclude sorrow, "even if strewn with many thorns," hence, the sorrow cannot be dismissed or ignored; "sorrow" remained part of the "path" to God. Pier Giorgio understood that God did not create the individual for a "sad" path. Writing to Luciana, "It is joyful even in the face of sorrow."

Pier Giorgio's fundamental understanding as he experienced his Catholic faith enabled him to embrace precisely that which was rejected by so many: sorrow. Pier Giorgio knew that to reject sorrow, in his remarkable sense of Christian spirituality, meant to reject the suffering of the cross. Even in sorrow, joy prevailed because with faith one transcends the human experience of sorrow and touches supernatural joy preparing for eternity.

Pier Giorgio associated the emotional void experienced in "sadness" especially with the spiritual void triggered by atheism, "This illness is nearly always caused by atheism."[17] The coherency in Pier Giorgio's argumentation as he wrote Luciana was well-thought out: a person without faith experienced sadness because the absence of faith creates a spiritual void. The atheist reflected nothing more than an emotional condition subjecting the will to deny God.

Pier Giorgio's joy also expressed being reunited with his beloved friend, Beltramo, who had been away at the Aeronautic Academy. Excited about Beltramo's arrival in the midst of emotional turmoil, the affectionate Pier Giorgio anxiously anticipated with joy Beltramo's arrival, as Pier Giorgio expressed in a letter to Beltramo late-January 1925, "I have been counting the days which still separate us. . . . I want to be among the first to hug you."[18]

17. See *ST*, IIa–IIae, q. 20, a. 4, on "sadness" and "spiritual sloth"/despair.
18. *Letters*, "To Marco Beltramo, January 26, 1925, 10:30 p.m.," 204.

The letter to Beltramo expressed the joy of seeing his very close friend, while in a spirt of sorrow, God offered Pier Giorgio the consolation of his close friend returning to Turin to visit his family. Beltramo proposed to visit Pier Giorgio at his home; but, Pier Giorgio replied that not only was he "counting the days" of Beltramo's return, but Pier Giorgio preferred to be right at Turin's Porta Nuova train station to welcome his friend. In fact, Pier Giorgio did not even wait for Beltramo to reach Turin, but he went to meet him in Asti, about one hour from Turin, so as to return on the last segment of Beltramo's trip together.[19] The "joy," *gioia*, Pier Giorgio experienced in Asti anticipating his friend's arrival was expressed in a letter sent to Beltramo two days before his arrival on February 10.[20]

Joy that results from a shared faith, uniting friends in prayer, focused on God, formed part of Pier Giorgio's eschatological vision. Through the experience of love and joy on earth, one can further anticipate their perfection, already with a foretaste that God allows according to his holy will.

5. Letter to Marco Beltramo—Turin, April 10, 1925[21]

Pier Giorgio wrote to Beltramo after his spiritual retreat at Villa S. Croce. Looking at the past, reminiscing, reflected Pier Giorgio's personality as he often returned with both joy and nostalgia of those "good days together." The long letter to Beltramo was the last of his long letters written to his close friend. Written in the spirit of the retreat, he reflected above all on the spiritual value of his friendships which made them true in the proper meaning of friend. He further recognized how he and their common friends had all been blessed "by the grace of God" because, they have "faith." The heart of the letter reflected how true friends helped Pier Giorgio grow in sanctity. Discussion of their exams, some details on the activities of their common friends were also included in the letter.

5.1. Faith

From the opening of the Holy Door to mark the beginning of the Jubilee Year on the Solemnity of Christ the King, Pier Giorgio wrote eight letters with reference to "faith": the first letter of the Holy Year contained the subject of "faith," January 15. The understanding of "faith" had changed from

---

19. *Letters*, 204n1.
20. *Lettere*, Ital. ed., "To Marco Beltramo, Asti, February 10, 1925," 304.
21. *Letters*, 224–25; Ital. ed., 329–31.

his earlier letters, from the confessional sense of "faith" in reference to Catholicism, evolving and maturing to that of "faith" offered by divine grace, the theological virtue. In this latter sense Pier Giorgio employed "faith" eight times in the Holy Year until his final use of the word in a letter to Beltramo on April 10. Four references to "faith" in letters sent to Bonini suggested a deep spiritual correspondence with Bonini besides Beltramo. Pier Giorgio also wrote about his "faith" in letters to Luciana, February 14, and the very last letter on "faith" to Clementina Luottto, May 3.

In his letter to Beltramo, Pier Giorgio employed both senses of "faith" in one sentence, "but we who, by the Grace of God, have the Faith, when we find ourselves in the presence of such beautiful souls, surely nourished by Faith." The significance, reflected the second use of "faith"—that virtue which "nourishes." Pier Giorgio understood that through one's "faith," in the presence of beautiful souls, Clementina—Laura—Ernestina, the "Existence of God" was grasped. "Faith," therefore, transformed friendship from sensory feeling and attachment moving outward to the Transcendent.

Were it not for Pier Giorgio's faith, and this was his intended message to Beltramo, he would not even be able to thank God for the goodness of his male and female friends who guided him during his whole life. His mind and heart responded to goodness not only in the human sense, but also at a supernatural level: these friends have been, one might say, spiritual guides to sanctity. Only from the vision of faith can this "goodness" be understood and acknowledged.

Pier Giorgio made a further link, one between goodness and grace: without the grace of God at work in the lives of individuals, the goodness that faith permitted him to witness, it would not have been possible, had these individuals not been moved by divine grace. In other words, Pier Giorgio interpreted his thought and relations at a supernatural level.

Was this the influence of Saint Paul's thought on faith? The readings of Saint Augustine on grace? St. Matthew's Gospel on the Beatitudes? Pier Giorgio appeared to have assimilated fundamental sources as a point of reflection, further drawing from his own experiences, constant in his receptivity to the work of God's grace in his life beginning with his baptismal faith.

Pier Giorgio did not diminish the fact that he was a sinner, but God in his mercy, as Pier Giorgio acknowledged, overlooked his sins. He thought of his own "ingratitude" in how he responded to the numerous graces God sent him with "so little." This reflection of having received so much, Pier Giorgio also applied to the upper-middle-class Italians, but whom he felt showed little appreciation for their blessings; instead, the poor, in all their misery and suffering, were far more grateful to God by the faith in which they lived. An observation which Pier Giorgio made and reflected upon:

why the ingratitude among the plentiful and the gratefulness among the poor? A paradox Pier Giorgio witnessed by the religious apathy if not hostility in the lives of the wealthy, and the piety and fear of God, among the poor. A pressing thought that disturbed Pier Giorgio and a reality which he did not separate from final judgment and the justice of God.

In his postscript, Pier Giorgio asked Beltramo for his prayers to strengthen his will. Praying for his family and friends as well as asking for their prayers represented an authentic testimony throughout Pier Giorgio's life of faith, knowing that God heard the prayers brought before him and these prayers were answered.

Faith, in Pier Giorgio's life, as he had written himself, began with his baptism. The guidance he received at home served as a foundation to his moral life. Later at the Social Institute, with the help of Jesuit formation, but especially with the encyclical of Pius X on frequent communion, Pier Giorgio's baptismal faith was nurtured and strengthened. His sacramental life, confession and communion, his active involvement in eucharistic and Marian confraternities, including all-night adoration, his apostolate with the Saint Vincent de Paul to reach out to the poor of Turin, his membership in Italian Catholic university clubs, his sociopolitical commitments, especially through the Savonarola and Cesare Balbo Clubs, *Milites Mariae*, as well as *Pax Romana*, using his ties especially to help poor German students, all served to demonstrate how faith in the life of Pier Giorgio was accompanied by actions, *i fatti*.[22] In his own writing, Beltramo identified three characteristics that nourished Pier Giorgio's spiritual life: his devotion to Mary, daily communion, and to love others as Christ loves.[23]

Pier Giorgio closed his letter to Beltramo offering the greatest gift to a friend, "peace," but peace, Pier Giorgio understood, expressed Christian charity. Faith manifested in acts as Pier Giorgio revealed in his own life reflected the inseparable relationship between faith and charity, the response to one's baptism.

6. Way to Eternal Salvation: "Notes for a Speech about Charity"[24]

Pier Giorgio's notes on charity offered the abundant fruit of his spiritual life—contemplative and active—delivered to the FUCI students. The notes served to encourage participation in the Saint Vincent Conferences.

---

22. See chapter 1, section 5.1.
23. Beltramo, "Il messaggio perenne," 95–97.
24. *Letters*, 239–41; Ital. ed., 353–55.

Elements in the notes drew from his previous letters and writing, "things re-hashed in poor words," generating a rich reflection on "charity." The notes concretized, proper to Pier Giorgio's personality, the value of action. Charity transformed individuals into how they lived their life of faith.

The relationship between Catholicism and charity Pier Giorgio asserted, "the foundation of our religion is Charity," and to be Catholic meant to adhere to two fundamental teachings of Christ drawing from the Scriptures, "to love God with all our strength and to love our neighbour as ourselves."[25] Pier Giorgio employed the biblical reference to "prove" that Catholicism was a religion built on "real love" and not on violence. The association of love with peace, or nonviolence was at the forefront of Pier Giorgio's thoughts, especially during the Jubilee Year of 1925. Violence led to hatred which bore "evil fruits," while charity brought peace. Pier Giorgio qualified "peace" not being the peace of the "world," but rather, the peace that only faith in Christ brought uniting individuals in "brotherly love." Pier Giorgio's message, therefore, Christ-centered, was not the peace according to the standards, values and ideas of people, but peace in conformity with the Catholic faith.

Human nature was not ignored in his discourse, violence might appear as an easier solution, "more satisfying," suggesting the route to peace involved greater difficulty, "full of thorns." The "perverse way of the world reflected the way of violence." Pier Giorgio clearly had the Fascists and their supporters in mind and the bloody violence caused by Communists. The immoral road of brutality and perversion which sharply contrasted with those who faced daily difficulties having "renounced material pleasures" so that they might follow God's laws. Pier Giorgio thought of the poor and suffering whom he had known both in Turin and Berlin, suffering injustices inflicted upon them, yet persevering in prayer seeking God's help. Pier Giorgio believed that God would hear their cry for help. He also knew that individuals strived to renounce the immoderate pleasures of the world, principles by which his own friends lived, and those committed to bring the love of Christ to the poor.

Pier Giorgio believed that a moral regeneration of society was necessary in the postwar period which had brought "material and moral" havoc. His language was filled with hope, and this reflected his Catholic faith, believing that a "radiant dawn," as he wrote in the spirit of the Encyclical, *Quas Primas*, which emphasized the sovereignty of Christ as King of the World. Pier Giorgio in a similar fashion believed nations were called to recognize Jesus Christ as King, stressing once again, "not only in words but in all their people's lives." Charity, as Pier Giorgio developed his discourse, necessarily

---

25. Mark 12:30; Luke 10:27.

entailed actions. He drew the example of the Florentine Republic, inspired by the religiopolitical writings of Fra Savonarola, who acted to establish a Christian state.

6.1. Love of Christ

The great plan Pier Giorgio desired to bring to "fulfillment" with his fellow Catholic university students was inspired by the encyclical of Pope Pius X and the Sacred Scriptures: that all nations recognize "Christ is King." The "fulfillment" meant students needed to "work generously." The Conferences of Saint Vincent, Pier Giorgio maintained, offered precisely the opportunity to work together to bring Christ the King into the lives of the people. Pier Giorgio conveyed how charitable acts through the Saint Vincent Conferences suited students because of the flexibility of the conferences requiring little commitment: "being in a particular place one day a week and then visiting two or three families every week." The meetings and visits reflected the importance of the conference members united in their common mission which had as the fundamental aim to visit Jesus in the poor, to bring Christ to the malnourished. These visits as part of the Saint Vincent apostolate in practical terms meant spending time with the poor in whatever conditions they were living, offering them not only words of comfort, but whatever assistance the members could provide. The love of Christ, Pier Giorgio explained, proclaiming Christ as King, recognized by the nations, as each individual baptized in the faith was engaged in acts of charity. Pier Giorgio appealed to the university students because he knew their involvement, their cooperation, paved the way for the future. Doing good to others, materially and spiritually, also helped the individual grow in sanctity, "how much good we can do to ourselves." Charity for Pier Giorgio was the work of divine providence so one could not take credit for one's charitable acts; members of the Saint Vincent Conference were "unworthy instruments of Divine Providence." In this way, the work of God's love was being continuously fulfilled.

In his experience with the poor, reflecting his own receptive personality, Pier Giorgio asserted, "As we grow closer to the poor little by little we gain their confidence." The poor were treated with respect growing "closer" which could only occur through a commitment of repeated visits, where they were not poor people any longer living in slum conditions, but individuals with their life stories. Pier Giorgio showed sensitivity being at their side, "in the most terrible moment of this earthly pilgrimage." In this extraordinary passage, Pier Giorgio conveyed the true meaning of love, its purification by grace to transform into acts of charity: to love a perfect stranger, who could offer nothing in return at a natural level, but supernaturally, the hungry stranger offered the presence of Jesus. This Pier Giorgio understood, "He instead took great interest. He did not limit himself to drop off the goods and say a few words of comfort or goodbye until next week. If there were children, he tried to attend to them the best he could; if they needed clothes, he made a note, and looked for them until he found them. I still see him now while asking with concern, 'What do you do? Do you need this or that?'"[26] Charity signified putting the interest of the other, the good of the other, before one's own; this openness to grace purified the individual of self-interested love. This was what Pier Giorgio meant by "how much good we can do to ourselves." Cleansed of ego-centeredness one could reach the heights of charity.

The reference to one's journey on earth as a "pilgrimage" reflected both the temporariness of the earthly life and its preparatory nature as one moves toward everlasting life. Pier Giorgio's discourse took on a moral character because the pilgrim journey required support and guidance "comforting words of faith," and again Pier Giorgio acknowledged that leading the individual to the "right road" was not accomplished out of one's own "merit," but inferred in the statement, the work of God's grace. Pier Giorgio offered support not only in the material sense, but his care was spiritually motivated, and therefore, inseparable from bringing Christ to those whom he visited. The nonjudgmental approach offering support to those who have "strayed," Pier Giorgio recognized, "not out of malice." So, the poor who deviated from the right road had not done so intentionally, but it would appear out of ignorance or circumstance.

Pier Giorgio developed a further reason for the visits to the poor, perhaps a surprising motivation, "to help curb our passions." Charitable work served as an incentive to "get on the right path." Not only were the poor being material and spiritually helped, but the conference members received support gaining spiritual strength. Given Pier Giorgio's sensitive disposition, the suffering testified the fragility of human existence in its condition of misery, a reminder of the pilgrim journey, the finite nature of the individual on this journey. Such experiences no doubt led to existential questions, as Pier Giorgio often asked himself. These experiences, therefore, purified passions so as to properly order them.

Being exposed to "atrocious sufferings," "constant sacrifices" that the families they visited must bear, Pier Giorgio underscored their faith, a

---

26. "Testimony of Zaccaria Negroni," Luciana Frassati, *La carità*, 259. The cause for Beatification of the Servant of God, Zaccaria Negroni, was opened in 2014. Pier Giorgio referred to him as the *buon Negroni*, "the good Negroni," in his letters.

significant point for him, when so many well-off people showed the complete opposite—indifference toward God and even criticism of the church. The poor Pier Giorgio considered an authentic testimony of faith. Pier Giorgio invited his FUCI listeners, Saint Vincent members, and potential members to question themselves: Pier Giorgio wanted the people to think and act, "then we resolve in our conscience to follow the way of the Cross from then onward, the only way that leads us to Eternal Salvation."

Continuing his discourse on charity, Pier Giorgio moved toward *fatti*, "deeds," which also meant sacrifice. The Saint Vincent conference in Turin drew university students made up especially of those preparing to leave and begin their adult life. He acknowledged that their members were "meager"; nevertheless, each could contribute to assist the suffering based on the teachings of Christ. The reward for such charity was heaven: "Jesus Christ had promised that all we do for the poor for Love of Him He will consider it as having been done to Himself."[27] Pier Giorgio emphasized the infinite love of Jesus for humanity offered in the sacrament of the Eucharist. This was the love that Pier Giorgio sought to convey: eucharistic Jesus as "our Consoler and as Bread of the Soul." Pier Giorgio suggested that the love of Jesus waited for a response, an invitation to love him in return, and this response was expressed in the choices that were made, to accept the love of Jesus, or to ignore this invitation of love. Pier Giorgio encouraged the students to participate in the conference but the motivation also reflected Pier Giorgio's eschatological vision. The human, sacramental, and eschatological for Pier Giorgio were inseparable.

7. Note for Grimaldi—Turin, July 3, 1925[28]

"Here are the injections for Converso. The pawn ticket is Sappa's. I forgot it, renew it in my name." Pier Giorgio's last act of charity was expressed in a note written during his final paralyzing moments of poliomyelitis.[29] He found barely enough strength to write a note to Grimaldi while he intended to make his usual visit to the poor that Friday. Even during his final hours, Pier Giorgio was more concerned about the well-being of his mother who had been attending her dying mother, nonna Linda Ametis.

Preoccupied with the weakening condition of nonna Linda Ametis, Pier Giorgio did not want to disturb his mother, in spite of his own rapidly

---

27. Matt 25:40.

28. *Letters*, 233–41; Ital. ed., 353.

29. For a detailed account of Pier Giorgio's final days and last hours, see Frassati, *My Brother*, 2002.

deteriorating and painful state. He appeared indifferent to his suffering, "His last days were sheer physical and moral torment, but he was too humble and self-denying to mind the indifference of others."[30] Nonna Linda Ametis died July 1. It was Pier Giorgio who had gone to the parish to call the priest for the sacrament of extreme unction.[31] The family did not realize that Pier Giorgio was dying because he suppressed his pain, so as "not to disturb."[32] On Friday, July 3, Pier Giorgio was paralyzed waist down. Nobody imagined his condition as he hid well his fragile state. On that Friday the family went to Pollone for the grandmother's funeral. Pier Giorgio's mother decided not to go to her mother's funeral due to her fatigue, and to remain at Pier Giorgio's side. With the urgent call from Turin the family hastened after the funeral rituals back to their Turin residence where they discovered Pier Giorgio's grave condition.

From his alpaca jacket, brought to him by Luciana, Pier Giorgio removed a pawn ticket from the *Monte di Pietà* as well as a small container of injections. He wrote the note himself, it was Friday, the day for the Saint Vincent Conference, a note to Giuseppe Grimaldi.[33] On the Saturday morning, Pier Giorgio received the sacrament of confession and holy communion from Don Formica. Sister Michelina helped Pier Giorgio make the sign of the cross at four in the morning; in the afternoon, he received extreme unction.[34] "Greater love has no man than this, that a man lay down his life for his friends."[35]

Pier Giorgio did not separate his apostolate among the suffering from his eschatological vision: preparing himself for God's absolute love, the fullness of life began on earth as a pilgrim, choosing acts of goodness each day and sacrifices, thanking God for the gift of his family, friends and creation. Baptized in the faith, Pier Giorgio prepared his soul for the perfection of love to be experienced in the fullness of God's presence for all of eternity.

Questions

1. In Pier Giorgio's letter to Willibald Leitgebl, how does Pier Giorgio express "Divine Justice" (§1; February 1923; 1.1)?

---

30. Frassati, *Beatitudes*, 140.
31. Frassati, *Beatitudes*, 140. Sacrament of anointing of the sick.
32. Frassati, *Beatitudes*, 141.
33. Frassati, *Beatitudes*, 142.
34. Frassati, *I giorni*, 188.
35. John 15:13.

2. How does Pier Giorgio suggest he is prepared for death in his letter to Villani (§2; July 1923)?

3. What is the subject of the papal document, *Quas Primas* (3.1)? Why does Pier Giorgio refer to this document in his letter to Bonini (§3; January 1925)?

4. What is the "joy of being Catholic" for Pier Giorgio when he writes to his sister, Luciana (§4; February 1925; 4.1)? How does Pier Giorgio describe faith in his letter to Beltramo (§5; April 1925)?

5. In Pier Giorgio's "Notes for a Speech about Charity," what is the way to eternal salvation (§6; 6.1)?

6. Describe Pier Giorgio's final act of charity (§7). What does Jesus teach about the supreme act of love (John 15:13)? How does Pier Giorgio put into practice what Jesus teaches in relation to the following? (a) His family; (b) prayer; (c) sacramental life; (d) his friends; (e) the poor; (f) chastity.

Bibliography

Angeloni, Italo Mario. *Ho amato così*. Turin: S. Lattes, 1925.
Aquinas, Thomas. *Summa Theologiae*. 2nd ed. Translated by English Fathers of the Dominican Province. 1920.
Armini, Michele. *Pier Giorigo Frassati*. Bergamo: Velar, 2007.
Arrighini, Angelo. Essay (untitled). In *Beato Pier Giorgio Frassati*, edited by Raimondo Spiazzi, OP, 117–19. Bologna: Edizioni Studio Domenicano, 2001.
Augustine of Hippo. *The Confessions of Saint Augustine*. Translated with introduction and notes by John K. Ryan. Garden City, NY: Image, 1960.
Bedouelle, Guy. *Saint Dominic: the Grace of the Word*. Translated by Mary Thomas Noble. San Francisco: Ignatius, 1987.
Bellusci, David Christian. "Pier Giorgio Frassati: Italian Nationalism, Mussolini and the Vatican." Paper given at the *Canadian Jacques Maritain Association*, Ryerson University, Toronto, May 20–21, 2017.
Beltramo Ceppi, Marco. "Il messaggio perenne di Pier Giorgio." In *Pier Giorgio Frassati: Echi di memorie*, edited by Luciana Frassati, 93–97. Genoa: Marietti, 1989.
Bosco, Giovanni, Saint. "Storia ecclesiastica ad uso delle scuole." In *Opere*. Prime serie: Libri e opuscoli. Vol. 1: 1844–1855. Rome: LAS, 1976.
Brady, Gerard K. *Saint Dominic: Pilgrim of Light*. Preface by Cardinal Lercaro, Archbishop of Bologna. London: Catholic Book Club, 1957.
Calloway, Donald H. *Champions of the Rosary*. Stockbridge, MA: Marian, 2016.
Capua, Raymond. *The Life of St. Catherine of Siena*. Translated by George Lamb. Rockford, IL: TAN, 2003. [Italian edition by the Dominican Priory of Siena, 1934.]
Casalegno, Carla. *Fra Terra e Cielo: Pier Giorgio Frassati*. Milan: San Paolo, 2011.
———. *Pier Giorgio Frassati*. Turin: Effatà, 2005.
Castronovo, Valerio. *Il Piemonte*. Turin: Enaudi, 1977.
Catella, Aceste. *La Vergine bruna di Oropa*. Milan: San Paolo, 2002.
Catherine of Siena. *The Letters of Saint Catherine of Siena*. Translated with introduction and notes by Suzanne Noffke. Binghamton, NY: Medieval and Renaissance Texts and Studies, 1988.
Cojazzi, Antonio. *Pier Giorgio Frassati: Testimonianze*. Turin: SEI, 1928.
Comíns Forcada, Vincente. *Il Beato Piergiorgio Frassati (laico domenicano 1901–1925)*. Translated and notes by Raimondo Sorgia. Melara, Italy: Roma, 2014.
Congregatio pro Causis Sanctorum. Canonizationis Servi Dei Petri Georgii Frassati. Positio super virtutibus. Vol. 1. Rome: Guerra, 1987.

De Biasio, Elisabetta. *Alfredo Frassati: Un conservatore illuminato.* Milan: Franco Angeli, 2006.

De Rosa, Gabriele. Introduction to *Un uomo un giornale*, by Luciana Frassati, XI-L. Rome: Edizioni di Storia e Letteratura, 1978.

D'Onofrio, Giulio. "Renaissance." In *History of Theology*, edited by Giulio D'Onofrio, vol. 3. Translated by M. J. O'Connell. Collegeville: Liturgical, 1997.

Frassati, Luciana. *Calendario di una vita.* Turin: La Salle, 1981.

———. *L'impegno sociale e politico di Pier Giorgio.* Preface by Giorgio La Pira, introduction by Carlo Trabucco. Rome: AVE, 1978.

———. *A Man of the Beatitudes.* Translated by Dinah Livingstone. Ottawa: Novalis, 2000. Revised edition adapted and edited by Patricia O'Rourke. [First published in Italian as *Pier Giorgio Frassati: i giorni della sua vita.* Roma: Edizioni Studium, 1975.]

———, ed. *Mio Fratello Pier Giorgio: La carità.* Turin: Effatà, 2013.

———, ed. *Mio fratello Pier Giorgio: La fede.* Milan: Paoline, 2004.

———. *My Brother Pier Giorgio: His Last Days.* Translated by H. G. Pérez. Foreword by Benedict Groeschel. New Hope, KY: New Hope, 2002.

———. *Pier Giorgio. I giorni della sua vita.* Studium: Rome, 2011.

———, ed. *Pier Giorgio Frassati: Echi di memorie.* Genoa: Marietti, 1989.

———, ed. *Un uomo un giornale.* Vol. 1, pt. 1. Rome: Edizioni di Storia e Letteratura, 1978.

Frassati, Pier Giorgio. *Pier Giorgio Frassati: Letters to His Friends and Family.* Translated by Timothy E. Deeter, edited by Timothy E. Deeter and Christine M. Wohar. New York: St. Pauls, 2009. [Originally published, *Pier Giorgio Frassati, Lettere (1906–1925)*, edited by Luciana Frassati. Milan: Vita e Pensiero, 1995.]

http://www.fuci.net/index.php/chi-siamo/storia

Ginoli, C. "Fra Girolamo Savonarola e 'Fra Girolamo' Pier Giorgio Frassati." *Sacra Doctrina* 5 (2003) 155–66.

Giuliani, Reginaldo. Essay (untitled). In *Beato Pier Giorgio Frassati*, edited by Raimondo Spiazzi, 92–95. Bologna: Edizioni Studio Domenicano, 2001.

Hinnebusch, J. F. "Peter Martyr, St." In *New Catholic Encyclopedia*, 11:192. 2nd ed. Detroit: Thomson/Gale, 2003.

Jørgensen, Johannes. *Saint Catherine of Siena.* Translated by Ingeborg Lund. New York: Longmans, Green, 1938.

La Pira, Giorgio. Preface to *L'impegno sociale e politico di Pier Giorgio*, edited by Luciana Frassati, 29–36. Rome: AVE, 1978.

"La Stampa." Year XL. January 27, 1906. In Valerio Castronovo, *Piemonte*, 164–65.

"La Tribuna Biellese. July 5, 1891." In *Un uomo un giornale*, edited by Luciana Frassati. Vol. 1, pt. 1. Rome: Edizioni di Storia e Letteratura, 1978.

Levi, Mario Attilo. "Al D'Azeglio Insieme." In *Pier Giorgio Frassati: Echi di Memorie*, edited by Luciana Frassati, 52–56. Genoa: Marietti, 1989.

Liber Constitutionum et Ordinationum: Fratrum Ordinis Praedicatorum. Curia Generalitia: Romae, 2010. [English publication: *The Book of the Constitutions and Ordinations of the Brothers of the Order of Preachers.* Dublin, 2001.]

Malgeri, Francesco."Pier Giorgio's World." In *Pier Giorgio Frassati: Letters to His Friends and Family*, edited by T. E. Deeter and Christine M. Wohar, xxiii–xxvii. New York: St. Pauls, 2009.

Maritain, Jacques. *Trois Réformateurs.* Paris: Plon, 1925.

Massetti, Francesco. V. *Pier Giorgio Frassati*. Milan: O.R., 1976.
"The Matteoti Crime." *London Times*. June 24, 1924.
Pierazzi, Maria Rina. *Così ho visto Pier Giorgio*. Brescia: Queriniana, 1955.
———. *Pier Giorgio Frassati*. Brescia, Italy: La Scuola, 1957.
Pinckaers, Servais. *Sources of Christian Ethics*. Translated by Mary Thomas Noble. Washington, DC: Catholic University of America Press, 1995.
Rerum Novarum. Encyclical letter of Pope Leo XIII. May 15, 1891.
Revised Standard Version (Catholic Edition), 1965, 1966. National Council of Churches of Christ in the United States of America.
Ridolfi, Roberto. *Life of Girolamo Savonarola*. Translated by Cecil Grayson. New York: Knopf, 1959.
Robotti, Filippo. Essay (untitled). In *Beato Pier Giorgio Frassati*, edited by Raimondo Spiazzi, 96–97. Edizioni Studio Domenicano: Bologna, 2001.
http://www.sanvincenzoitalia.it/chi-siamo/la-famiglia-vincenziana/congregazione-della-missione-padri-della-missione/
Savonarola, Iieronimo. *Crica il reggimento e governo della citta di Firenze*. Florence, 1494. [Republished in 1847 by Tommaso Barrachi, Florence. Reprinted by Elibron Classics, 2006.]
Seton-Watson, C. *Storia d'Italia dal 1870 al 1925*. Rome: Laterza, 1967.
Siccardi, Cristina. *Pier Giorgio Frassati*. Milan: San Paolo, 2014.
Soldi, Primo. *Verso l'assoluto*. Rome: Jaca, 1991.
Spiazzi, Raimondo, ed. *Beato Pier Giorigo Frassati*. Bologna: Edizioni Studio Domenicano, 2001.
Taylor, Charles. *A Secular Age*. Cambridge: Belknap, of Harvard University Press, 2007.
Thomas à Kempis. *Imitation of Christ*. Translated by William C. Creasy. Notre Dame: Ave Maria, 1989.
Tocco, Felice. *Savonarola: Profeta e Ribelle*. Genoa: Mariette, 1998.
Torrell, Jean-Pierre. *Saint Thomas Aquinas. The Person and His Work*. Vol. 1. Translated by Robert Royal. Washington, DC: Catholic University of America, 2005.
Trabucco, Carlo. Introduction to *L'impegno sociale e politico di Pier Giorgio*, edited by Luciana Frassati, 5–27. Rome: AVE, 1978.
Weisheipl, James. *Friar Thomas D'Aquino: His Life, Thought, and Work*. New York: Doubleday, 1974.

Index

action, 17–19, 26–29
Agnelli, Giovanni, 7
agnostics, 5
Agricultural Institute, 84
agriculture studies, 84, 96
Albert, Charles, 77
Albert of Cologne, Saint, 169
Alexander VI, Pope, 176
All Night Youth Adoration, 91
Allamano, Joseph, Blessed, 9
Amadeus, Victor, 77
Ametis, Adelaide (later Frassati), 9–28
Ametis, Elena (aunt), 9, 10, 12, 43–46, 62–67, 64n54, 122, 123
Ametis, Emilia (aunt), 5, 9, 10n42
Ametis, Francesco (maternal grandfather), 2, 10, 15, 42
Ametis, Linda (maternal grandmother), 10, 38–42, 53, 220–21
Angelic Warfare Confraternity, 184
Angeloni, Italo, 193
Anti-Blasphemy Law (1930), 164n88
anti-Communist FIAT club, 91, 177
apologetics training for youth, 158–59
Apostolate of Payer, 62, 64, 78
Aquinas. *See* Thomas Aquinas, Saint
architecture, 103–4
Ariosto, Ludovico, 95
Arrighini, Angelo (Father), 173
art, 11–12, 40, 43–44, 103–5
Assisi, Italy, 96–97
Association of the Blessed Sacrament, 62, 78
Association of the Holy Eucharist, 64
atheism, 5, 213

Augustine, Saint, 95, 185, 196, 211, 215
Auxiliary Sisters of the Souls in Purgatory, 55, 55n21
Axerio (friend), 63, 86

Balbo, Enrico Luigi, Count di Vinadio, 64n54
baths of Caracalla, 93–94
Baumgarten, Clara (housekeeper), 17
Bellingeri, Carlo, 63n51, 72–85, 145, 153
Beltramo, Marco, 120, 124–28, 125n37, 135–39, 198–201
Benedict XII, Pope, 184
Benedict XV, Pope, 151
Benedictine monastery, Monte Cassino, 182
Berlin, Germany, 85, 90, 100–101, 142–46
Bernard of Clairvaux, Saint, 94, 104
Berro, Benedetto (Friar), 173
Bertagna, Francesco, 153
Bertini, Gian Maria, 125n37, 146–52, 159, 174–78
Besnate (Father), 63
"The Betrothed," *Promessi Sposi* (Manzoni), 114
Bianchetti, Caterina, 31
"Black Virgin," 65, 65n62
Bobola, Enrico (Father), 150
Bodoni, Mario Lobetti, 28
Bolshevik Revolution (1917), 151, 165
Bonafous Institute, 84, 144
Bonelli, Ernestina (Tina), 125, 125n37, 126, 130–34

Bonini, Checchi, 120, 201–2
Bonini, Isidoro, 120, 125n37, 185, 193–98
Bonomi, Ivanoe, 146n23
Bonous, Guido, 73
Borla (Don), 56
Bosco, Giovanni, (Bosco, John), Saint, 8n35, 9, 32–33n8, 64, 71, 71n6
Busatto, Rosina, 28, 51, 69–70

Calvin, John, 8
Cane, Felice (Don), 53, 64
Cargnino, Giuseppe, 133, 139
Castrale, Costanzo (Monsignor), 64
Catechism of Saint Pius X, 48, 57
Cathar heresy, 171
Catherine of Siena, Saint, 95, 168, 178–81
Catholic Action (AC) club, 91, 123–24, 155–59
Catholic Church, in Turin, 8–9
Catholic Youth movement, 123, 157
Cavagna, Celeste, 18
Cerutti, Giuseppe, 135
Cesare Balbo Board of Directors, letter to, 159–62
Cesare Balbo Club, 88, 89, 147–50, 152–53, 158, 171, 175, 201
    See also Federation of Italian Catholic Universities
charity, 5, 5n23, 60–62, 75, 80, 216–20
Charles VII, King of France, 176
Christ, love of, 218–20
Christ the King, Feast day, 209–10
Christian democracy, 162–64
Christian principles, 8
Christian responsibility, 61–62
Church of Corpus Domini (Turin), 52n11
Club Alpino Italiano (CAI), 79n38
Coda-Conati, Giuseppina (later Frassati,), 2
Cojazzi, Antonio (Don), 21, 28, 32, 35n18, 56–57, 56n27, 57n29, 63, 71–72
Comments on Catholic Morality (Manzoni), 95

communion, sacrament of
    first reception of, 54–57, 56n25
    frequency of, 57–60, 79, 202
    receiving for someone, 123
communion of saints, 123, 202
Communism, 124, 155, 163–65, 217
Conference of Saint Vincent de Paul, 152–54, 201, 218, 220
Confessions (Augustine), 95, 196, 211
Confirmation, sacraments of, 64–65, 64n52
Confraternity of the Holy Rosary, 79, 170
conscience-formation, 51
Contarini, Gasparo, 8n34
Copello, Linda. *See* Ametis, Linda
Cottolengo, Giuseppe Benedetto, (Cottolengo, John Benedict), Saint, 9, 32n8, 153

dancing, 106
Dante Alighieri, 92, 93, 94–95, 104, 113, 169
de Paul, Vincent, Saint, 33n8, 152–54, 201, 218, 220
de Sales, Francis, Saint, 9, 71
death, preparation for, 206–7
democracy
    Christian, 162–64
    social, 163
Descartes, René, 8
Dezani, Serafino (Professor), 177
Dialogue of Divine Providence (Jørgensen), 181n56
Divina Commedia (Dante), 93, 95, 104
divine intervention, 17–19
divine justice, 205–6
Dominic, Saint, 9, 169–70
Dominican Office of Our Lady or the Rosary, 170, 174
Dominican Order, 172n17, 173
"The Dominican Rule," 89
Dominican spirituality, 184
Dominicans, Third Order (Lay Dominicans), 170–74, 170n6, 176–77
Don Bosco College/Institute, 54, 63

Eiffler, Emil (Reverend Doctor), 99, 100, 146
Emanuele, Vittorio, 149
Emilian Youth Convention, 144, 156
Emmanuel, Victor (King), 77, 150–51, 164
empathy, 16–17
Enlightenment humanism, 4, 8
Erasmus of Rotterdam, 8n34
eschatological vision
    belief in, 119, 155
    charity, 216–20
    death, preparation for, 206–7
    divine justice, 205–6
    faith, 214–16
    hope, 207–8
    "indissoluble bond" and, 130
    joy, of being Catholic, 212–14
    love of Christ, 218–20
    peace, 210–12
    Quas Primas encyclical, 209–10
    salvation, 216–20
Eucharistic League, 79
Eucharistic miracle, 112–13
Eusebius, Bishop of Vercelli, 65
Eymard, Peter Julian, Saint, 62, 62n47

Facta, Luigi, 146n23, 155
faith, 201–2, 214–16
Falchetti, Alberto, 103–7
family life, 34–38, 105–7
Fascists and Fascism
    anti-Fascist views, 119, 123–24
    breaking into family home, 162, 163
    in Italian government, 164
    La Stampa and, 163
    Matteotti's kidnapping and killing, 162n84
    Mussolini and (*See* Mussolini, Benito)
    violence and, 217
Federation of Italian Catholic Universities (FUCI)
    anti-Catholic environment and, 157–58
    Catholic Youth movement and, 123
    female members, 175
    letter to parents, 88

Milites Mariae Club and, 156–58
Pax Romana and, 115
Ravenna Convention (1921), 113–14
sacredness of the flag, 148, 159–61, 175
See also Cesare Balbo Club
feelings, subjective, 50n8
Felice, Charles, 77
Ferdinand, Franz, Archduke of Austria, 144
FIAT, automobile company, 7
FIAT club, 91, 177
Filiberto, Emanuel (Duke), 77
first communion, 54–57
Fischer, Maria, 52n11, 107–9, 112–16
flowers and the garden, 33–34, 41
Formica (Don), 221
Formica, Giorgio, 156
Forzano, Giovacchino, 125
Foscolo, Niccolò, 95
Francis de Sales, Saint, 9, 71
Francis of Assisi, Saint, 97
Frassati, Adelaide Ametis (mother)
    exchange with Alfredo, 12
    family background, 10
    first baby, Elda, 14
    letter from Pier Giorgio, 9–10, 15–25, 53–60, 188–91
    letter to Pier Giorgio (1922, July 28), 189–91
    marriage, 13, 193
    moral values, 13–14
    mountain trips, 20, 21, 131–32
    painting, 11–12, 40, 43–44
    personality, 11, 24, 36, 189
    Pier Giorgio's birth and baptism, 14–15
    Pier Giorgio's final days, 220–21
    reaction to Laura Hidalgo, 212
    relationship with Elena, 43
    values passed to Pier Giorgio, 51, 51n10
Frassati, Alberto (brother), 72–76
Frassati, Alfredo (father)
    as agnostic, 5, 51
    birth, parents, studies, 2

Frassati, Alfredo (father) (continued)
  career expectations for Pier Giorgio, 59
  characteristics, 36, 37, 37n32
  death, view on, 5
  exchange with Adelaide, 12
  Germanophile influences, 3, 53, 92, 95
  Hamlet (articles written on), 94n3
  humanist values, 51, 51n10
  as Italian ambassador to Germany, 85, 90, 100, 101
  Italian society and politics, 6–9
  journalism career, 2–6
  La Gazzetta Piemontese newspaper, 4
  La Stampa, newspaper, 4, 4n15, 144, 152
  La Tribuna Biellese, biweekly newspaper, 4
  La Tribuna newspaper, 3
  letters from Pier Giorgio, 1–2, 25–29
  secular humanism and, 4
  social values of, 4–5
  Varazze accusations, publication of, 72
  on the Versailles Treaty, 145–46
Frassati, Emma (aunt), 5–6
Frassati, Giuseppina Coda-Conati (paternal grandmother), 2, 15, 192, 201
Frassati, Luciana (sister)
  childhood, 31–38
  first communion, 54-56, 56n25
  Jan Gawronski, engagement to, 119
  law degree gift from Pier Giorgio, 179–80
  Leitgebel family visit, 118
  marriage, 193, 198–201, 199n45
  Pier Giorgio's affection for, 2
  on Pier Giorgio's response to helping others, 18–19
  schooling, 28
  on Sonnenschein, 143–44n7
  Tipi Loschi and, 125n37
Frassati, Pier Giorgio
  action, 17–19
  anti-Fascist views, 119, 123–24
  art, 11–12, 40, 103–5

associations and memberships, 62, 64, 78–80, 90–91
birth and baptism, 14–15
Catholic associations, membership in, 62
childhood companions, 30–31
dancing, 106
death of, 220–21
empathy, 16–17
eschatological vision, 119, 130, 155
family homes, 18n61
family life, 34–38, 105–7
flowers and the garden, 33–34
as "Fra Girolamo," 169, 170, 177–78
Germanophile influences, 3, 53, 92, 95
on his mother's absence, 23–25
on his sister's birth, 31–32
languages learned, 70, 90, 92
letter from mother (1922, July. 28), 189–91
literature, 93, 94–95
mining vocation, 109
mountain climbing, 20, 21, 83, 130–32
music, 102–3
outdoor activities, 45–46
personality, 82–84
political purity, 165–66
on the Pope, 150
poverty, awareness of, 60–61, 88
poverty, personal, 97–98
prayer, 17, 54
recreation with family friends, 86–87
relationship with his mother, 188–91
religious activities, 88–89
school failure, 25–29
sensitivity, 32–33
social activities, 88–89
social culture, 105–7
sociopolitical issues, 123–24, 151–52, 164
St. Thomas parallel, 182–83
as Third Order Dominican, 173–74
trust, 19–22
World War I, reaction to, 144–46

INDEX

See also sacramental life
Frassati, Pier Giorgio, letters to
    Alberto Falchetti (Oct. 14, 1921), 103–7
    Antonio Villani (Aug. 17, 1924), 120–24
    Antonio Villani (Aug. 31, 1923), 168–74
    Antonio Villani (Jul. 18, 1922), 152–55
    Antonio Villani (Jul. 19, 1923), 206–8
    Antonio Villani (June 23, 1924), 162–66
    Antonio Villani (Mar. 17, 1921), 142–46
    aunt Elena (Alassio, Aug. 16, 1916), 62–67
    aunt Elena (Alassio, Aug. 16, 1924), 122, 123
    aunt Elena (Apr. 1912), 43–46
    Bonini, Isidoro (Dec. 28, 1924), 193–98
    Bonini, Isidoro (Mar. 6, 1925), 201–2
    Carlo Bellingeri (Aug. 15, 1917), 82–85
    Carlo Bellingeri (Oct. 26, 1917), 76–82
    Carlo Bellingeri (Sept. 23, 1916), 72–76
    Cesare Balbo Board of Directors (Oct. 26, 1923), 159–62
    father (Perugia, Sept. 6, 1919), 95–98
    father (Pollone, 1906), 1–2
    father (Pollone, Oct. 1913), 25–29, 60–62
    father (Rome, Oct. 10, 1915), 93–98
    Franz Massetti (Jan. 4, 1925), 181–84
    Laura Hidalgo (Aug. 11, 1924), 191–93
    Marco Beltramo (Jan. 25, 1925), 198–201
    Marco Beltramo (Nov. 1924), 135–39
    Marco Beltramo proclamation (Aug. 1924), 124–28
    Maria Fischer (Dec. 28, 1922), 107–9
    Maria Fischer (May. 17, 1922), 112–16
    maternal grandmother, 38–42
    Milites Mariae Club (Oct. 30, 1922), 155–59
    mother (Dec. 20, 1910), 53–60
    mother (Freiburg im Breisgau, Oct. 7, 1921), 188–91
    mother (Freiburg im Breisgau, Oct. 12, 1921), 98–103
    mother (Pollone, Dec. 19,1907), 15–22
    mother (Pollone, Nov. 7, 1907), 9–10
    mother (Pollone, Sept. 25,1913), 22–25
    parents (1908), 48–53
    parents (1922, Apr. 6), 89–91
    parents (1922, Feb. 28), 85–89
    Tina Bonelli (Sept. 13, 1924), 130–34
    Willibald Leitgebel (Feb. 3, 1923), 205
    Willibald Leitgebel (Jan. 28, 1923), 116–20
Frassati, Pietro (paternal grandfather), 2
Frassati, Pietro (uncle), 4n13, 169, 192, 207–8
Frederick II, Emperor, 182
Freemasons, 146, 147, 148–49, 165
Freiburg im Breisgau, Germany
    letter to Alberto Falchetti (Oct. 14, 1921), 103–7
    letter to Gian Maria Bertini (Oct. 23, 1921), 146–52
    letter to Gian Maria Bertini (Oct. 31, 1923), 174–78
    letter to mother (Oct. 7, 1921), 188–91
    letter to mother (Oct. 12, 1921), 98–103
Friends of Catholic University of the Sacred Heart, 91
friendship, 129–30

INDEX

Gamba, Giuseppe, Archbishop, 199
gardening, 33–34, 41
Garibaldi, Giuseppe, 150
Gautrelet, Francis Xavier, 78
Gawronska, Wanda, 35n18, 59n41, 125n37, 190n3
Gawronski, Jan, 118, 199, 199n40
Gérard, Cesare (Don), 132
Gillet, Stanislaus (Father), 173
Giolitti, Giovanni, 4, 6–7, 144n10, 146n23, 164–66
Girolamo, Fra, 169, 170, 177–78
    See also Savonarola, Girolamo, (Friar)
Giuliani, Reginaldo (Friar), 173
Giuliano, Emilia, 56, 56n27
God
    judgment, 207, 216
    love for, 202
    love of, 218–20
    will of, 196–98
Goethe, Johann, 95
Gola, Giuseppe, 41–42, 84
goodness of faith, 215
grace
    goodness and, 215
    sacrifice and, 197–98
Grassi (Professor), 121
Gregory XI, Pope, 179, 182
Grimaldi, Giuseppe "Figaro," 125n37, 126, 135, 220–21
Grossi, Giovanni, 52, 55, 56n27
Guardia-Riva, Constantino, 175
Guglielmini, Maddalena, 125n37, 126
guilt, sense of, 48–50

Hamlet (Shakespeare), 93
Heine, Heinrich, 95
Helpers of the Souls in Purgatory, 54–55
Henry, Abbot, 131
Hidalgo, Laura, 125, 125n37, 131, 134, 191–93
Holy Year, 210–11
Honorius III, Pope, 169
hope, 207–8, 217
humanism, 4, 7–8, 8n34
humanist, defined, 5
humanist values/virtues, 51, 51n10, 59

Hume, David, 8
I Loved That Way (Angeloni), 193–96
Ibertis, Enrico (Friar), 173
Ignatius of Loyola, Saint, 79
Il Momento (newspaper), 152
Il Popolo d'Italia (newspaper), 144
The Imitation of Christ (Kempis), 69, 80–82
International Catholic Congress, 143
International Exhibition of Venice in April 1912, 43–44
"intrinsic value," 3
Italian Alpine Club, 79, 79n38, 138
Italian Catholic Convention, 158
Italian nationalism, 150–51
Italian Popular Party (PPI), 90
Italian school system, 74n20, 74n22

Jesuit Social Institute (*l'Istituto Sociale*), 57–59, 62, 74, 77–78, 152
John the Baptist, 49
Jørgensen, Johannes, 180–81, 181n56
joy
    of being Catholic, 212–14
    "Eternal Joy," 82
    gift from the Holy Spirit, 64
justice, divine, 205–6

The Kaiser in Exile, 104

La Consolata "Saint Mary the Consoler," 65
La Crocetta parish, 14, 106, 124, 156, 157, 166
La Stampa, newspaper, 4, 4n15, 144, 152, 163
Leitgebel, Nisse, 119
Leitgebel, Willibald, 116–20, 205
Leo XIII, Pope, 7, 141, 143, 147–48, 151, 170
Liceo Massimo D'Azeglio. See Massimo D'Azeglio
Life of Saint Catherine of Siena (Jørgensen), 181, 181n56
literature, 93, 94–95
Lombardi, Pietro, 57, 59, 62, 64, 78
Loreto, Italy, 96–97

INDEX

love
  of Christ, 218–20
  fundamental teaching of Christ, 217
  for God, 202
  for Laura, 191–93
  natural love and charity, distinctions, 5, 5n23
  that Catholics possess, 201–2
Luotto, Clementina (Tina), 125, 125n37, 131, 196, 204, 215
Luther, Martin, 8

"manifold evils in the world," 209–10
Manzon, Luca, 157n67
Manzoni, Alessandro, 95, 114
Marian Confraternity, 79
Marian Congregation, 77
Marian shrines, 65–67, 96–97
Marian spirituality, 170
Maritain, Jacques, 8n35
marriage, sacrament of, 198–201
Masoero, Carolina, 37, 65
masons. *See* Freemasons
Massetti, Franz, 120, 125n37, 181–84, 197
Massimo D'Azeglio (middle-secondary school/liceo), 25, 25n83, 54, 56, 57, 61, 73–76
Matteotti, Giacomo, 162n84
Mazzarello, Maria, Saint, 9
meaning of life, 206–7
Mechanical Engineering, 85, 88
Mère, Catherine, Sainte, 54, 55n21, 56
Mexican churches (1920's), 165
Micheli (family friend), 86
Michelina, Sister, 221
Midsummer Night's Dream (Shakespeare), 104
Milites Mariae (Catholic Action Club), 91, 123–24, 155–59
mining, 88, 109
Monti, Augusto (Professor), 145
morally questionable lifestyles, charity for, 153–54
More, Thomas, Saint, 8n34
Mount Grivola ("Forbidden Fruit"), 130–32
mountain climbing, 20, 21, 83, 130–32, 135–39

mountains, Catholic masses on, 132–34
Mozart, Wolfgang, 103
music, 102–3
Mussolini, Benito, 101, 124, 144, 155, 159–62, 164–65

namesday, 16
nationalism, 150–51
natural love and charity, distinctions, 5, 5n23
nature and the senses, 40–42
Negroni, Zaccaria, 219n26
neighbor, defined, 52n13
Non expedit decree (Pius IX), 151
Novo, Natalina, 84, 145

orphans, 32–33
Our Lady of Loreto, 96–97
Our Lady of Mount Carmel parish, 152–53
Our Lady of Oropa, 65–66, 66n64
Our Lady of Peace parish, 152–53
outdoor activities, 45–46

paintings, 11–12, 40, 43–44, 103–5
Papini, Giovanni, 95
Paradiso (Dante), 92, 95, 169
Partito Popolare Italiano (PPI), 151–52
Paschetto, Felice (Don), 65
pasta, cooking for guests, 121
Pax Romana, 91, 113–16
peace, 210–12
penance, sacrament of, 52–53
Perugia, Italy, 96–97
Peter Martyr, (Peter of Verona), Saint, 171, 171n11, 171n12
philosophers, Salesians rejection of, 71–72
Pierazzi, R. M. (cousin), 6, 15, 35
pilgrim's journey, 219
Pinardi, Giovanni Battista, Monsignor, 160, 160n81
Pinckaers, Servais (Friar), 4n18
Pini, Giandomenico (Monsignor), 88, 148, 158, 178
Pius VII, Pope, 77
Pius IX, Pope, 150–51
Pius X, Pope and Saint, 48, 57, 67, 202, 218

INDEX

Pius XI, Pope, 71n6, 139, 155, 164–65, 165n93, 209–10
Pius XII, Pope, 55n21
Pol, Carlo, 139
Poland, 107–9
political purity, of Pier Giorgio, 165–66
politics
    scripture and, 161–62
    social justice and, 154–55
Pollone residence, description of, 39–40
Popular Party of Italy, 146, 151–52, 155, 164–66
poverty, 60–61, 88, 97–98
prayers
    asking for, 122–23
    as a child, 17
Prodigal Son, 49
Promessi Sposi, "The Betrothed" (Manzoni), 114
Protagoras (Greek philosopher), 50n8
Providence de la, Mère Marie, 55n21
Province of Saint Peter Martyr, 171
public schools, corrupt instructions, 158, 165n93
purgatory, 123, 207

Quas Primas (Pius XI encyclical), 209–10, 217

Rahner (Professor), 101–2
Randone, Cesare, 138
Randone, Emilio, 125n37, 126
Ravenna Convention (1921), 113–14, 156
Raymond of Capua, 179
relationships, 42
    See also chapter 6 and "Shady Ones" (*Tipi Loschi*). Also, chapter 9
religious congregations, persecution of, 72
Renaissance humanism, 7–8, 8n34
repentance, 49–50
Rerum Novarum (Leo XIII encyclical), 7, 141, 143, 147–48, 151
responsibility, 26–29
Richelmy, Agostino, Archbishop, 177
Richetto, (Father), 133
Rizzetti, Luigi, 6

Robespierre, Maximilien, 125
Robotti, Filippo (Friar), 89, 168, 171–72, 173, 177–78
Robotti, Francesco (Friar), 171n13, 172, 173–74
Roccati, Alessandro (Monsignor), 14, 64, 91, 106, 156
Rome
    geopolitical status, 141, 149–50
    Italian nationalism and, 150–51
    Vatican, 94, 150
    visit to, 93–94
Rome Convention (1921), 144, 156
Rosaries, 65, 114, 170
Rousseau, Jean-Jacques, 8n35
Roux, Luigi, 4
Royal Turin Polytechnic, 85, 87, 87n63, 152
Rule of Dominicans, 89
Rule of Saint Augustine, 169, 185
Russian Revolution (1917), 151

sacramental life
    Christian responsibility and, 61–62
    communion, 54–60, 79, 123
    confirmation, 64–65, 64n52
    conscience-formation, 51
    devotion to Blessed Virgin Mary, 65–67
    penance, sacrament of, 52–53
    repentance, 49–51
Sacramentine Fathers, Turin, 62, 62n47
sacrifice, 195–98, 201–2
sadness, 213
"Saint Mary the Consoler" *La Consolata*, 65, 67
Saint Paul Outside the Walls (Papal Basilica), 94
Saint Paul's Hymn to Charity, 95
Salesian College, Alassio, 71–72
Salesians, congregation of, 71–72
salvation, 216–20
San Sebastian Club, 158
Santa Pece de' Pazzi, 127–28
Saturday Charity, 4, 153
Savio, Dominic, Saint, 9, 169–70
Savonarola, Girolamo, (Friar), 8n34, 89, 89n72, 168, 172, 176–78, 217

INDEX

Savonarola Club, 89, 91, 156, 171–72, 178
Schiller, Friedrich, 102
scripture, politics and, 161–62
secular humanism, 4, 8
secularization, 8, 158, 165n93
sensitivity, 32–33
Severi, Antonio, 120, 125n37, 126
"Shady Ones" Club, (*Tipi Loschi*) 91, 120–28, 125n37
Shakespeare, William, 93, 104
sin, forgiveness of, 49
sinners, charity for, 153–54
Smet, Eugene, 55n21
Smetana, Bedrich, 103
social culture, 105–7
social democracy, 163
Social Institute (*l'Istituto Sociale*), Jesuit, 57–59, 62, 74, 77–78, 152
social justice, politics and, 154–55
social problems, in Italy, 6–7
social values, of Frassati, Alfredo, 4–5
socialism, 147, 162n84, 165
Society of the Most Holy Sacrament, 79
socioeconomic crisis, post WWI, 151–52, 164
sociopolitical issues, 123–24
Sonnenschein (Reverend Doctor), 100, 101, 118, 142–44
sorrow, 213
spiritual exercises, Ignatius, 79
spiritual growth, 42
studies
    agricultural, 84, 96
    attitude toward, 121–22
    home tutor, Busatto, 69–70
    struggle with, 28, 70, 74–75
    See also specific colleges and institutions by name
Sturzo, Luigi (Don), 91, 151, 163, 166
suffering, unjustly, 117–18
Summa Theologiae (St. Thomas Aquinas), xvii, 5n23, 41n48, 50n9, 97n17, 111, 127n44, 183n64

Taylor, Charles, 8n36
Thérèse of Lisieux, Saint, 78n37

Third Order Dominicans (Lay Dominicans), 170–74, 170n6, 176–77
Thoma, Hans, 103
Thomas Aquinas, Saint, 5, 5n23, 50n8, 95, 105, 111, 169, 181–84
Tipi Loschi, ("Shady Ones" Club), 91, 120–28, 125n37
Toniolo, Giuseppe, 143, 165, 166n96
Treaty of Versailles, 145
trust, 19–22
Turin Polytechnic, 85, 87, 87n63, 152, 171
Turkish baths, 94

Unterrichter, Guglielmo, 139

vanity, 81–82
Varazze accusations, publication, 72
Vatican, 94, 150
    See also Rome
Venchi, Innocenzo, 177n38
Versailles Treaty, 100, 115, 117, 146, 205
Vianney, Jean-Marie, Saint, 55n21
Victor Emmanuel III, King, 43–44
Villani, Antonio, 120–24, 142–46, 152–55, 162–66, 168–74, 197
Vincent de Paul, Saint, 33n8, 152–54, 201, 218, 220
violence, 217
Virgin Mary
    Marian shrines, 65–67, 96–97
    Our Lady of Oropa, 65–66, 66n64
    rosary, 65
    Saint Mary the Consoler, 67
Vittoriano Monument, 149

Wagner, Richard, 102
will of God, 196–98
William II, Kaiser, 104
Wilson, Thomas Woodrow, 145
World War I
    Italian post politics, 151–52, 154–55
    reaction to, 144–46

Young Mountaineers, 138
Young Mountaineers (GM), 91
Young Workers Adoration, 91

Zanatta family, 153–54

www.ingramcontent.com/pod-product-compliance
Lightning Source LLC
Chambersburg PA
CBHW050349230426
43663CB00010B/2056